T0355481

OXFORD TEXTUAL PERSPECTIVES

*Materializing Englishness in Early Medieval Texts*

GENERAL EDITORS

Elaine Treharne          Greg Walker

# Materializing Englishness in Early Medieval Texts

JACQUELINE FAY

OXFORD
UNIVERSITY PRESS

# OXFORD
### UNIVERSITY PRESS

Great Clarendon Street, Oxford, OX2 6DP,
United Kingdom

Oxford University Press is a department of the University of Oxford.
It furthers the University's objective of excellence in research, scholarship,
and education by publishing worldwide. Oxford is a registered trade mark of
Oxford University Press in the UK and in certain other countries

© Jacqueline Fay 2022

The moral rights of the author have been asserted

First Edition published in 2022

Impression: 2

All rights reserved. No part of this publication may be reproduced, stored in
a retrieval system, or transmitted, in any form or by any means, without the
prior permission in writing of Oxford University Press, or as expressly permitted
by law, by licence or under terms agreed with the appropriate reprographics
rights organization. Enquiries concerning reproduction outside the scope of the
above should be sent to the Rights Department, Oxford University Press, at the
address above

You must not circulate this work in any other form
and you must impose this same condition on any acquirer

Published in the United States of America by Oxford University Press
198 Madison Avenue, New York, NY 10016, United States of America

British Library Cataloguing in Publication Data

Data available

Library of Congress Control Number: 2021952311

ISBN 978-0-19-875757-3 (hbk.)
ISBN 978-0-19-875756-6 (pbk.)

DOI: 10.1093/oso/9780198757573.001.0001

Printed and bound by
CPI Group (UK) Ltd, Croydon, CR0 4YY

Links to third party websites are provided by Oxford in good faith and
for information only. Oxford disclaims any responsibility for the materials
contained in any third party website referenced in this work.

# SERIES EDITORS' PREFACE

*Oxford Textual Perspectives* is a series of informative and provocative studies focused upon texts (conceived of in the broadest sense of that term) and the technologies, cultures, and communities that produce, inform, and receive them. It provides fresh interpretations of fundamental works, images, and artefacts, and of the vital and challenging issues emerging in English literary studies. By engaging with the contexts and materiality of the text, its production, transmission, and reception history, and by frequently testing and exploring the boundaries of the notions of text and meaning themselves, the volumes in the series question conventional frameworks and provide innovative interpretations of both canonical and less well-known works. These books will offer new perspectives, and challenge familiar ones, both on and through texts and textual communities. While they focus on specific authors, periods, and issues, they nonetheless scan wider horizons, addressing themes and provoking questions that have a more general application to literary studies and cultural history as a whole. Each is designed to be as accessible to the non-specialist reader as it is fresh and rewarding for the specialist, combining an informative orientation in a landscape with detailed analysis of the territory and suggestions for further travel.

*Elaine Treharne* and *Greg Walker*

# CONTENTS

# Introduction

## *Materializing Englishness*

In illuminating how a group of people with diverse origins came to be English, the surviving textual record is full of significant moments described with extreme brevity and usually with a focus on matters other than identity. What is very difficult to discern within this record, as within almost every realm of inquiry in early medieval studies, is what the everyday experience of becoming and being English consisted of for most people. The markers that modern readers understand as constitutive and expressive of identity—such as language, dialect, dress, or food— are very rarely addressed by early medieval English writers in what might be recognized as their day-to-day contexts. The effect of important historical events on the lives of regular people are similarly difficult to gauge, preserved as they are in treaties, annals, and historical texts. Consider, for example, a moment in 1052 when, according to the *Anglo-Saxon Chronicle*, war almost broke out between the forces of Earl Godwine and Edward the Confessor. Godwine and his sons had been exiled a year before for reasons that are variously reported by the different *Chronicle* versions, and the reluctance of both sides to decide the situation by battle is attributed by the text to their shared identity as English men.

> [H]it wæs heom mæst eallon lað þæt hig sceoldon fohtan wið heora agenes cynnes mannum, for þan þar wæs lyt elles þe aht mycel

*Materializing Englishness in Early Medieval Texts.* Jacqueline Fay, Oxford University Press.
© Jacqueline Fay 2022. DOI: 10.1093/oso/9780198757573.003.0001

> myhton buton englisce men on ægþer healfe, 7 eac hig noldon þæt
> utlendiscum þeodum wære þes eard þurh þæt þe swiðor gerymed, þe
> hi heom sylfe ælc oðerne forfore.[1]

> (It was hateful to almost all of them that they should fight against
> their own kinsmen, because there was little else of much worth except
> English men on either side, and also they did not want this country to
> become more open to foreign peoples on account of this, because
> they themselves had destroyed each other.)

Had it been fought, the *Chronicle* suggests, this battle would have
constituted a civil war, rather than the expulsion of an invading force
or a conflict between rival kingdoms for territory, which is how the
*Chronicle* describes preceding battles. In this account, *englisce men* are
represented as a group counterbalanced by those *utlendisc þeod* who
may overrun the *eard*, the territorial homeland, should the English
eradicate each other. Sometimes, as in this example, being English was a
question with life-and-death urgency. But most of the time, just like
now, it would have been an everyday matter, part of the lived experience of individuals that barely registered on their consciousness at all.

The 'taken-for-grantedness' of English identity is, of course, discern-
ible in this passage in the way that it presents the reasons for not
fighting the battle. The annal suggests that three components are
fundamental to being English: first, the idea of kinship; second, the
mutual responsibility for the protection of a homeland against foreign
forces; and finally, that English men share a common history, interestingly expressed here in terms of the collective future perfect of what
'will have happened' should all the English have killed each other. All
three components are taken to be self-evident, although none of them
is. Godwine and Edward's forces cannot all have been kin in the sense
of being able to trace a familial relationship, and their concerns about
*utlendisc* men are sustained notwithstanding that their own ancestors
originally came to the island from the Continent or from Scandinavia.
The associations of Englishness are, however, powerful: being English
assigns value to those potentially participating in the battle—*lyt elles þe
aht mycel* exists on either side—and also encourages resolution of the

---

[1] Quoted in the original from *The Anglo-Saxon Chronicle 5: A Collaborative Edition*,
vol. 5, *MS C*, edited by Katherine O'Brien O'Keefe (Cambridge: D.S. Brewer, 2001), p. 113.
Translation is my own.

situation through diplomacy rather than violence. The apparently self-evident nature of being English, the way in which its fundamental lineaments are assumed here rather than questioned or asserted, gives it this power. This passage is thus a good example of the components that this book identifies as fundamental to Englishness during the early medieval period: an essential tie to the land, a shared history, a perceived embodied bond between members, and the fusion of these components in such a way that they seem to occur naturally and in a realm below, beyond, or additional to that of texts and ideas.

While previous scholars have recognized that these same elements are important in the formation of ethnic groups, limitations exist when it comes to imagining how the fusion between them occurs. For example, Anthony Smith argues that an ethnic community has a reality that is explicitly social, resulting 'from the meanings conferred by a number of men and women over some generations on certain cultural, spatial and temporal properties of their interaction and shared experiences'.[2] These meanings serve to lend presence to an ethnic group, both for its own members and for outsiders, and all require constant iteration, even if such repetition eludes conscious attention.[3] Much scholarship on Englishness within medieval studies, where the topic has been of sustained interest for at least two decades, has also concentrated primarily on tracking the terminology used by and for groups and on story-telling in texts, with an additional focus on attributing a date to the emergence of social formations.[4] While this work is very helpful in conceptualizing the workings of ethnic groups, and underpins what is to

[2] Anthony Smith, *The Ethnic Origin of Nations* (Oxford: Blackwell, 1986), p. 22.

[3] Ibid., p. 183. See also John Hines, 'The Becoming of the English: Identity, Material Culture and Language in Early Anglo-Saxon England', *Anglo-Saxon Studies in Archaeology and History* 7 (1994): pp. 49–59, at pp. 51–2.

[4] Thorlac Turville-Petre, *England the Nation: Language, Literature and National Identity, 1290–1340* (Oxford: Clarendon Press, 1996). For studies specific to early medieval England, see Kathleen Davis, 'National Writing in the Ninth Century: A Reminder for Post-Colonial Thinking about the Nation', *Journal of Medieval and Early Modern Studies* 28 (1998): pp. 611–37; Sarah Foot, 'The Making of Angelcynn: English Identity before the Norman Conquest', *Transactions of the Royal Historical Society* 6 (1996): pp. 25–49; and the selected essays in Kathy Lavezzo, ed., *Imagining a Medieval English Nation* (Minneapolis: University of Minnesota Press, 2004). Only one book concentrates on this topic in early medieval England in particular: Stephen Harris, *Race and Ethnicity in Anglo-Saxon Literature* (New York: Routledge, 2003). See also Harris's 'An Overview of Race and Ethnicity in Pre-Norman England', *Literature Compass* 5 (2008): pp. 740–54.

follow in this book, it does rely on the primacy and inertness of 'action' and 'experience', which become significant only through the retroactive and repeated attribution of meaning in oral or written narratives. This model of ethnic community thus conceptualizes the material interactions of lived experience and texts as belonging to separate realms.

The goal of this book is to restore to the story of Englishness the lively material interactions between words, bodies, plants, stones, metals, and soil, among other things, that would have characterized it for the early medieval English themselves. In particular, each chapter aims to demonstrate how a productive collapse, or fusion, between place and history not only happens in the intellectual realm—in ideas—but is also a material concern, becoming enfleshed in encounters between early medieval bodies and a host of material entities. Through readings of texts in a wide variety of genres—such as hagiography, heroic poetry, medical and historical works—the book argues that Englishness during this period is an embodied identity emergent at the frontier of material and textual interactions that serve productively to occlude history, religion, and geography. The early medieval English body thus results from the rich encounter between the lived environment—climate, soil, landscape features, plants—and the textual-discursive realm that both determines what that environment means and is also itself determined by the material constraints of everyday life. Rather than relying on those binaries of mind/body, interiority/exteriority, language/matter, native/foreign that have organized later fields, the book aims to be alive to the entangled matter of Englishness in early medieval England, where an imported textual culture and practices mingle with and mark lived experience. The book therefore engages with the long-lasting discussion of cultural syncretism within scholarship focusing on this period, but radically extends the contours of this discussion through its focus on materiality.

The approach is perhaps best explained by way of another example, one focusing not on a single event like a battle but on a complex and slower-moving set of interactions between plants, animals, people, water, and other materials during settlement and population movement. Resulting from just such a set of interactions is Watling Street, a road that features at several important moments in the early medieval historical record. For instance, Watling Street is mentioned in the description of the boundary between the Scandinavian and English portions of England in the treaty of Alfred and Guthrum in the late ninth century. The bounds coincide first with rivers and then with the established course of Watling Street:

> Ærest ymb ure landgemæra: up on Temese, & ðonne up on Ligan, & andlang Ligan oð hire æwylm, ðonne on gerihte to Bedanforda, ðonne up on Usan oð Wætlingastræt.[5]

> (First about our land-boundaries: up the Thames, and then up the river Lea to its source, then straight to Bedford, then up the river Ouse to Watling Street.)

Although the date and circumstances of this treaty are far from certain, it is generally understood to be the act that founded what would later be labelled the Danelaw, that north-eastern portion of England that was settled by Scandinavians in the ninth century and that retained some measure of independence into the tenth and even eleventh centuries. Following years of fierce fighting between the English and the Danes that had eradicated all the independent English kingdoms other than Wessex, the treaty is clearly important in paving the way for England to become a political and territorial unit with contours roughly coinciding with those it currently has. The description of the boundaries, however, has a homely familiarity, employing as it does the type of naturally occurring and manmade landmarks regularly invoked in charter bounds, a number of surviving examples of which also mention Watling Street.

Watling Street is a material entity with a complex and interactive relationship with English people during the period (and beyond, if we consider that it lives on in the form of the A5). Originally a trackway used by a native British tribe known as the Catuvellauni, Watling Street was worn into the vegetation and soil by the hooves of cattle, wending their way from pasture to water source. It was lent more permanence due to the material properties of stone added to the route by the Romans around AD 43. Because it was made of stone, Watling Street

[5] For description of the terms of the treaty, which is preserved in two vernacular versions, see Patrick Wormald, *The Making of English Law: King Alfred to the Twelfth Century* (1999; repr. Oxford: Blackwell, 2000), pp. 285–6. See also Simon Keynes, 'Royal Government and the Written Word in Late Anglo-Saxon England', in *The Uses of Literacy in Early Medieval Europe*, edited by Rosamund McKitterick (Cambridge: Cambridge University Press, 1990), pp. 226–57, at pp. 233–4.

must have been a prominent site for the early English. Nicholas Howe has called it a spectral survival of the marvels of Roman engineering and its 'imperial will to power over the terrain', but it is more immediately a lithic and explicitly material expression of history.[6] As Bede puts it in his *Historia Ecclesiastica*, the Roman occupation of Britain was made present for succeeding inhabitants because of its effects on the landscape:

> Habitabant autem intra uallum, quod Seuerum trans insulam fecisse commemorauimus, ad plagam meridianum, quod ciuitates farus pontes et stratae ibidem factae usque hodie testantur.[7]
>
> (They had occupied the whole land south of the rampart already mentioned, set up across the island by Severus, an occupation to which the cities, lighthouses, bridges and roads which they built there testify to this day.)

Whereas it appears not to have been named by the Romans, the early medieval English called it either *Wætlinga* or *Wæclinga stræt* after the *Wæclingas*, or Wacol's people, about whom we know nothing.[8] St Alban, the hugely popular Romano-British saint, was martyred near Watling Street (at Wæclingaceaster, the Old English name for Roman *Verulamium*) and, 700 years later in 1013, the road was to become the threshold of a different kind of violence when Swein Forkbeard held back from ravaging the English until he had crossed Watling Street.[9] As the *Anglo-Saxon Chronicle* tells us:

---

[6] Nicholas Howe, *Writing the Map of Anglo-Saxon England: Essays in Cultural Geography* (New Haven and London: Yale University Press, 2008), p. 77 and p. 83. In *The East Midlands in the Early Middle Ages*, Pauline Stafford notes that burials along the course of such roads, including Watling Street, suggest that they may not have been busy throughout the early medieval period, and underlines that they functioned as boundaries, since graves were often placed on the margins of communities (Leicester: Leicester University Press, 1995), p. 11.

[7] *Bede's Ecclesiastical History of the English People*, edited by Bertram Colgrave and R. A. B. Mynors (Oxford: Clarendon Press, 1969), i.11.

[8] Kenneth Cameron, *English Place-names* (London: B. T. Batsford, 1961), p. 154. All that we do know of these people is that they gave their name to this road and to the settlement at *Wæclingaceaster*. See also A. Mawer and F. M. Stenton, *The Place-Names of Bedfordshire and Huntingdonshire*, English Place-Name Society 3 (Cambridge: Cambridge University Press, 1926), pp. 5–7.

[9] Simon Keynes argues that Swein landed at Sandwich but began his campaign from Gainsborough because 'he expected that the men of the Danelaw, remembering their parentage, would prefer to submit to a Danish army under a Danish king rather than

7 þa sona beah Uhtred eorl 7 ealle Norðhymbre to him 7 eal þæt folc on Lindesige 7 siððan þæt folc into Fifburhingum 7 raðe þæs eall here be norðan Wæclinga stræte, 7 him man sealde gislas of ælcere scire. Syððan he undergeat þæt eall folc him to gebogen wæs... he ða wende syþþan suðweard mid fulre fyrde...7 syððan he com ofer Wæclinga stræte, worhton þæt mæste yfel þæt ænig here don mihte.[10]

(And then Earl Uhtred and all the Northumbrians submitted to him, and all the people of Lindsey, and afterwards those of the Five Boroughs, and soon all of the *here* [Scandinavian armed groups] north of Watling Street, and he was given hostages from every shire. After he understood that all the people had submitted to him... then he went southwards with a full army... and after he came over Watling Street, they inflicted the greatest evil that any invading army might do.)

In crossing, not crossing, or in talking across Watling Street, the early medieval English enter into and are changed by participation in the discursive and material network that is Watling Street. For example, during a revolt by northern landowners against their southern overlord in 1065, the rebels stop at Northampton and talk with the court across Watling Street, no doubt aiming to engage and refer to its role as a divide between the north and the south of England. As Matthew Innes puts it, they talk, 'across a political marker rich in redolence. Watling Street was not only a physically visible marker, but it was also embedded in the cultural landscape, as a mnemonic for past relationships.'[11]

---

resist so powerful a force, and he was not disappointed'. See Keynes' *The Diplomas of King Æþelred 'The Unready'* (Cambridge: Cambridge University Press, 1980), p. 226. Dawn Hadley argues that Swein was probably aiming for regional support, arguing that 'Swegn may possibly have harboured notions of mobilizing ethnic support in the region, but if he did we should not suppose that he simply called on the descendants of earlier Scandinavian settlers... if Swegn wanted to draw on "Scandinavian" support, it would have to be from a people who had become firmly welded to native society'. See ' "Cockle amongst the Wheat": The Scandinavian Settlement of England', in *Social Identity in Early Medieval Britain*, edited by William O. Frazer and Andrew Tyrrel (London: Leicester University Press, 2000), pp. 111–35, at p. 119). See also Dawn Hadley, *The Vikings in England: Settlement, Society and Culture* (Manchester: Manchester University Press, 2006), p. 129.

[10] *Anglo-Saxon Chronicle*, p. 97.

[11] 'Danelaw Identities: Ethnicity, Regionalism, and Political Allegiance', in *Cultures in Contact: Scandinavian Settlement in England in the Ninth and Tenth Centuries*, edited by Dawn M. Hadley and Julian D. Richards (Turnhout: Brepols, 2000), pp. 65–88, at p. 70.

Watling Street is part of the story of Englishness during the early medieval period, but its role in this narrative is not solely the province, or entirely under the control, of the discursive realm of texts and ideas. The road was made by the allied agencies of cattle, looking to satisfy their species' needs, and those humans who were farming them, looking to satisfy theirs, and the perambulations of both cattle and humans occur in response to the land in the distribution of soil type, vegetation, and water sources. Hundreds of years later, stone brings longevity to Watling Street because of its resistance to erosion. The approach adopted in this book accounts for the role of these material elements as integral, rather than contextual and background, parts of the narrative that welds history to geography and forges Englishness. This is not to deny that people aim to assign and manipulate the meanings of material objects, but to acknowledge that matter itself participates in this process, although not in the wilful, conscious modes that humans have traditionally recognized as agential—to explore, in other words, how the narrative of Englishness is actively shaped by the material interactions of cattle, people, plants, soil, and stone, rather than conceiving of these as passive elements waiting to be assigned meaning in the discursive realm of texts.

## Defining matter in early medieval England

What counts as matter varies a great deal over time, with the boundary between the material and immaterial having more or less prominence as a constitutive factor depending on the historical period, the dominant cosmology, and changing technologies. Many examples exist from early medieval England demonstrating that the distinction between material and immaterial entities is very differently configured during the period than it would be in later centuries. For instance, in contrast

---

Versions D and E of the *Anglo-Saxon Chronicle* give an account of this revolt by the northern landowners against Tostig, a Godwin and a southerner. Innes argues that their actions demonstrate 'the intricate balance between regional and national allegiances within mid-eleventh-century England' (p. 69), and serve to recall earlier regional political structures.

to the later medieval church, early medieval English writers espouse a vernacular theology in which matter is not opposed to an immaterial and inward spirituality, as Leslie Lockett, in her 2011 study of *Anglo-Saxon Psychologies in the Vernacular and Latin Traditions*, has shown.[12] Lockett carefully demonstrates that the Platonic notion of the incorporeal and immaterial soul was accessible only to very few pre-Conquest authors and was unlikely to have permeated popular religion at all until the eleventh century. Instead, early medieval English texts, both prose and poetry, favoured a tripartite structure of mind-body-soul in which thought and emotion are not absolutely distinguished but are both experienced as constriction or expansion accompanied by heating or cooling of the chest cavity—what scholars have called a hydraulic model. While it is eternal, the soul (*sawol* in Old English) is nonetheless beholden to the actions of the body, which determine its long-term health. The body, conversely, is not an inherently inferior entity lectured to and castigated by the spiritually superior and virtuous soul. Because the mind somatically manifests in the chest, the body can make choices and is not necessarily predisposed to a life of vice and the pursuit of worldly desire; neither is the soul by definition predisposed to virtue. As Lockett carefully shows, this tripartite hydraulic model is not metaphorical in early medieval English culture—as it is, for example, in contemporary expressions such as 'burning love' or 'think with your head, not your heart'—but is a literal understanding based on experience. Unlike Cartesian and post-Cartesian models of thought, in which mind and body are strictly separated from each other in terms of active (mind) and passive (matter), early medieval English culture exhibits a psychosomatic system in which the body is valorized and endowed with agency.

Matter and the body, while they are connected in modern understanding, are not as intimately associated as they are in early medieval thinking. As Carolyn Walker Bynum describes, medieval writers understood body to mean '"changeable thing": gem, tree, log, or cadaver, as well as living human being. . . . To explore "the body" was to explore stars and statues, blood and resin, as well as pain, perception,

---

[12] (Toronto: University of Toronto Press, 2011).

and survival.'[13] In Old English the concept of matter is etymologically linked to timber: according to *A Thesaurus of Old English*, *ontimber*, *ontimbernes*, and *timber* represent half of the available vocabulary words for 'substance' or 'material'.[14] The Latin equivalent, *materia*, also originates with the meaning 'timber' but has an additional association with *mater*, or 'mother', which the *Oxford English Dictionary* suggests is a way of referring to the main trunk of a tree as the origin of a system of branches.[15] This maternal connotation is interestingly not present in Old English equivalents for the Latin word; other Old English terms for 'matter', such as *andweorc* and *geteoh*, are instead explicitly connected to work and tools. While the nature of these terms betrays the importance of wood as a building material for the pre-Conquest inhabitants of England, their extension to refer to matter in general ultimately provides a more concrete and embedded diction than is suggested by the more abstract modern English *matter*.

The aesthetic and scientific dimensions of this system of integrated matter are evident in a diagram from Oxford, St John's College MS 17 that is associated with Byrhtferth of Ramsey (Figs 1a and 1b). Such diagrams built upon the Galenic theory of the four bodily humours—in which blood, yellow bile, black bile, and phlegm are associated with the four seasons, elements, winds, and properties of nature—by adding the four ages of man, the signs of the zodiac, and the four evangelists. The fabric of the human body is not isolable from the other components of this multi-layered system but will respond differently depending on the time of year, direction of the wind, or place at which it is located. Although lacking a full treatise on the principles of humoral medicine, the Old English medical corpus clearly shares with much Graeco-Roman medicine a sense of the human body as integrated within a fabric also containing non-human bodies, plants, and what we would

---

[13] *Christian Materiality: An Essay on Religion in Late Medieval Europe* (New York: Zone Books, 2011), p. 32.

[14] Jane Roberts, Christian Kay, and Lynne Grundy, *A Thesaurus of Old English in Two Volumes* (Atlanta, GA: Rodopi, 2000), p. 135.

[15] See Walker Bynum, *Christian Materiality*, and Anne F. Harris, 'Hewn', in *Inhuman Nature*, edited by Jeffrey Jerome Cohen (Washington, DC: Oliphaunt Books, 2014), pp. 17–38.

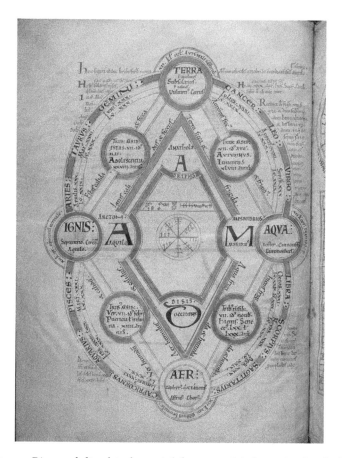

FIG 1A  Diagram believed to be copied from an original associated with the eleventh-century monk Byrhtferth of Ramsey and showing the synthetic relationships between the four humours, the four elements, the four ages of man, the seasons, the two equinoxes, the twelve months, the twelve astrological signs, and the twelve winds. A facsimile of the entire manuscript is available online at http://digital.library.mcgill.ca/ms-17/index.htm. Oxford, St John's College MS 17, fo. 7v, by permission of the Master and Fellows of St John's College, University of Oxford.

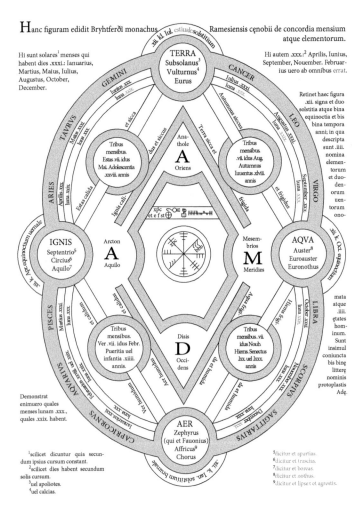

FIG 1B  Peter Baker's rendering of Byrhtferth's diagram into modern English. An interactive version of the diagram is available at http://babelstone.blogspot.it/2008/12/byrhtferths-ogham-enigma.html, archived at http://web.archive.org/web/19961025235309/http://www.engl.virginia.edu/OE/Editions/Decon.pdf. By permission of Peter S. Baker.

recognize as environmental factors.[16] In other words, the early medieval English understand the body to be part of an ever-changing and interconnected material system, which mandates holistic treatment options, such as remedies made from plants and animal parts, charms, and petitioning of saints. The Old English medical corpus is one example among many from early medieval England providing evidence that the body is not conceived of separately from an immaterial entity like a soul or mind, and is also more profoundly engaged with other forms of matter than it will be understood to be after Descartes.

## The matter of method

This book points out that, despite being thought of as natural, there is nothing inevitable about the entwined nature of place, history, and people that characterizes notions of Englishness in early medieval culture. In other words, in early medieval England just as now, simply being born in a certain place did not alone provide individuals with a connection to the history and topography of that place in such a way that they would understand themselves to have a special connection to it. Because the body is frequently represented as the ground of this entanglement between individual, place, and history, it is often thought that such linkage is natural, in the same way that other bodily features like size or eye colour are thought of as natural. Asserting such a natural or inherent connection between people and place is a strategy of many oppressive regimes throughout history, represented perhaps most

[16] Conan Doyle, *Anglo-Saxon Medicine and Disease: A Semantic Approach* (Unpubl. PhD dissertation, University of Cambridge, 2011) has recently shown that terms for the humours are used purposefully and consistently within Old English medical texts. For a slightly different conclusion, see Lois Ayoub, 'Old English *wæta* and the Medical Theory of the Humours', *Journal of English and Germanic Philology* 94 (1995), pp. 332–46. Also on the question of the humours in Old English medicine, see: M. L. Cameron, *Anglo-Saxon Medicine* (Cambridge: Cambridge University Press, 1993); Helen King, 'Female Fluids in the Hippocratic Corpus: How Solid Was the Humoral Body?' in *The Body in Balance: Humoral Medicines in Practice*, edited by Peregrine Horden and Elisabeth Hsu (New York: Berghahn Books, 2013), pp. 25–52; Debby Banham, 'A Millennium in Medicine? New Medical Texts and Ideas in England in the Eleventh Century', in *Anglo-Saxons: Studies Presented to Cyril Roy Hart*, edited by Simon Keynes and Alfred P. Smyth (Dublin: Four Courts Press, 2006), pp. 230–42.

obviously in the Nazi slogan 'Blood and Soil' used to fabricate a racial link between people and land. To return a role to matter in the production of identity, as this book does, is a project absolutely distinct from such ideological projects of racial oppression, which actually work entirely within the realm of discourse—that is, partial and biased discourse *about* matter that would in fact be undermined by matter's unpredictable agencies. The book is therefore aligned with Kate Rigby's comments in her ecocritical exploration of the Heideggerian concept of dwelling, a related concept which is helpful to consider while making clear the falsity of any material claims made within ideological cults of belonging.[17] As Rigby notes, while 'dwelling involves an attunement to the given, it is itself not given, either by place of birth or ancestral belonging, even if your dwelling place does in fact happen to be that of your forefathers'.[18] Instead dwelling must be learned over and over, and is thus better conceived of as an 'achievement' resulting from 'commitment' and 'not something that is in any sense "in the blood"'.[19] The approach taken here makes the same assertion that no one is 'born English' but rather is in a process of always continuing to become so through a series of encounters with innumerable entities such as landscape, stories, plants, animals, and microbes. The book thus emphatically upholds the point that, as Stephen Harris puts it in a related discussion of race in pre-Norman England, '[t]here is nothing one can point to, dissolve in a beaker, or grind into a powder that reveals an English race.'[20]

Instead my approach emphasizes that, while material (dissolved, ground up, or in other ways encountered by an early medieval person) cannot make someone English, its interactions with words and ideas do play a role in the story. Serenella Iovino and Serpil Oppermann put it aptly in their 2014 collection *Material Ecocriticism*, writing that, 'discourses about the *living* world, though necessary, are per se insufficient, if separated from their broader material substratum of inanimate

[17] 'Earth, World, Text: On the (Im)possibility of Ecopoiesis', *New Literary History* 35 (2004): pp. 427–42.

[18] Ibid., p. 432.      [19] Ibid., p. 432.

[20] 'An Overview of Race and Ethnicity in Pre-Norman England', *Literature Compass* 5 (2008): pp. 740–54, at p. 740.

substances and apersonal agencies'.[21] Their concept of 'storied matter' indicates that the world we inhabit is alive with stories that develop both within bodies and by means of ideas, arising in co-evolutionary collectives that include matter and signs. If we concentrate only on the human-generated narratives housed within the linguistic realm of texts, we are missing a large part of the plot; this book, by working with a more expansive, and less anthropocentric, definition of narrative agency, aims to open up a fuller story. In this story Englishness is not natural, and nor is it a solely ideological product of texts that promote a sense of the interconnectedness of people, place, and history. Although texts do work to disseminate these ideas, they also offer models in which the body is fabricated from, or materializes out of, history and place. For example, since all food at this time is by definition local (transforming nutrients in the soil, air, and water into plant and animal matter), ingestion provides a simple model by which to understand how the body is made from place.[22] However, how are we to understand the examples of ingestion in hagiographical literature that I will discuss in the first chapter, in which people are healed by consuming earth infused with the blood of a local saint? These examples, since they involve blood and soil, might seem to suggest that a connection to a place is biologically transmitted in some simple, self-evident and exclusionary manner. But to assume this would be to completely miss the point that the soil exists in a highly complex amalgam with many other elements, all of which are required for it to do its work. This earth that renews the bodies of those who consume it is both material and textual, in that ideas about its efficacy are disseminated in historical narratives that tell of the deeds of English saints. But while this earth could not 'work' without such stories, neither is its effectiveness 'made up' by texts. Such models are not in any simple sense fictionalized accounts of a physicalized Englishness, accounts that use the body and bodily processes to *represent* conceptual associations between events, individuals, and the place that they occupy. They serve to show how historical events (such as the death of well-known saints) fuse with place (the

---

[21] 'Introduction: Stories Come to Matter', in *Material Ecocriticism*, edited by Serenella Iovino and Serpil Oppermann (Bloomington: Indiana University Press, 2014), p. 3.

[22] For all questions about what the early medieval English ate, and when, see Debby Banham, *Food and Drink in Anglo-Saxon England* (Stroud: Tempus Publishing, 2004).

earth) and then grow and nourish the fabric of the consuming body, and it is in this unique combination that Englishness materializes. Nothing about the process is simple or given, and it cannot be reduced to either culture or biology alone.

As this example makes clear, *Materializing Englishness* is centrally concerned with the preoccupations of New Materialism, a theoretical field that acknowledges that humans 'inhabit an ineluctably material world' that has not been adequately addressed in the history of philosophy.[23] As Dianna Coole and Samantha Frost put it in their useful introduction to *New Materialisms: Ontology, Agency, and Politics*, new materialists argue that 'foregrounding material factors and reconfiguring our very understanding of matter are prerequisites for any plausible account of coexistence and its conditions in the twenty-first century'.[24] More broadly, New Materialism is part of posthumanism, a movement to dismantle the centrality and universality assigned to 'man' during humanism and the attendant species hierarchy that places humans above other entities.[25] As part of this broader movement, New Materialism has expansive interconnections with feminist science studies, ecocriticism, critical plant studies, and animal studies, among other areas. At its root, New Materialism posits the simultaneity and inseparability of being and knowing, ontology and epistemology, asserting that all being fundamentally occurs within a process of ever-shifting relations between physical matter and ideas. New Materialism thus profoundly reconfigures our understanding of the relationship between language and matter, rejecting the core ideas of both essentialism—that language is belated and descriptive of a physical world characterized by self-identity and stability—and the premise advanced during the linguistic turn that language de facto constitutes the world because it mediates an inert and inaccessible materiality. Because it is process-oriented, New Materialism refutes binary thinking—in terms of dichotomies like male/female, nature/culture, inside/outside, mind/body, etc.—emphasizing instead the fluid and shifting nature of being

[23] Dianna Coole and Samantha Frost, *New Materialisms: Ontology, Agency, and Politics* (Durham, NC: Duke University Press, 2010), p. 1.

[24] Ibid., p. 2.

[25] For the breadth of posthumanism, see the introduction and entries in *The Posthuman Glossary*, edited by Rosi Braidotti and Maria Hlavajova (London: Bloomsbury, 2018).

and those categories that are used to describe it and characterizing this dynamic process by terms such as volatility, transcorporeality, intra-activity, vibrant matter, viscous porosity, and viscosity.[26] The early medieval body that *Materializing Englishness* posits, then, is not a primarily cultural product, as it has been analysed within much medieval scholarship upon which this study builds; rather it should be understood as being porous and involved with other entities in a process of mutual constitution.[27]

New Materialism has been critiqued for its claim to newness. Not only is this type of framing familiar from other movements seeking to distinguish themselves from theoretical progenitors such as New Historicism, but bringing the theory to the analysis of material from far distant time periods raises certain questions and problems. In particular, to what degree is New Materialism yoked to a contemporary context and in what ways is it anachronistic to bring its insights to bear on early medieval England? As Kyla Wazana Tompkins points out, even though New Materialism has been around for two decades, it 'still seems speculative, emergent, and contestatory', prompting us to ask 'what is the heroic narrative that…putative "newness" seeks to

---

[26] See Elizabeth Grosz, *Toward a Corporeal Feminism* (Bloomington: Indiana University Press, 1994); Stacy Alaimo, *Bodily Natures: Science, Environment, and the Material Self* (Bloomington: Indiana University Press, 2010); Karen Barad, *Meeting the Universe Halfway: Quantum Physics and the Entanglement of Matter and Meaning* (Durham, NC: Duke University Press, 2007); Jane Bennett, *Vibrant Matter: A Political Ecology of Things* (Durham, NC: Duke University Press, 2010); Nancy Tuana, 'Viscous Porosity: Witnessing Katrina', in *Material Feminisms*, edited by Stacy Alaimo and Susan Hekman (Bloomington: Indiana University Press, 2008), pp. 188–213; Arun Saldanha, 'Reontologising Race: The Machinic Geography of Phenotype', *Environment and Planning D: Society and Space* 24 (2006): pp. 9–24.

[27] The 1990s saw a florescence of interest in the body in many fields (Caroline Bynum, 'Why All the Fuss about the Body? A Medievalist's Perspective', *Critical Inquiry* 22 [1995]: pp. 1–33, at p. 3). Much scholarship on this topic within medieval studies leaps from late Antiquity, with its panoply of tortured martyrs, to the affective piety of twelfth- and thirteenth-century Europe, treating the early medieval context as an invisible middle. Notable exceptions include: Clare Lees and Gillian Overing, 'Before History, Before Difference: Bodies, Metaphor, and the Church in Anglo-Saxon England', *Yale Journal of Criticism* 11.2 (1998): pp. 315–34; *Naked Before God: Uncovering the Body in Anglo-Saxon England*, edited by Benjamin C. Withers and Jonathan Wilcox (Morgantown: West Virginia University Press, 2003); Katherine O'Brien O'Keeffe, 'Body and Law in Late Anglo-Saxon England', *Anglo-Saxon England* 27 (1998): pp. 209–32.

instantiate?'[28] Much of New Materialism is not actually new. Its focus on the liveliness of matter; its refusal of human-centred definitions of growth, narrative, and agency, among other qualities; its emphasis on the process-oriented nature of being and the entangled nature of matter and ideas—all are familiar from other contexts, cultures, and times, including but not limited to early medieval England. As Tompkins observes, many of these ideas can be found in the work of black and Indigenous thinkers, feminists, and also are characteristic of non-Western philosophies and medicine. She finds the New Materialist insistence on the agential and lively qualities of matter quite familiar as a scholar of the nineteenth century, causing her concern about 'how the non-white or otherwise minoritarian subjects and indeed history itself, haunt the edges of certain veins within New Materialist thought'.[29]

As a scholar of not the nineteenth but the ninth century, I understand and share Tompkins and others' sense of the familiarity of New Materialism, and part of the intent of *Materializing Englishness* is to contribute to and advance the wider theoretical conversation about materiality by means of historical analysis rather than just passively apply theoretical insights to a presumptively dead past. New Materialism is a temporally situated discourse, in that it emerges specifically after the linguistic turn and responds explicitly to the global environmental crisis, capitalism, and the various toxicities of the contemporary moment.[30] And yet the ideas developed by new materialists have so much affinity with the lively and proximate world of early medieval England, a time 'when food and shelter were precarious and human connections to natural sources constantly foregrounded by daily living

---

[28] Kyla Wazana Tompkins, 'New Materialisms', *Lateral* 5.1 (2016), https://doi.org/10.25158/L5.1.8. Listen also to the panel on 'What's New About New Materialism? Black and Indigenous Scholars on Science, Technology and Materiality' hosted by the Center for Race and Gender at the University of California Berkeley https://www.crg.berkeley.edu/podcasts/whats-new-about-new-materialism-black-and-indigenous-scholars-on-science-technology-and-materiality/.

[29] Ibid.

[30] For a very compelling explanation of how toxicity is profoundly modern, not because toxic chemicals are distinctive to the contemporary moment, but because the notion of immunity as an individual phenomenon capable of being attacked by an outside agent is a modern concept, see Mel Y. Chen, *Animacies: Biopolitics, Racial Mattering, and Queer Affect* (Durham, NC: Duke University Press, 2012), pp. 189–221.

conditions', as Heide Estes suggests, perhaps allowed people 'to understand human entanglements with natural objects and non-human
living beings more easily than humans in developed urban areas can
today in our movements among climate-controlled homes and work-
spaces by way of climate-controlled conveyances and our easy access
to food in packages of plastic and metal rather than on the hoof or in
the field'.[31]

Estes's 2017 *Anglo-Saxon Literary Landscapes: Ecotheory and the
Environmental Imagination* is among a number of recent works of
scholarship with which *Materializing Englishness* is in conversation
that address the topic of materiality in early medieval England. Medieval studies has long cultivated a material understanding of 'text', in
which every manuscript utterance is individual and particular meth-
odologies are required that relate these individual expressions to larger
cultural notions of textuality.[32] But more recent work like Estes's, while
being apt to a manuscript culture in which books are specifically
material entities, goes much further in its consideration of materiality,
bringing radical new insights to the relationship between people and
non-human entities, whether objects, animals, plants, or buildings.
Through readings of literary and documentary texts, Estes explores
how the early medieval English understood 'their relationship to the
land and its nonhuman creatures', arguing that 'the ideas that enabled
the Industrial Revolution and the climate crisis of today were already in
circulation' during this early period.[33] Corinne Dale, in *The Natural
World in the Exeter Book Riddles*, also draws on ecocriticism in addition
to ecotheology to argue that the vernacular riddles undertake 'a program of resistance to anthropocentrism...whereby the riddles challenge human-centred ways of depicting the created world'.[34] The
Exeter Book riddles, along with other vernacular poetry, also feature

---

[31] Heide Estes, *Anglo-Saxon Literary Landscapes: Ecotheory and the Environmental
Imagination* (Amsterdam: Amsterdam University Press, 2017), p. 150.
[32] See, for example, Gerald Bruns, 'The Originality of Texts in a Manuscript Culture',
*Comparative Literature* 32 (1980): pp. 113–29; Katherine O'Brien O'Keeffe, *Visible Song:
Transitional Literacy in Old English Verse* (Cambridge: Cambridge University Press,
2006); Thomas Bredehoft, *The Visible Text: Textual Production and Reproduction from
Beowulf to Maus* (Oxford: Oxford University Press, 2014), especially pp. 48–9.
[33] Estes, *Anglo-Saxon Literary Landscapes*, p. 10 and p. 32.
[34] Corinne Dale, *The Natural World in the Exeter Book Riddles* (Woodbridge:
D.S. Brewer, 2017), p. 2.

centrally in two further important volumes focusing on the interactions of people and objects: James Paz's 2017 *Nonhuman Voices in Anglo-Saxon Literature and Material Culture* and Denis Ferhatović's 2019 volume *Borrowed Objects and the Art of Poetry: Spolia in Old English Verse*.[35] Paz's work on materiality is wide ranging, with articles also on medicinal charms and sections of the book dedicated to the Franks Casket and the Ruthwell Cross. Building on thing theory, he argues that the talking non-human things in the literature and the material culture of early medieval England possess their own agency and are not just anthropomorphized objects. He thus rethinks the concept of voice as a quality distinctive to humans, and also challenges conventional distinctions between animacy and inanimacy. Ferhatović uses *spolia*, material that is taken from one context and reused in another, to guide his investigation of the way that animacy is transported between human and non-human entities to create points of connection between people across time, or what he describes as 'temporal and spatial layers'.[36]

This recent work shares certain principles of analysis, in particular contesting the distinctiveness, primacy, and boundedness of human beings to instead identify a world where humans are processually constituted through their permeability to other elements that are themselves agential, vocal, and affective. The scholarship is differentiated, however, by how much it prioritizes the 'natural world', even while critiquing the self-evidence of that concept, or the material world more generally. Estes and Dale specifically identify their work as ecotheoretical, although they differ quite a bit in the degree to which they assert that the ecological ethics of reading medieval texts are de facto involved in contemporary environmental activism. Attentiveness to the non-human world involves green readings, or those overlooked representations of 'the created world as an entity in itself'.[37] Paz's and Ferhatović's work is located more toward the object-oriented side of posthumanism, focusing specifically on the voice and agency of non-human things. The most stable factor amongst all this recent work,

---

[35] James Paz, *Nonhuman Voices in Anglo-Saxon Literature and Material Culture* (Manchester: Manchester University Press, 2017); Denis Ferhatović, *Borrowed Objects and the Art of Poetry: Spolia in Old English Verse* (Manchester: Manchester University Press, 2019).

[36] Ferhatovic, *Borrowed Objects*, p. 2.      [37] Dale, *The Natural World*, p. 22.

however, is the archive, which characteristically and meaningfully centres on the Exeter Book riddles, with other vernacular poetry, the Franks Casket, and the Ruthwell Cross also featuring prominently. The special nature of the riddles is explored directly by Benjamin C. Tilghman in his article 'On the Enigmatic Nature of Things in Anglo-Saxon Art', where he argues that the riddles advance 'a kind of early medieval "thing" theory' that provides us insight into the onto-logical systems governing what objects were to the cultures that made them.[38] James Paz also asserts that one of the three ways in which his own work advances new materialist scholarship on premodern culture is by recognizing 'the significance and relevance of Old English riddles and riddling culture to the role that things play in this early period'.[39] Corinne Dale's book is of course entirely about the riddles, with significant portions or chapters dedicated to them also in Ferhatović's and Estes's monographs.

I mention this focus on the riddles, vernacular poetry, and inscribed 'speaking objects' not because I disagree with any of its conclusions, from which my own work has profited greatly, but only because it helps limn one distinctive point about *Materializing Englishness*.[40] The arch-ive here is fairly diverse, linguistically, temporally, and generically, and includes hagiography, history, documentary texts, and poetry, as well as unnamed (in the sense of not having a title assigned by scholars) things like grave markers and metalwork. The argument is founded on the work of historians, literary scholars, archaeologists, and palaeograph-ers, but also engages research from disciplines such as pedology, plant science, and parasitology, among others. In defining what it is that brings this material together, I am drawn to and inspired by Mel Y. Chen's discussion of the feral, a term she uses for her own 'shifting archive' and her approach to the usual proprietary constraints of disciplinarity.[41] In describing the reasons why she analyses the particu-lar twentieth- and twenty-first-century cultural productions that she

---

[38] Benjamin C. Tilghman, 'On the Enigmatic Nature of Things in Anglo-Saxon Art', *Different Visions: A Journal of New Perspectives on Medieval Art* 4 (2014): pp. 1–43, at p. 2.

[39] Paz, *Nonhuman Voices*, p. 5.

[40] See my 'Becoming an Onion: The Extra-Human Nature of Genital Difference in the Old English Riddling and Medical Traditions', *English Studies* 101.1 (2020): pp. 60–78.

[41] Chen, *Animacies*, p. 18.

does, she writes: 'it is my intention and design that the archives themselves feralize, giving up any idealization about their domestication, refusing to answer whether they constitute proper or complete coverage'.[42] Tracing a 'rangy, somewhat unruly construct' with 'a capacity to romp through, under, and over...hierarchical knowledges'—like animacy—requires feral disciplinarity that, in turn, yields a feral archive unrecognizable or nameable by the conventional terms of scholarly investigation and resistant to the myth of comprehensiveness that often serves to authenticate our investigations.[43] Unlike interdisciplinarity, which remains within the proper space between disciplines, or the (explicitly masculine) *bricoleur* who fabricates from what is at hand, 'feral transdisciplinarity' ranges widely and a little bit wildly but does not just wander. Following the traces of clustered affinities, a feralized argument is entirely logical on its own terms but does not look so from traditional vantage points about the way that material for study is related, leading to groupings being designated by terms like 'eclectic' and posing the risk that a feral argument will be misrecognized or discredited. In attempting to provide the 'fuller treatment of materiality in Old English texts' that Estes among others has noted would be of interest to the field of early medieval studies, *Materializing Englishness* aims to track its subject through a wide disciplinary landscape, admitting unusual combinations into the archive of primary and secondary material, despite the risk.[44]

The first chapter focuses on early English hagiography, a genre with very particular links to place. In early medieval England, as elsewhere in Europe, association with a local saint gave a place an identity, while the practice of pilgrimage created a conceptual network in which towns and cities could be linked along itineraries. For example, if we are to believe Ælfric, hundreds visited St Swithun's tomb at Winchester (Wulfstan of Winchester even claims that it was thousands). Texts such as the *Lives of Saints*, Bede's *Historia ecclesiastica*, and the *Old English Martyrology* worked to disseminate information about saints

---

[42] Ibid., p. 18.     [43] Ibid., p. 18 and p. 234.

[44] Estes, *Anglo-Saxon Literary Landscapes*, p. 185. In his very favourable review of Estes's book, Michael Bintley agrees that an area for further study is 'better understanding and representation of the material contexts of early medieval literature and documentary historical sources' (Review of Heide Estes, *Anglo-Saxon Literary Landscapes: Ecotheory and the Environmental Imagination, TMR* 18.11.06).

and the places that held their relics. However, hagiographical texts are not simply vehicles for content about saints and the places where they are interred. This chapter argues that early English saints' lives, particularly those of Oswald and Cuthbert as popularized by their inclusion in Bede's *Historia ecclesiastica*, productively fused geography and history by means of miracles of saintly earth. It also asserts that, via reading or hearing the story, this fused product could be intruded into the body of the reader or auditor. More particularly, these saints' lives provide a model of ingestion in which the event of the saint's martyrdom permeates the landscape in the form of blood, and is then absorbed into the body of the worshipper who ingests a portion of this sacralized earth. As the chapter shows in close readings of posthumous miracles mentioned by Bede and the compiler of the *Old English Martyrology*, the soil, which nourishes both physically and spiritually, literally composes part of an English body connected, in its fabric, to land and history.

Where the first chapter is concerned with how place and history infuse the matter of the English body through ingestion of a rapidly changing substance—soil—the second chapter examines what is in a way the opposite process: marking the dissolution of the dead and decaying body into the landscape by means of a very slow-changing substance—stone. This chapter contextualizes changing practices of treating the dead body in late ninth-century England, and particularly the growing use of inscribed grave markers, within what I call more broadly 'mortuary discourse'. While written texts in this period in England are a relatively novel mode for preserving the details of historical events, these works also frequently register anxieties about the permanence of the record at the very same time that they include it. In a wide-ranging reading of lapidary and textual examples, the chapter demonstrates that tombstone inscriptions are a particularly interesting case of this phenomenon, because at the same time that their locative language ('here lies . . .') insists on a stable connection between textual record, matter (the dead body), and land (the burial place), the propensity to move and to recopy them always offers the possibility that this link will be truncated or reassigned. As much as tombstone inscriptions uphold the promise that writing will combat the disappearing matter of history, they also offer a model of text that is authorized and underpinned, quite literally, by the fecund body of the historical agent beneath the marker. The second half of the chapter turns to the *Anglo-Saxon Chronicle*, arguing that the locative *'her'* that opens almost every annal intrudes itself into this circuit, borrowing from the logic of tombstones to insist on a material link between the embodied act of reading and the insular history recorded in the text. By revealing the *Chronicle*'s links to what the first half of the chapter has identified as mortuary discourse, I argue that it also borrows a specific historio-graphic logic from tombstones, one capable of materially linking the past of events to the present space of reading.

Where the first two chapters focus on the earlier part of the period, the final half of the book concentrates on the eleventh century, in particular the strains placed upon an embodied model of English identity by the Scandinavian invasions of the late tenth and early eleventh centuries. I argue that Æthelred's reign witnesses a movement toward an English identity that is in some respects precipitated by Scandinavian invasions that simultaneously strengthen and complicate notions of what it means to be English. As the English imaginary flexes to accommodate Scandinavian invaders, the very notion of an embodied English subject at the meeting point of history and geog-raphy receives certain challenges. It is evident from contemporary discussion of hairstyles, for instance, and from surviving metalwork, that people in England at this time are experimenting with new Scan-dinavian fashions in personal appearance. These experiments would seem to 'empty out' or confuse any sense of the body as capable of manifesting a distinctively English identity. However, beyond these brief discussions of hairstyles, contemporary texts do not engage in much sustained discussion of the effect of Scandinavian invasions and migration. In the absence of robust textual evidence for acculturation, the final two chapters take up the question of how ethnic identity might have been experienced and lived in the early eleventh century by establishing new and perhaps surprising contexts for reading and understanding those English narratives that do feature Scandinavians.

In particular, the third chapter reconstructs the larger network within which surviving textual accounts of the St Brice's Day Massacre would have functioned, in an attempt to understand how this violent and still largely opaque event would have resonated at the time. Central to the chapter is the closest and most direct source on the massacre, a charter issued in 1004 by Æthelred to St Frideswide's monastery,

Oxford, which describes the killing in terms borrowed from Matthew 13:24-30, the parable of the cockles among the wheat. The chapter considers the specific effect of this comparison—of the English to wheat and the Scandinavians to weeds—on an audience familiar with real cornfield weeds, their growth habits, and the controlled dangers of ingesting them. The comparison that the charter draws between invasive plants and people is not just figural within the predominantly agricultural community of early eleventh-century England, but part of a material continuum including actual encounters with weeds. By necessity these encounters would have involved paying close attention to the physical characteristics of weeds, in order to identify their differences from crop plants, and may also have involved bodily illness caused by accidentally eating them. Adequately understanding the meaning of the charter, then, involves acknowledging that encounters with weeds, reading about weeds, and encounters with people represented as weeds mingle together on a continuum involving both discursive and material modes of being English. And as much as the author(s) of the charter might wish to harden the boundaries of the identity position 'English' in response to a perceived porosity to 'Scandinavian-ness', representing the English and Scandinavians as cockles and wheat always troublingly returns the idea that one can be mistaken for the other. Rather than determining the metaphor, the botanical matter both reinforces and challenges in interesting ways that would not have been lost on an early medieval English audience.

The final chapter turns to the most well-known text copied during Æthelred's reign, *Beowulf*, arguing that the poem's focus on fragmented bodies resonates with the type of volatility explored in the previous chapter as characterizing the English body at the opening of the eleventh century. Understanding the ways that *Beowulf*, a poem set in sixth-century Scandinavia, relates to the embodiment of English identity in the eleventh century raises complex questions about chronology and method that are distinctive to the material of this chapter. However, the chapter argues that *Beowulf* refracts, in a removed or altered state, the same kinds of concern with the precarity and instability of embodied identity that were discussed in the previous chapter. In particular, by closely reading the use of body parts in the poem through the lens of museum theory, this chapter argues that *Beowulf* functions as a type of manual of the ways that the body can be harnessed to political and identificatory structures, and also of the ways that it resists full co-optation by these systems. Unlike the previous chapters, then, this last focuses on poetry's value for modelling ways of using, reacting to, and understanding the body; but it also argues that poetry registers the body's resistance to the discursive systems in which it is pressed to serve, and within which poetry itself resides.

Taken together, the four chapters aim to recognize the way that bodies congeal flesh, imaginary systems, elements, chemicals, words—to take seriously, in other words, early medieval English notions of the transformative interactions between people and world.

# The Workings of Soil in Early English Hagiography

When in the early fifth century Bishop Germanus of Auxerre visits England, Bede tells us that he takes back with him a somewhat unusual souvenir: blood-infused soil from St Alban's death-site. Bede writes that 'de loco ipso, ubi beati martyris effusus erat sanguis, massam pulueris secum portaturus abstulit, in qua apparebat cruore seruato rubuisse martyrum caedem persecutore pallente'[1] (he collected a heap of soil from the place where the blood of the blessed martyr had been shed, to take away with him. In it the blood still showed, pointing to the contrast between the scarlet tide of martyrdom and the pale visage of the persecutor.) This detail of the blood-red earth, which originates in the anonymous *Passio S. Albani*, clearly struck Bede as an arresting way to supplement his main source for this section, Constantius's *Vita*

---

[1] Bede, i.18. All quotations from the *Historia* in both Latin and English translation are drawn from *Bede's Ecclesiastical History of the English People*, edited by Bertram Colgrave and R. A. B. Mynors (Oxford: Clarendon Press, 1969). A number of terms for soil exist in Latin and Old English, including *pulvis*, *humus*, *solum*, *terra*, and *lutum*, and, in the vernacular, *dust*, *mold*, *lam*, and *eorþ*. Of these, *pulvis* and *dust* are the most commonly used for saintly earth. Both also connote the material of the human body, from which it is made and to which it returns. In addition, the semantic range of these words indicates something about the texture and content of the soil, with *dust* being used for drier soil with small particles, *lam* often indicating high moisture content, and *eorþ* denoting both soil and the totality of soil ('the earth'), as it still does in Modern English.

*Materializing Englishness in Early Medieval Texts.* Jacqueline Fay, Oxford University Press.
© Jacqueline Fay 2022. DOI: 10.1093/oso/9780198757573.003.0002

*S. Germani*, which treats the episode much more allusively.[2] Where the *Vita S. Germani* only notes that Germanus visited the place where Alban was venerated, the anonymous *vita* and other sources indicate that he performed a relic exchange while he was there, taking the earth and leaving relics of the apostles and martyrs; upon returning to Auxerre, he used the soil to dedicate a church there to St Alban. Unlike the sand or stones that contemporary visitors might perhaps take home from a beach they have visited, Germanus of Auxerre takes this particular soil because it is special, not to him alone as a reminder of a place but to others as a tangible manifestation of the saint and, as Bede notes, as a healing remedy. Because of its miracle-working properties, soil infused with the blood of saints was highly desired by the sick, who would introduce it to their bodies by topically applying it to the skin, keeping it in their clothing in a bag, or drinking a solution of it in water. No wonder then that desire for the soil at a host of locations associated with saints—not only the place where they violently met their deaths but also where the water used to wash their translated bones is poured, and all their burial sites—becomes so immoderate that, in a number of cases, a large hole remains from the removal of earth.

The appetite for saintly soil is not surprising given the immense importance of the cult of saints to medieval communities throughout Europe. As Peter Brown memorably and aptly described them, saints were the 'special dead', deceased people whose life, works, or mode of death had earned them a privileged place in heaven next to the divine.[3] After death, they embarked on a second career as mediators for living Christians looking for guidance or miraculous intervention in situations where few other remedies presented themselves, such as illness, poverty, temptation, failure of the harvest, or a host of other material, spiritual, or emotional challenges. Saints served as conduits between

---

[2] For the relationship among the sources, see Richard Sharpe, 'Martyrs and Local Saints in Late Antique Britain', in *Local Saints and Local Churches in the Early Medieval West*, edited by Alan Thacker and Richard Sharpe (Oxford: Oxford University Press, 2002), pp. 75–154, at pp. 113–18.

[3] Peter Brown, *The Cult of the Saints: Its Rise and Function in Latin Christianity* (Chicago: University of Chicago Press, 1981). For an introduction to saints in early medieval England, see Michael Lapidge, 'The Saintly Life in Anglo-Saxon England', in *The Cambridge Companion to Old English Literature* (Cambridge: Cambridge University Press, 2006), pp. 243–63, and David Rollason, *Saints and Relics in Anglo-Saxon England* (Oxford: Blackwell, 1989).

the earthly world and the divine realm, which was otherwise not directly accessible to medieval Christians. And relics—body parts of saints or objects that they had touched during their life or after their death—served as portals by which this line of contact was most immediately and powerfully opened.[4] Pathways, those worn by pilgrims journeying to visit relics and by the relics themselves as they found new homes through trade, gift or theft, formed trans-European networks linking medieval communities. None of this would have been possible, however, without a popular and standardized textual form for disseminating information about the lives of these special dead: a genre, hagiography, that authenticated these individuals by shaping the details of their lives within a well-established narrative arc, including a selection of expected, even required, elements such as miraculous healings, prescient childhood behaviour, extreme resistance to temptation, the ability to survive with little or no food and water, and many others.

Advertising is a crude analogue for hagiography, but both do employ stories to craft perception and to reach a wide audience. Like advertising, the norms of hagiography did not only record but also influenced how saints lived, and this collapse between life and art is indicated in the designation 'saints' lives', the term for this type of text. Such works also addressed themselves to authenticating relics by including predictable stories about their discovery or the miracles they had engendered as part of the narrative of a saint's life, which was especially necessary since most relics were visually unremarkable objects like small bones or cloths. So quotidian were the forms of relic objects, and so subject to decay and dissolution, that all were often referred to by the general descriptor 'dust', forcefully reminding medieval Christians of the relic's position on the border of life and death.[5] Many early relics, as Cynthia Hahn notes in her study of medieval reliquaries, literally were dirt or small pebbles, just like the earth pocketed by Bishop Germanus.

The particular treatment of such a diffuse material as saintly soil— how individuals find it, interact with it, preserve it, and whether and

---

[4] For information about relics, see Alexandra Walsham, 'Introduction: Relics and Remains', *Past and Present* 5 (2010): pp. 9–36, and the other essays in this collection, as well as Cynthia Hahn, *The Reliquary Effect: Enshrining the Sacred Object* (London: Reaktion Books, 2017).

[5] Walsham, 'Relics and Remains', pp. 19–22. See also Michael Marder, *Dust* (London: Bloomsbury, 2016), for the ways that dust troubles ontological boundaries.

how they write about it in early medieval England—will be the topic of this chapter. As much as interaction with such saintly earth, including the grisly detail of its visible infusion with blood, is a material phenomenon involving digging, touching, and eating, this interaction is also simultaneously a symbolic act. The blood in the soil taken from Alban's death-site is not 'just' blood, but also refers to the role of martyrdom within Christian history, which Bede makes obvious by noting that it 'in qua apparebat cruore seruato rubuisse martyrum caedem persecutore pallente' (points to the contrast between the scarlet tide of martyrdom and the pale visage of the persecutor).[6] Bede's comment indicates how tangled are the material and discursive elements that inform and compose saintly earth, which is both subject to sensory consumption (viewing, touching, and tasting) but also representational (gesturing toward types, 'martyr' and 'persecutor', in a universal narrative of good and evil). Neither element, the materiality of the soil and blood or the discursive interpretive layer, is separable from the other, which begs the question of exactly what people are eating when they consume saintly earth.

While such interactions with sacred soil are happening all over Europe, and are based on scriptural precedent, those associated with early English saints are distinctive in several respects that warrant further examination. The way that the saint's dead body is treated in England is the result of an idiosyncratic combination of European practices and popular devotion, the constellation of which encourages a uniquely intimate and hands-on encounter with the corpse in various stages of post-mortem preparation and care. In addition to this, Bede's careful propagation of certain native saints in the *Historia ecclesiastica* preserves stories of sacred soil and makes them a central part of lives told and retold in the pre-Conquest hagiographical tradition. Alban, Oswald, and Cuthbert, among other early island saints, are associated with numerous local sites and miracles resulting from sacred earth that, in the earliest hagiographical texts associated with them, would have served to foster their regional followings among a community somewhat familiar with the places themselves. But the enduring popularity of these saints throughout the period, and the continuing re-

---

[6] Bede, i.18.

narrativization of their lives, made practices of creating, collecting, and consuming saintly soil part of a much larger materialized sanctity that served to infuse history and place into the bodies of worshippers and readers.

It is easy to dismiss these practices of collecting and consuming saintly soil as simply a well-accepted part of the cult of saints, and therefore while peculiar, perhaps superstitious from a modern point of view, understandable from the perspective of hagiographers searching for miracles by which to authorize their subjects, or sick people desperate for a cure for their many ailments. But to do so is to set aside, as Stephen Justice observes in his essay 'Did the Middle Ages Believe in their Miracles?', the question of faith entirely.[7] If we emphasize how hagiographers like Bede write about miracles of sacred earth they have not witnessed, but which are useful to their project of narrating the lives of saints, we assume a self-conscious pursuit of the benefits that such stories could bring but short circuit the question of whether hagiographers believed what they were writing. Similarly, if we understand those who used sacred earth as a healing remedy as being either naive or desperate, we reinstate the opposite notion of the childish medieval consciousness, creating a polarity between conniving hagiographers and the credulous 'ordinary' subjects of their stories. To bring Justice's point to bear upon miracles of sacred earth in particular, to rest at the level of the text and the hagiographer is to sidestep the question of the soil's materiality and, notwithstanding the many textual records of its efficacy, the complex question of how sacred earth worked and what its effects were (on place, on the worshipper, on the community, on the body, etc). But approaching these questions is extraordinarily difficult, since soil is always changing. Defined by the National Soil Resources Institutes as a combination of mineral material, organic material, air, and water, soil 'is made from the breaking down of rocks and organic matter by physical, chemical and biological processes' that never cease.[8] The matter of medieval earth has thus long been consumed by worms or penitents, its component elements broken down many times over by

[7] *Representations* 103 (2008): pp. 1–29.
[8] 'Glossary of Soil-related Terms', Cranfield University, National Soil Resources Institute (2011), http://www.landis.org.uk/sitereporter/glossary.pdf.

weathering and transformed into other substances or buried under successive soil horizons.

Given that soil never stays the same, it makes particularly obvious what is a general problem of the attempt to recover some connection with the lost material world of the past. Looking to the cult of saints, as a place where the material and the discursive are thoroughly enmeshed, proves useful in this effort. Comprising both devotional practices and complex sets of texts, both oral and written, that authorize, record, and promote these practices, it is hard indeed to say where the textual 'edge' of the cult of saints ends and the material begins. And far from being a discourse entirely controlled by the church, the worship of saints very clearly receives impetus from popular devotion, and thus mingles official and unofficial discourses. The cult of saints, in early medieval England as elsewhere in Europe, is thus multiple and discontinuous in nature, a compendious set of practices and texts that refuses easy categorization and that sustains mutually contradictory thinking about important concepts such as place and time.

This chapter will pursue an interdisciplinary approach to the question of saintly soil in early medieval England, using scholarship on landscape history, knowledge about contemporary practices of pica (or the consumption of non-food substances), and research in geobiology to investigate how such earth was made, how it worked, and what its effects were. This approach allows for a recognition of the agency of soil as a material substance both independent of and part of the fabric of the human body, and as existing outside of a discourse that also partially constructs it. New ways of understanding the role of sacred earth in hagiographical texts open from taking this 'view from the soil' or, as Michael Marder puts it, from re-experiencing texts *sub specie pulveris*, under the aspect of dust'.[9] Once sacred soil is viewed as having a symbiotic relationship with the various components that contribute to its production and that receive its effects—namely, the saint, the *vita*, the caretakers of the saint, and those who seek healing—it becomes possible to observe the ebb and flow of this material-discursive trajectory through bodies, earth, and texts. Stories about sacred soil allow us to discern at some remove the desires and needs of that soil's original

---

[9] Marder, *Dust*, p. 33.

users, who took it in hope of receiving some beneficial effect that would ameliorate their cares, illnesses, poverty. By focusing on the soil itself, this chapter will recover the unrecognized agency of this soil in organizing and disorganizing human intentions, desires, and groups. More specifically, the chapter will trace the material and narrative networks that establish the properties of very particular, localized soils and then subsequently build potential for all soil in early medieval England to become porous to historical events that it served to transform into a consumable substance.

## Sacred earth and early English saints

The association of a number of important early English saints with sacred earth is cemented by the *vitae* provided for them by Bede in his *Historia Ecclesiastica*, the widespread readership for which is well attested and needs no further rehearsal here. However, while his text shapes and disseminates narratives about saintly soil, Bede is unlikely to have been inventing these episodes wholesale. There is no reason to suppose that he is not describing (albeit in a complicated and mediated fashion) real practices of taking and consuming soil, and the actual holes in the ground that were the result of such practices. As John Blair notes, Bede here 'recycles material that is recognizably vernacular folklore' into passages that are often treated by scholars as though they were exceptional, but in fact record behaviours that were likely widespread and normal at the time.[10] Blair writes that the relationship between 'the stable (often aridly stable) idiom of saints' lives' and what he aptly calls the 'kaleidoscopic fluidity of folklore' is very hard to determine when it can only be approached through texts.[11] And '[y]et the attempt is worth making', because within saints' lives may lie 'fossilized' the perceptions of seventh- to ninth-century lay people about saints and, I would add, the lost material transactions involved in their veneration. While I will return to the question of origins at greater length in the next section, it is important to remember, before

[10] John Blair, *The Church in Anglo-Saxon Society* (Oxford: Oxford University Press, 2005), p. 148.
[11] Ibid., p. 148.

turning to those saints about whom Bede writes, that these particular
stories of saintly earth concern only a small portion of the soil that was
taken, consumed, and which left behind holes in the ground.

While the use of saintly soil was likely to have been somewhat
commonplace, those saints with whom it is associated in the *Historia*
are anything but ordinary. Ultimately, while many other saints no
doubt provoked similar miracles of sacred earth but were later forgot-
ten, at least outside of their local communities, the saints promoted by
Bede were not. The prominence and longevity of Bede's text is worth
bearing in mind, because it significantly broadens the effect that saintly
earth can be assumed to have had on the early medieval English in
general, rather than just those who consumed it in the environs of each
cult site. Within the *Historia*, saintly earth is associated with a particular group of saints connected to each other and/or to the monastery of
Lindisfarne, and all of whom died within a half-century span coinciding with the explosive growth of monasticism at the close of the seventh
century[12]: Oswald (d. 642), the king of Northumbria who was responsible for inviting Aidan from Iona and appointing him first bishop of
Lindisfarne; Chad (d. 672), a pupil of Aidan at Lindisfarne, and subsequent bishop of Lichfield; Cuthbert, Lindisfarne's most famous bishop
(d. 687); and Hædde (d. 705), bishop of Wessex. Of these, the latter is
by far the least well known, being perhaps best recognized for preceding
Aldhelm in the episcopate. However, he is named in the life of Oswald
as the person responsible for translating Bishop Birinus, whom Oswald
and Cynegils of Wessex appointed to his see, from Dorchester to
Winchester. Although these four saints receive very different treatment
in the *Historia*—from a brief mention to the rendition of numerous
posthumous miracles—all four *vitae* gesture to the appetite at the close
of the seventh century and into the eighth for saintly earth. Newly
established minsters and their surrounding communities strongly
manifest a desire for their own saints at this time and, with a fluid set
of conventions on how to make these saints, miracles of saintly earth
serve to forge potent local connections between people, place, and saint.
This first section will review the details of these saints' lives and their
associations with sacred soil; the following portion of the chapter will

[12]  Ibid., pp. 79–100.

be dedicated to understanding how such saintly earth works; and the final part will consider the implications for a material understanding of Englishness as, due to their inclusion in Bede's *Historia*, these originally local saints gradually become English saints.

The most intense exploration of the concept of saintly place in the *Historia ecclesiastica* concerns Oswald, with seven chapters devoted to his reign and a further five to his death and posthumous miracles. Bede's text is the primary source for the life of Oswald, although its fantastic elements have long caused scholars to question its veracity; as Clare Stancliffe observes, 'one cannot help wondering about the artificiality of the role which the History assigns to Oswald'.[13] In depicting Oswald as a saint, Bede is breaking new ground, as Alan Thacker, Clare Stancliffe, and others have noted, because as a Germanic warrior king, Oswald made for a somewhat unusual male saint, since he hardly embodied humility and pacifism.[14] While early medieval England has a higher concentration of royal saints than other countries, later candidates conform more closely to the paradigm of saintliness, either by being martyred or by withdrawing into monastic life.[15] That Oswald did neither is probably one of the reasons for the particular density of spatial concerns in his *vita*, as stories about places provide a pragmatic method to supplement the lack of miracles, as well as to detract from the violence he committed, in his life.

The political circumstances of Oswald's reign identify him as a key figure, for Bede and others, of a fledgling notion of English political and territorial unity. He came to the throne at a tumultuous time in Northumbria's history, when the death of Edwin at the hands of the British

---

[13] Clare Stancliffe, 'Oswald, "Most Holy and Victorious King of the Northumbrians"', in *Oswald: Northumbrian King to European Saint*, edited by Clare Stancliffe and Eric Cambridge (Stamford: Paul Watkins, 1995), pp. 33–83, at p. 35, n. 8.

[14] Alan Thacker, '*Membra Disjecta*: The Division of the Body and the Diffusion of the Cult', in *Oswald*, pp. 97–127, at p. 106; Stancliffe, 'Oswald', pp. 41–2.

[15] Rollason, *Saints and Relics*, pp. 124–8. For a study of pre-Conquest regal saints, see Susan J. Ridyard, *The Royal Saints of Anglo-Saxon England* (Cambridge: Cambridge University Press, 1988). Although Ridyard notes that Bede never explicitly refers to Oswald as a martyr (p. 93, n. 80), she believes that Bede was portraying him as such (p. 243). For the contrasting view that Bede represents Oswald gaining sanctity because of his faith during his life, rather than because of the circumstances of his death, see Victoria A. Gunn, 'Bede and the Martyrdom of St Oswald', *Studies in Church History* 30 (1993): pp. 57–66.

had broken apart the union of the kingdoms of Deira and Bernicia that Edwin had cemented.[16] Oswald—no friend of Edwin, whose kingship was achieved by killing and supplanting Oswald's father, and driving his sons into exile—nevertheless realized the unifying political and spiritual goals that had characterized his predecessor's reign, but that had been abandoned by Edwin's immediate successors, those apostate kings whom Bede wanted struck from the historical record.[17] Fragmentation of the combined Christian kingdom of Northumbria was an especial fear of both Edwin and Oswald, because their expansionist ambitions had created a common enemy of the pagan Britons and Mercians, led by Cadwallon and Penda. Both Northumbrian kings chose to make alliances with southern rulers in order to combat this threat, Edwin forging links with Kent and Oswald with Wessex.

Oswald, having successfully defeated Cadwallon at the battle of Heavenfield in 634 and decisively laid to rest British claims to the northern kingdoms, ruled his combined Northumbrian kingdom for eight years. During his early years as king, he invited an Ionan bishop, Aidan, to evangelize and establish the Christian faith in his kingdom. Having lived in exile for seventeen years among the Irish community of Dál Riada in western Scotland before taking the throne, Oswald was himself familiar both with Christianity and with the Irish language, and acted on several occasions as Aidan's interpreter. Both Aidan and Oswald became, and were closely associated as, saints, but the nature of Oswald's death, as Alan Thacker puts it, 'offered exceptional opportunities to the impresarios of his cult', beyond those available for Aidan.[18] Killed by a familiar combined force of Britons and Mercians, Oswald's head and arms were severed and hung on stakes after his death, allowing for the dispersal of his relics and subsequent wide

---

[16] The following account of the historical background to Oswald's reign is based on Rosemary Cramp, 'The Making of Oswald's Northumbria', in *Oswald*, pp. 17–32, and Clare Stancliffe, 'Oswald.'

[17] Bede notes of these kings, Osric of Deira and Eanfrith of the Bernicians, that '[V]nde cunctis placuit regum tempora computantibus ut, ablata de medio regum perfidorum memoria, idem annus sequentis regis, id est Osualdi uiri Deo dilecti, regno adsignaretur' (So all those who compute the dates of kings have decided to abolish the memory of those perfidious kings and to assign this year to their successor Oswald, a man beloved of God), Bede, iii.1.

[18] Thacker, '*Membra Disjecta*', p. 101.

dissemination of his cult within England.[19] The play between fragmentation and unity in the role of Oswald's dead body, the dissolution of which enhanced its potential to unite devotional communities, replicated the central concerns of his life as king, during which time he was concerned to hold together a previously divided Northumbrian kingdom and to make new alliances with southern rulers. Both his life and afterlife, therefore, were very much shaped by the themes of territorial and communal consolidation.

As several scholars have astutely observed, probably because of his overt adherence to the Roman custom of keeping saints' bodies intact, Bede seems a little uncomfortable with Oswald's fragmentary post-mortem state and, although the severing of his head and arms is mentioned twice in the *Historia*, the saint is generally presented as entire.[20] While the Britons may have put Oswald's body on show, Bede thus refuses to, highlighting instead the saint's links to various places contacted by his living and dead body. The first of these, at Heavenfield, is the site at which Oswald erected a cross and prayed before his victory against the Britons in 634; the second, at Maserfelth, is the location of his death in 642.[21] The *inventio* and *translatio* of his body to Bardney between 679 and 697, engineered by his niece Osthryth of Mercia, generated two further holy sites, one at the new tomb and another at a place where water, used to wash the bones, was poured away.

Because Oswald died in battle, Bede dedicates a considerable amount of narrative attention to the discovery of his death-site, providing two accounts of its miraculous discovery. In the first of these, a sick horse fortuitously rolls onto the exact spot where Oswald had died and is immediately cured. As luck would have it, a 'uir sagacis ingenii' (intelligent man) happens to be passing by at this exact moment and realizes that what he has witnessed must be due to a holy man having died at the place in the past. After marking the spot, a paralysed girl is brought

---

[19] See Clare Stancliffe and Eric Cambridge, 'Introduction', in *Oswald*, pp. 1–12, at p. 2, for Oswald's importance as a saint in early medieval England and on the Continent.

[20] Bede, iii.6, 12.

[21] Bede describes Oswald's death occurring 'in loco qui lingua Anglorum nuncupatur Maserfelth' (in a place called in the English tongue *Maserfelth*), iii.9. There is no modern English version of *Maserfelth* and the site is generally associated with Oswestry, Shropshire, for reasons summarized and discussed by Clare Stancliffe, 'Where Was Oswald Killed?', in *Oswald*, pp. 84–96.

to the site and cured, thus confirming the perceptive passer-by's supposition. In the second account, a Briton notices the intense greenness and lush growth of the place where Oswald had died, and removes some earth, which is subsequently miraculously preserved through a fire at the house where he spends the night. Subsequently, Bede notes, so much earth was removed from the place, where miracles continue up to the moment of his writing, that a large hole remained:

> Vnde contigit ut puluerem ipsum, ubi corpus eius in terram conruit, multi auferentes et in aquam mittentes suis per haec infirmis multum commodi adferrent. Qui uidelicet mos adeo increbruit, ut paulatim ablata exinde terra fossam ad mensuram staturae uirilis altam reddiderit.[22]

> (It has happened that people have often taken soil from the place where his body fell to the ground, have put it in water, and by its use have brought great relief to their sick. This custom became very popular and gradually so much earth was removed that a hole was made, as deep as a man's height.)

Even though such ready proliferation of holy places, and particularly the detail of holes in the landscape, has often been seen as marking a cult's popular orientation, they are also a feature of large-scale cult complexes, such as those associated with Cuthbert.[23] Cuthbert was born around a year after the beginning of Oswald's reign, c.635, and lived forty-five years after its end. Even though the pair travelled together after death, when Oswald's head was placed in Cuthbert's coffin, Cuthbert was a much more conventional saintly figure than Oswald had been. He famously was both a hermit and a bishop, and thus his life had enormous potential for reconciling the eremitic and pastoral strands of previous hagiographical models, including Benedict, Anthony, and Martin.[24] A prior at Melrose and Lindisfarne, Cuthbert

---

[22] Bede, iii.9.

[23] Alan Thacker, 'The Making of a Local Saint', in *Local Saints and Local Churches in the Early Medieval West*, edited by Alan Thacker and Richard Sharpe (Oxford: Oxford University Press, 2002), pp. 45–72, at p. 71.

[24] Clare Stancliffe, 'Cuthbert and the Polarity between Pastor and Solitary', in *St Cuthbert, his Cult and his Community to AD 1200*, edited by Gerald Bonner, David Rollason, and Clare Stancliffe (Woodbridge: The Boydell Press, 1989), pp. 21–44. For a summary of Cuthbert's life, see the 'Introduction' to this volume, pp. xxi–xxiii. Sulpicius Severus's *Vita S. Martini* and Athanasius's translation of Evagrius's *Vita S. Antonii* were

spent much of his life as a hermit on the island of Farne, where he performed a number of miracles. He reluctantly became bishop of Lindisfarne in 685, but retired to his island hermitage shortly before his death in 687. Having lived a deeply engaged life of religious and public service, Cuthbert was just as active after his death as he had been when alive. He was translated twice before the Lindisfarne community left the monastery around 875 for Chester-le-Street, taking Cuthbert's body with them, and he was moved from there to Durham in 995. During the tenth century, veneration of Cuthbert became, as Gerald Bonner puts it, 'diffused throughout England', and Cuthbert was to remain one of the most important medieval saints throughout the period.[25]

Cuthbert's prominence as a saint was fomented by a steady stream of hagiographical works focusing on his life and providing updates on his posthumous career of miracle-working. An anonymous monk of Lindisfarne produced a prose life of the saint around 700, very shortly after the body was first translated in 698.[26] This Latin *vita*, as Clare Stancliffe has argued, shares similarities with the *Vita Columbae* that Adomnan was writing around the same time, and thus offers up Cuthbert as the same type of founding saint for Northumbria as Columba was for Iona.[27] At the same time, however, the anonymous author rigorously asserted Cuthbert's adherence to Roman practices, even when that meant making slight changes to the historical record, such as claiming

---

being used as school texts by Theodore and Hadrian at Canterbury in the late seventh century. Michael Lapidge and Rosalind Love note that the prestige of the Canterbury school probably significantly elevated the preference for these hagiographical texts, particularly in England as models. See Lapidge and Love, 'The Latin Hagiography of England and Wales (600–1550)', in *Hagiographies: Histoire internationale de la littérature hagiographique latine et vernaculaire en Occident des origines à 1550/International History of the Latin and Vernacular Hagiographical Literature in the West from Its Origins to 1550*, vol. III, edited by Guy Philippart (Turnhout: Brepols, 1994–2006), pp. 203–325.

[25] 'St Cuthbert at Chester-le-Street,' in *St Cuthbert*, pp. 387–95, at p. 389.

[26] For the anonymous and Bede's prose lives, see *Two Lives of Saint Cuthbert: A Life by an Anonymous Monk of Lindisfarne and Bede's Prose Life*, edited and translated by Bertram Colgrave (Cambridge: Cambridge University Press, 1940). Following the practice established in *St Cuthbert, his Cult*, pp. xx, the anonymous life will be referred to below as *VCA* and Bede's prose life as *VCP*, with both cited by chapter.

[27] Stancliffe, 'Cuthbert, Pastor and Solitary', pp. 22–3.

that Cuthbert first received the Petrine tonsure in Ripon rather than, as was more likely the case, the Irish tonsure at Melrose.[28] Closely following the anonymous prose *vita*, Bede composed a metrical life for Cuthbert around 705, according to Michael Lapidge, which he then revised during the 720s, but certainly before 721 when he produced his own prose life of Cuthbert.[29] Bede also assigns Cuthbert an important place at the close of the fourth book of the *Historia*, indicating the growing recognition of the cult and the significance of the saint for Bede as a hagiographer and historian. As Walter Berschin points out, Bede likely composed the poetic *vita* in order to elevate Cuthbert to a status equivalent to St Martin, 'whose life the Latin public was accustomed to read in prose and in verse', while his prose *vita* was intended as a structural pair for the metrical version.[30] The paired metrical and prose lives allowed audiences to encounter Cuthbert's story on different levels: narratively in the prose *vita* and more contemplatively in the poetic work.[31]

In addition to having variant purposes, the growing corpus of Cuthbert lives includes an expanding number of tomb miracles, as would be expected with the increase in veneration and the spread of information outward from the cult centre. Bede, in his prologue to the prose life, explains at length that his information about Cuthbert derived from investigation and interviews with witnesses, and was reviewed both by Herefrith, a contemporary of Cuthbert, and the Lindisfarne monks.[32] Both the anonymous and Bede's prose *vitae* for Cuthbert include the miracle of a demoniac boy cured by drinking a solution of earth taken from the place where water used to wash Cuthbert's body had been poured.[33] Bede's version, which is typically more expansive and colourful than that of the anonymous author, also includes a fairly detailed description of the pit still evident at this site:

> Ostenditur usque hodie fossa illa cui memorabile infusum est lauacrum quadrato scemate facta, ligno undique circundata, et lapillis

---

[28] Stancliffe, 'Cuthbert, Pastor and Solitary'.

[29] Michael Lapidge, 'Bede's Metrical *Vita S. Cuthberti*', in *St Cuthbert*, pp. 77–93.

[30] Walter Berschin, '*Opus deliberatum ac perfectum*: Why Did the Venerable Bede Write a Second Prose Life of St Cuthbert?' in *St Cuthbert*, pp. 95–102.

[31] Lapidge, 'Bede's Metrical.'    [32] *VCP*, Prologue.

[33] *VCA*, IV: v; *VCP*, xli.

intus impleta. Est autem iuxta aecclesiam in qua corpus eius requiescit, ad partem meridianum. Factumque est ex eo tempore, ut plures sanitatum operationes per eosdem lapides uel eandem terram Domino donante fierent.[34]

(The pit is still shown today into which that memorable bath of water was poured—it is in the form of a square with a border of wood on all sides and filled up with pebbles; and it is moreover near the church in which his body rests, on the south side. And it happened from that time, by God's permission, that many miracles of healing took place by means of those same stones or with some of that earth.)

Bede does not mention this pit in the chapters dedicated to Cuthbert in the *Historia*, which is perhaps not surprising since he intends the posthumous miracles related there as an update to his earlier prose work on the saint.[35] Because Cuthbert is found incorrupt at his first translation, a broad range of miracle-working objects are associated with him, including shoes, vestments, hair, and other items, along with sacred earth. However, the *Historia* does reference another hole from the removal of saintly earth at the death-site of Bishop Hædde of the West Saxons:

Denique reuerentissimus antistes Pecthelm...referre est solitus, quod in loco quo defunctus est ob meritum sanctitatis eius multa sanitatum sint patrata miracula, hominesque prouinciae illius solitos ablatum inde puluerem propter languentes in aquam mittere atque huius gustum siue aspersionum multis sanitatem egrotis et hominibus et pecoribus conferre; propter quod frequenti ablatione pulueris sacri fossa sit ibidem facta non minima.[36]

(Bishop Pehthelm...used to relate that many miracles of healing happened on the spot where Hædde died, through the merits of his holiness. He said that the men of that kingdom used to take soil from the place and put it in water for the benefit of the sick, and both sick men and cattle who drank it or were sprinkled with it were healed. As a result of the constant removal of the sacred soil, a hole of considerable size was made there.)

As the description of the pit associated with Cuthbert's wash water indicates, some architectural effort was expended in order to maintain such sites and to allow worshippers easy access to the sacred dust they contained. In the case of the site associated with Cuthbert, the provision was a simple rigging of wood and stones; at St Chad's burial place, in contrast, Bede describes a much more elaborate house-like shrine with a hole in the side for pilgrims to gain access to saintly dust.[37] As John Blair observes, although the house-tomb is generally thought to have been constructed post-translation over Chad's new burial site, Bede actually states that it was built over the vacated grave, indicating that even sites empty of the saint's body were the subject of veneration and consumption.[38] In the cases of both Cuthbert and Chad, the maintenance of these places indicates that the border between popular and ecclesiastical practice was porous, and access to sacred earth was both controlled and encouraged by the church and also desired by a laity eager to heal themselves and their animals. The surviving hagiographical literature of early medieval England, and the practices it records, associate a number of important early English saints—Oswald, Cuthbert, Hædde, Chad—with healing soil so effective that the miracles it performs continue perpetually and its removal results in large holes in the landscape.

# Christian background to saintly earth

Scriptural texts circulating in early medieval England provide a number of sometimes contradictory models for saintly earth; it is important to understand these models since, while distinctive, English practices surrounding sacred soil do not come about independent of Continental tradition. For the idea that soil was profoundly changed by contact with a holy body, readers could look to the life of John the Evangelist and, of course, Christ himself. The life of John was available in early medieval England in several versions in both Latin and Old English. The ninth-century *Old English Martyrology* entry for John—which draws on the

---

[37] *Historia ecclesiastica*, iv.3.
[38] John Blair, 'A Saint for Every Minster? Local Cults in Anglo-Saxon England', in *Local Saints and Local Churches*, pp. 455–94, at pp. 490–4.

full-length life, Aldhelm's *Prosa de virginitate*; the Hiberno-Latin Pseudo-Isidore *De ortu* (a summary of the lives of scriptural people); and Scripture itself—is a useful summary of the details known in early medieval England about his tomb. The Martyrologist observes that

> æt þære byrg`i'ne bið wellmicel wundor gesewen/ and gehired: hwilon heo eðað swá lifiende man slape, hwilon þonne man þa byrgine sceawað, þonne ne bið þær nan lich(o)ma gesewen, ác bið micel swetnisse stenc. Forþam nat nænig man hwæþer sé Iohannes sí þe cwicu þe dead.[39]

> ([A]t the tomb are a great many wonders seen and heard: sometimes it breathes as though a living man were sleeping, sometimes when someone examines the tomb, then no body is seen there, but there is a very sweet smell. Therefore no one knows whether John be alive or dead.)

As Cross demonstrates, this entry blends the tradition that John was still alive, which led to the common convention of the breathing grave, with an alternative notion that he had already been resurrected, and that his grave would thus be found empty. In addition, the Martyrologist layers in a reference to miracles occurring at the possibly empty gravesite (the 'wellmicel wundor') found elsewhere only in the full life.[40] While the particularities of this situation derive from the peculiar mythology surrounding John's death, this entry ends up literalizing the conventional notion that a saint is simultaneously present in his or her grave and in heaven, as well as gesturing toward the notion that saints died only to be born into eternal life. The play between presence and absence of the body and that between life and death, however, leads to confusion of that further boundary between saintly body and place, with the grave understood to be sentient and alive. The grammatical gendering of Old English makes this particularly clear; in describing how 'hwilon heo eðað swá lifiende man slape', it is 'heo', or the feminine-gendered noun 'byrgine', that takes on attributes of the saint by breathing as though a living, sleeping man. This represents an extension of the

---

[39] *The* Old English Martyrology: *Edition, Translation and Commentary*, edited and translated by Christine Rauer (Rochester: Boydell and Brewer, 2014), ii.7. See also J. E. Cross, 'The Apostles in the Old English Martyrology', *Mediaevalia* 5 (1979): pp. 15–59, at p. 37.
[40] Cross, 'Old English Martyrology', pp. 35–6.

description provided by both Aldhelm and Pseudo-Isidore, who note that the dust on the surface of the tomb is moved 'quasi', as if by the breath of a living man within.[41] The source texts underlying the *Martyrology* entry, therefore, retain a notion of place as inert container for the body, whereas the rich grammatical and semantic confusion between these categories seems to be original to the Old English version, and underlies the production and capabilities of saintly earth.

Traditional and authorized accounts like the life of John the Evangelist inform early medieval Christians that the use of sacred earth in healing remedies makes sense because soil materializes place, saintly person, and events, usually miracles, and that this soil-matter can then serve to transform and repair the ailing fabric of the worshipper's body. Gregory's *Dialogi*, which includes an influential collection of miracle stories, provides one such example of earth removed from a holy place being used for its healing properties, when a man is returned from the dead after dust taken from the base of the altar is rubbed over his face.[42] This type of miracle performed by means of sacred earth may have been based on that described in John 9:1–12, where a blind man is healed after his eyes are anointed with a paste Jesus had made by spitting on dust. Most influential in shaping this trope of holy earth, however, were common stories of the Ascension site, which emphasize that, although the faithful remove dust from the place, the level of earth there is miraculously never diminished. As Bede writes in the *Historia ecclesiastica*:

> Interior namque domus propter dominici corporis meatum camerari et tegi non potuit, altare ad orientem habens angusto culmine protectum, in/ cuius medio ultima Domini uestigia, caelo desuper patente, ubi ascendit, uisuntur. Quae cum cotidie a credentibus terra tollatur, nihilominus manet, eandem que adhuc speciem ueluti inpressis signata uestigiis seruat.[43]

---

[41] For the text of these sources, see Cross, 'Old English Martyrology', p. 35, and Aldhelm, *The Prose Works*, edited and translated by Michael Lapidge and Michael Herren (Ipswich: D.S. Brewer, 1979), p. 81.

[42] Gregory the Great, *Dialogues*, edited by Adalbert de Vogüé, translated by Paul Antin, Sources Chrétiennes, 260 (Paris: les Éditions du Cerf, 1979), p. 338.

[43] *Historia ecclesiastica*, v.17. See also the *Old English Martyrology*, ii.85.

(The interior of the church could not be vaulted or roofed because the Lord's body passed up out of it. To the east it has an altar roofed in with a narrow canopy, and in the centre of the church are to be seen the last footprints of the Lord as He ascended, being open to the sky above. Although the earth is daily carried away by the faithful, yet it still remains and preserves the same appearance of having been marked by the impress of His feet.)

This important narrative demonstrates how an event, the Ascension, can both be in the past, as registered by the impress of Christ's feet, and yet in some sense be permanently in process, meaning that the church can never be enclosed with a roof. While the Ascension itself is extraordinary, the details of the account are paralleled elsewhere in saintly narratives that manifest the same powerful confusion of the categories of time, place, and person.

While places contacted by the body of Christ provide the model for these potent connections between the saint, the events of his life, and the landscape, significant details are distinctive to the English context, resulting in an expanded degree of interconnection between soil and saintliness. The origin of these practices, and the degree to which they represent a continuation of Romano-British customs, native innovation, or a Continental import are debated by scholars. The association of saintly earth with Alban as early as the fifth century indicates that removing and using such soil was actively practised during the period of Romano-British Christianity, and that it may have continued unabated as a popular custom through the disruption of religious traditions in Britain following the collapse of the Roman Empire. Richard Sharpe writes of the complicated genealogy underpinning the shift from late Roman to early medieval practices of venerating the saints, noting in particular the frequency with which martyrial sites in England developed around a secondary relic, such as a death-site or a place where water used to wash the body had been poured.[44] He notes that the presence of such sites in Roman and post-Roman Britain should be recognized as an equally important exemplar for the late Antique, and subsequently the early medieval, context as are imported models from the Continent. As he writes, 'the interest in venerating the

---

[44] Sharpe, 'Martyrs and Local Saints', p. 135.

martyrs and other saints of their own communities was neither a foreign import nor a literary construct: it was learnt through continuity of practice across Britain and Gaul.'[45] John Blair agrees, noting that the kind of cult practice surrounding Alban and other less well-attested Romano-British saints indicates a 'thread of influence from mainstream late Roman Christianity' that endures into the early medieval period.[46] Given the decline of Roman cities in Britain, as opposed to their continuation on the Continent, such practices seem likely to have drawn equally on the nature of the post-Roman British church as both a mainstream structure and a 'decentralized and rural' entity relying more on 'grass-roots support' than did its Continental counterparts.[47]

This continuity of practice in the treatment of saints and their secondary place-based relics would be reinforced in the seventh century by the importation to England from Francia of what Alan Thacker has described as a culture of 'intrepid interference' with the saintly body: handling, washing, removing and re-clothing the remains, as well as providing architectural access to saintly earth, become normative components in the rituals of saintly care-taking.[48] Moreover, while Francia largely abandons these physical practices in the treatment of saints under the Carolingian regime, preferring instead Roman customs, early medieval England maintained this focus on handling saints until at least the eleventh century.[49] Importantly, this set of practices allowed for increased proliferation of sites associated with the saint, especially those created by pouring away the wash water. In turn, these sites are subject to appetitive and immoderate desires for saintly earth. Thus, customs imported from a variety of geographical and textual contexts are combined in England into a procedure with an especially high degree of physicality, which in turn leads to the creation of many more sites generating saintly earth than would be available on the Continent.

---

[45] Ibid., p. 135.

[46] Blair, *The Church in Anglo-Saxon Society*, p. 13.

[47] Ibid., p. 10.

[48] Thacker, 'Making of a Local Saint', p. 57; John Crook, 'The Enshrinement of Local Saints in Merovingia and Carolingian Francia', in *Local Saints and Local Churches*, pp. 189–224.

[49] Crook, 'The Enshrinement of Local Saints', especially pp. 206–24.

This is remarkable, because despite the validation of sacred earth in association with Christian sites such as the Church of the Ascension, other biblical texts negatively associate such activities with subservience and punishment. Most famously, God issues punishment on the serpent in Genesis by saying, 'Đu gæst on ðinum breoste and ytst ða eorðan eallum dagum ðines lifes' (You will go upon your breast and eat earth for all the days of your life). Following this paradigmatic pronouncement, Psalm 72:9, Isaiah 49:23, and Micah 7:17 make reference to subduing enemies so completely that they will lick the dust at your feet. These biblical texts reinforce that, rather than a transcendent and healing experience to be sought out, having an intimate bodily encounter with soil is a mark of humiliation. The existence of such injunctions against eating earth, on one hand, indicates the special nature of saintly soil, since it provokes the opposite response. On the other hand, these narratives rely on the same sense of fundamental kinship between human and soil—that mankind comes from and will return to dust—also informing at some level those narratives of healing saintly earth in which soil is eaten or applied to the body. That people have a kinship to earth would be clear from texts such as Ælfric's homily for the First Sunday after Easter, which addresses the related topics of bodily resurrection from dust and God's creation of mankind from soil. Ælfric writes:

Nu is geðuht þæt him sy sumera ðinga eaðelicor to arærenne ðone deadan of ðam duste, þonne him wære to wyrcenne ealle gesceafte of nahte... He worhte Adam of lame. Nu ne mage we asmeagan hu he of ðam lame flæsc worhte, and blod ban and fell, fex and næglas. Men geseoð oft þæt of anum lytlum cyrnele cymð micel treow, ac we ne magon geseon on þam cyrnele naðor ne wyrtruman, ne rinde, ne bogas, ne leaf: ac se God þe forðtihð of ðam cyrnele treow, and wæstmas, and leaf, se ylca mæg of duste aræran flæsc and ban, sina and fex.[50]

---

[50] Ælfric, 'The First Sunday After Easter', edited and translated by Benjamin Thorpe, *The Homilies of the Anglo-Saxon Church: The Sermones Catholici or Homilies of Ælfric*, 1 (London, 1844; repr. New York, 1971), pp. 236–7. This passage is also quoted by Karen Jolly in 'Father God and Mother Earth: Nature-Mysticism in the Anglo-Saxon World', in *The Medieval World of Nature: A Book of Essays*, edited by Joyce E. Salisbury (New York: Garland, 1993), pp. 221–52, at p. 239, and in 'Magic, Miracle, and Popular Practice in the Early Medieval West: Anglo-Saxon England', *Religion, Science, and Magic: In Concert and*

(Now it seems that it is somewhat easier to him to raise the dead from the dust, than it was to him to make all creatures from naught...He wrought Adam from loam. Now we cannot investigate how of that loam he made flesh and blood, bones and skin, hair and nails. Men often see that of one little kernel comes a great tree, but in the kernel we can see neither root, nor rind, nor boughs, nor leaves: but the same God who draws forth from the kernel tree, and fruits, and leaves, may from dust raise flesh and bones, sinews and hair.)

Homilies on this topic, while making it clear that we cannot examine or discern exactly how God made flesh from soil, nonetheless clearly assert their shared properties. In this climate, the healing properties of saintly soil may be equally due to the special nature it derives from contact with a saint and to a material affinity between earth and flesh that allows these substances to reinvigorate and supplement each other.

# Pica and geophagy

Much of what scriptural precedents suggest about the workings of sacred earth in early medieval England agrees with insights derived from a very different area of scholarship: anthropological and scientific studies of the phenomenon of geophagy, or eating earth. Geophagy is a subtype of pica or, as Sera L. Young defines it, 'the craving and purposive consumption of items that the consumer does not consider to be food for more than a month', and has been practised for the whole of human history and on all six inhabited continents.[51] Although Young does not classify religious geophagy as pica in the strict sense of the term, she notes that non-religious and religious geophagy have much in common, particularly as spiritually prescribed earth shares the healing properties of geophagic earth more generally. In her review of contemporary religious geophagy, Young includes examples from Christianity, Islam, and Hinduism covering a wide geographical area

---

*In Conflict*, edited by Jacob Neusner, Ernest S. Frerichs, and Paul Virgil McCracken Flesher (Oxford: Oxford University Press, 1989), pp. 166–82, at p. 169.

[51] Sera L. Young, *Craving Earth: Understanding Pica* (New York: Columbia University Press, 2011), pp. 3–4.

from the United States to the Middle East and a range of desired outcomes, not only healing but also pregnancy or fidelity. Because this type of geophagy is promoted by a religious institution, the reasons motivating its practice can seem more obvious than those governing pica in general which, despite being so widely observed, is not entirely understood either by those who eat earth or by those scholars studying the phenomenon. But to suggest that religious geophagy can be explained as an ideological practice whereas 'ordinary' geophagy cannot is to impose a material/cultural binary that is too rigid to accommodate the complexity characterizing the field of geophagic behaviours. As Young writes,

> Pica has deep roots both in the microscopic world of cells and tissues that make up our bodies as well as in the complex workings of the macroscopic world, the culture that is the foundation of our societies. In essence, studying pica is a way to study what it means to be *us*.[52]

If non-religious geophagy is partly cultural, in other words, then religious geophagy is partly material and not simply a spiritual panacea or a fully symbolic practice that works, as in mind over matter, because of belief alone.

Geophagy has been widely studied for its potential medicinal and nutritional value or, more specifically, eating earth has been approached as a practice that is motivated by a bio-material deficit in the body rather than by cultural or psychological reasons apprehensible by those practising or observing it. While hunger alone is an insufficient explanation, since many of those who eat earth have other food sources at their disposal, deficiencies in the iron, zinc, and calcium content of geophagists' diets could explain the urge to eat earth, particularly among the pregnant women and children who make up a disproportionate number of the practitioners.[53] The field of data is complex, because while the need for these nutrients does correlate with the life stages of those who most often practise geophagy, their consumption of earth does not cease with the advent of adulthood, the cessation of pregnancy, or after the missing micronutrients are supplied by regular dietary supplements. In addition, even though certain types of earth do contain the micronutrients required, upon consumption

---

[52] Ibid., p. 140.      [53] Ibid., chs. 7 and 8.

these soils actually inhibit the body's ability to absorb these substances, thus having the opposite effect of causing rather than curing micronutrient deficiency.[54] However, a relationship does exist between those who consume earth and iron deficiency and, in addition, much soil that is eaten appears to be high in iron; it is not clear, though, that the iron is bioavailable during the digestive process.

Even though contradictory evidence exists for whether geophagy is practised because of micronutrient deficiencies—and certainly it appears inadequate as an overall explanation for the phenomenon—the connection to iron-deficient diets is compelling in relation to early medieval England. As Robin Fleming shows, iron-deficiency anaemia was prevalent among the early medieval English, and increased with the nucleation of villages and towns in the ninth through the eleventh centuries.[55] The deficiency is evident in skeletons that demonstrate porotic hyperostosis or cribra orbitalia, bone lesions on the skull or eye sockets, respectively, that form between the ages of six months and twelve years as a consequence of the overproduction of bone tissue that creates red blood cells and the underproduction of the outer bone layer.[56] Because anaemia is caused by poor diet but also by chronic blood loss associated with diarrhoea or infections, it is exacerbated in early medieval England as the population becomes concentrated in urbanized settlements. In both the early (sixth and seventh centuries) and later periods (tenth and eleventh centuries), however, iron deficiency occurs at much greater levels than in contemporary populations. It is compelling, therefore, to understand the urge to eat saintly earth in early medieval England in relation to endemic iron deficiencies, or at least to suggest that its effectiveness may be related to high iron content.

The relation between geophagy and calcium intake has received far less attention than have iron deficiencies, and what evidence is available presents a somewhat mixed picture.[57] Sera Young notes that geophagic practices do not correlate to those periods of life when calcium is most required by the body, which seems to suggest that micronutrient

[54] P. S. Hooda et al., 'The Potential Impact of Soil Ingestion on Human Mineral Nutrition', *Science of the Total Environment* 333 (2004): pp. 75–87.

[55] Robin Fleming, *Britain after Rome: The Fall and Rise, 400–1070* (London: Penguin, 2010), pp. 345–66.

[56] Fleming, *Britain after Rome*, pp. 349–50.

[57] Young, *Craving Earth*, pp. 102–13.

deficiency does not motivate the eating of calcium-rich items. In addition, although calcium is more easily absorbed by the body than are zinc and iron, it seems that many soil types do not provide a significant amount of the substance in a bioavailable form. In short, calcium deficiency could motivate the eating of certain soils in particular, but the evidence does not exist to support this hypothesis because insufficient studies have been completed.

An alternate explanation of the reasons for geophagy involves the protective and detoxifying potential of certain soil types. Most common materials for pica, including chalk, starch, paper, flour, and baby powder, are dry, powdery, crunchy, and adsorptive—that is, permeable by other molecules.[58] Because earth is the most commonly eaten pica substance, the biological consequences of adsorption have been particularly well studied for clay soil, in particular. The fine texture of clay, which is defined by the National Soil Resources Institute as that 'mineral fraction of the soil with particles smaller than 0.002mm in diameter', makes it a popular choice for geophagists, who in general avoid humus soils rich in organic matter.[59] Clay functions in two ways to prevent the absorption of toxic elements into the body: first, by reinforcing the mucosal barrier of the intestinal wall, ensuring that pathogens cannot move through it, and second, by binding molecules of harmful chemicals within the microscopic crystalline structure of the clay itself, thus moving them out of the gut before they can do any harm.[60] Since gastrointestinal distress is a marker of exposure to toxins and pathogens, geophagy occurs more frequently during periods of diarrhoea or abdominal pain and is also systemic in tropical regions where foodborne bacteria multiply more quickly. This latter is particularly interesting in application to early medieval England, a situation where, as I have discussed, chronic iron deficiency was probably the result of severe intestinal problems caused by parasites and infections thriving in a pathogen-rich environment. In such an environment, the urge to eat earth can be explained as a preventative measure allowing the consumption of otherwise unsafe foodstuffs.

---

[58] Ibid., p. 5.     [59] 'Glossary of Soil-related Terms'.
[60] Young, *Craving Earth*, pp. 119–35. Also L. B. Williams et al., 'What Makes Natural Clays Antibacterial?' *Environmental Science and Technology* 45 (2011): pp. 3768–73.

An additional advantage of clay soils is currently undergoing investigation by scientists searching for alternative treatments for so-called antibiotic-resistant superbugs such as MRSA and *E. coli*. A study funded by the US National Science foundation and led by Lynda Williams at Arizona State University found that certain clays, in particular blue and white, killed harmful bacteria by flooding the cells with iron and, in addition, lowering the pH level at the site of wounds to the slightly acidic range that is associated with healthy skin capable of eliminating incoming bacteria.[61] This explains why clay soils are effective when topically applied to the skin, as well as when ingested. Interestingly, these effects are produced when elements in clay are transferred to a cell through water, so the clay must be either in solution or in a wet poultice in order to be effective.

Despite some fundamental differences, geobiological studies of healing earth share some common ground with those experiences of saintly soil narrated by authors such as Bede, which is perhaps not surprising given that the science acknowledges a long folk history of effective geophagic praxis. Geobiology allows us to see that the ingestion of soil for healing is sometimes effective because of a 'reaction between the minerals and the human body or agents that cause illness' that is only now being recognized.[62] This reaction involves clays, in particular, supplementing or enhancing the body's own mechanisms for protection (such as strengthening the mucal membrane in the intestines, or restoring the normal pH level of skin) when these are either temporarily damaged or face the excessive threat of toxins, pathogens, or bacteria. As such, ingested and applied soils function as temporary parts of the human biological system, prosthetic agents that improve the functioning of that system and exist in a network with cells and the substances that inhabit and challenge them. Only certain soils have this capability, however, just as only that special soil associated with saints can perform miracles. Thus, both contemporary popular and ancient religious injunctions against 'eating dirt' function to instruct potential consumers about the special nature of certain soils that are permissible

---

[61] 'New Answer to MRSA, Other "Superbug" Infections: Clay Minerals?' US National Science Foundation, 17 July 2014, https://www.nsf.gov/discoveries/disc_summ.jsp?cntn_id=132,052&org=NSF.

[62] 'New Answer to MRSA'.

to eat and effective when eaten. Moreover, in their different ways, both geobiology and Christian discourse describe a certain kinship between the human body and these soils, on the one hand by demonstrating how healing earth works as part of a network including bodies and bacteria and, on the other, informing its converts that 'ðu eart dust and to duste gewyrst'. This kinship is apparently closer than science can yet fully account for, since no definitive explanation has been found for the growth of human tissue that occurs simultaneously with the use of antibacterial clays.[63]

## A new view of saintly soil

What can bringing recent geochemical research to bear on saints' lives written in early medieval England reveal? How can it allow us to get at the lost materiality of saintly soil and its effects on early medieval users? In answering these questions, I want to emphasize first that the role of contemporary science is not as a mechanism for enlightenment that will strip away the 'primitive' explanatory structure appended to healing soil by the early church and get to the 'reality' of its mineral content. This conclusion would explain why only certain soil works—which for a contemporary geophagist is a matter of taste but from the perspective of the hagiographer is due to its association with saints, while biochemically it would actually be because of its particular content—and why the texts specify that the earth be dissolved in water before being applied or ingested. The blood that Germanus of Auxerre observed in the soil from Alban's death-site, for example, might more logically refer to the colour of the earth than to actual blood, since much of St Albans is located on what is identified by the National Soil Resources Institute

---

[63] Williams et al., 'What Makes Natural Clays Antibacterial?' p. 3772. Nhiem Tran et al., 'Bactericidal Effect of Iron Oxide Nanoparticles on *Staphylococcus Aureus*', *International Journal of Nanomedicine* 5 (2010), pp. 277–83, at p. 281, show that iron oxide (magnetite) is antibacterial against *Staphylococcus aureus*, one of the most common human pathogens causing local infections. As the authors note, osteoblast (bone-forming cells) growth was enhanced by the presence of iron oxide nanoparticles during the study. This latter finding could begin to explain why healing clays, rich in iron, cause the proliferation of human tissue.

as soil series 5.54 'St Albans', which has a dark, reddish-brown colour.[64] However, the recorded site of Alban's death at Holywell Hill is currently composed of a different soil type entitled '812a Frome', a highly calcareous and loamy mix. But given that the saint's *vita* itself specifies that the stream at this site arose with the martyrdom of Alban, the original soil of Holywell Hill would in fact have been '571m Charity 2', a brown, calcareous soil with a fine and flinty texture. Because the genealogy of soil, as I mentioned at the outset of this chapter, is as complicated as that of saints' lives—and in this case the two are imbricated in each other—it is difficult to determine exactly what Germanus picked up when he took some saintly soil from Verulamium. It seems likely, though, that the colour of the earth, and even its healing potential, could be related to its geological profile as a calcareous or even clay-based soil. This fascinating possibility, however, does not overwrite the early medieval English understanding of saintly soil— or, to put this another way, it does not negate the blood in the soil—as much as it enables us to recognize the ways that early medieval English hagiographical texts are themselves part of a material discourse of saintly soil. That is to say, where geobiology is dedicated to explaining the interactions of human tissue and soil, using the language of bacteria and pathogens, pre-Conquest English hagiography reveals a different but analogous understanding of the material-discursive interrelations of bodies and earth. This section will, by exploring early medieval English hagiographies of sacred soil as such a material discourse, ultimately argue that these texts record how a people develop an essential connection to the land they occupy, when they have the potential to eat and apply special earth from that land to their bodies.

How materiality constrains and governs the production of saintly soil is revealed by comparing earth to other secondary relics and the common understanding of how they work. As Peter Brown delineates in his foundational work, secondary relics are created through the transmission of *praesentia,* a force that he analogizes to a virus, from

---

[64] Cranfield University Land Information System, 'LandIS *Soils Guide*', Cranfield University, accessed 8 November 2016, http://www.landis.org.uk/services/soilsguide/index.cfm. For help in interpreting the soil profile of this site, I am grateful to Caroline Keay, Senior Information Scientist at the School of Water, Energy and Environment at Cranfield University (personal email communication).

the saint's body into the object.[65] Those who handle the object are then able to access *praesentia* and are provided with a physical conduit to the divine. Numerous medieval texts indicate that *praesentia* produces a material change in the object itself—for example, stories of cloths that, after being touched to the saint's tomb, bleed profusely when cut.[66] If the relic has been infused with the presence of the saint by physical contact with the remains, it then serves as a conduit to the saint and in that sense becomes the saint. At the same time, as these stories indicate, secondary relics still maintain their particular materiality as objects— they might bleed like a person, but yet they are not people—and this governs how they are interacted with, displayed, and transported. Saintly soil, as a type of secondary relic, shares these characteristics. Typically created by spilling fluids, such as blood, and not only by touch, its miracle-working properties are attributed by medieval authors to the character of the saint him or herself, and their actions while alive. For example, Bede repeatedly explains the miracle-working prowess of places associated with Oswald by reference to the king's piety during his life: as he puts it, '[n]ec mirandum in loco mortis illius infirmos sanari, qui semper dum uiueret infirmis et pauperibus con- sulere, elimosynas dare, opem ferre non cessabat[67] ([n]or is it to be wondered at that the sick are cured in the place where he died, for while he was alive he never ceased to care for the sick and the poor, to give them alms, and offer them help).

Similarly, Bede writes of the place where water, used to wash the king's body, was poured: 'Nec mirandum preces regis illius iam cum Domino regnantis multum ualere apud eum, qui temporalis regni quondam gubernacula tenens magis pro aeterno regno semper laborare ac deprecari solebat.' (It is not to be wondered at that the prayers of this king who is now reigning with the Lord should greatly prevail, for while he was ruling over his temporal kingdom, he was always accustomed to work and pray most diligently for the kingdom which is eternal.)[68] Of the miracles attested at Heavenfield, he likewise observes that '[i]n

[65] Brown, *The Cult of the Saints*, especially 'Praesentia', pp. 86–105.
[66] A faculty famously referred to by Gregory the Great in his letter to the Empress Constantina (cited in Alan Thacker, '*Loca Sanctorum*: the Significance of Place in the Study of Saints', in *Local Saints and Local Churches*, pp. 1–43, at p. 17).
[67] Bede, iii.9.  [68] Bede, iii.12.

cuius loco orationis innumerae uirtutes sanitatum noscuntur esse patratae, ad indicium uidelicet ac memoriam fidei regis' ([i]nnumerable miracles of healing are known to have been wrought in the place where they prayed, doubtless as a token and memorial of the king's faith).[69] Bede, like hagiographers in general, attempts to shut down potential doubt in his readers by using language that asserts the self-evident nature of the events he describes and the obviousness of the explanation he provides for them, hence the repetition of 'nec mirandum.' Nevertheless, these healing events precisely are, by their nature as miracles, to be wondered at. Nor, if we pay attention to Bede's comments, is he explaining events by means of personification or anthropomorphization of the soil: although saintly earth might function *because of* the saint, it is not actually the saint. Wondering at and about the soil—looking beyond Bede's 'nec mirandum', in other words—allows us to account for the ways and degree to which saintly soil, like other secondary relics, has undergone a material transformation and what other such transformations it can effect.

In fact, place-based miracle stories make it clear that saintly soil is still soil; while the carnality of the earth touched by a saint's body is important, so is its essential 'soil-ness'. This soil-ness emerges in the narratives as a problem of recognition that must be explored and dispelled again and again. That is, if saintly soil is fundamentally soil, even though it is hybridized with the saint, then how are worshippers to find and perceive it? After all, saintly soil does not look any different from ordinary soil. Since most of the places associated with saints, with the exception of their shrines, are casually or inadvertently created (for example, by pouring away wash water), it is necessary to account for their discovery by means of *inventio* narratives. These can be read as extended explorations of materiality, because the special nature of saintly earth can only show itself through a non-linguistic medium, usually some sort of observable physical change. Bede provides a number of such narratives concerning Oswald's death-site. In the second of these, a Briton is said to have been passing by the place of Oswald's death when, 'uidit unius loci spatium cetero campo uiridius ac uenustius' (he noticed that a certain patch of ground was greener and

---

[69] Bede, iii.2.

more beautiful than the rest of the field), and concluded that 'nulla esset alia causa insolitae illo in loco uiriditatis, nisi quia ibidem sanctior cetero exercitu uir aliquis fuisset interfectus' (the only cause for the unusual greenness of that part must be that some man holier than the rest of the army had perished there).[70] On one level this story renders nature in culturally legible terms: while many other reasons for the greenness could in fact exist (such as pooling water, changes in the soil profile, etc.), these are all superseded by a governing religious interpretation in which nature has been improved by human action. From another point of view, the narrative asserts that the soil has been materially changed by contact with the saint's blood, becoming more fertile, which is registered by means of a visually apprehensible physical change in the vegetation it supports. Rather than becoming something else by means of its hybridization with saintly blood, however, sacred earth has enhanced properties *as* earth, making it hard to determine whether the soil has become more like the saint or the saint has become very much like soil. This latter reading recognizes that neither the materiality of the soil nor the religious discourse, the natural and the cultural elements of the narrative, is ascendant here, but both are required for the production of saintly soil to happen.

A sceptical reader might be tempted to observe at this point that the beauty of places associated with saints is not real, in the sense of an observable characteristic that existed outside of the written work, but instead is the manifestation of a popular medieval textual convention known as the *locus amoenus* trope. Catherine Clarke, in her study of *Literary Landscapes and the Idea of England, 700-1400,* defines the *locus amoenus* as 'any literary landscape of delight which is formed self-consciously out of conventional rhetorical elements or motifs'.[71] Although she notes that the particular conventions may change based on genre or context, 'they are always primarily pastoral and foreground natural beauty, fertility, delight and order'.[72] Typically they will include verdancy and fecundity, manifested in a multitude of flowers or fruit, and often the presence of running water and sweet odours. Clarke finds

[70] Bede, iii.10.
[71] Catherine Clarke, *Literary Landscapes and the Idea of England, 700–1400* (Cambridge: D.S. Brewer, 2006), p. 2.
[72] Ibid., p. 2.

the *locus amoenus* motif influential on Bede's descriptions of the death-sites of Alban and Oswald, and also, in his prose life of Cuthbert, on his representation of the saint's hermitage on the island of Farne.[73] For Clarke, these lush, green places filled with flowers represent miniature narrative reprisals of the *Historia*'s central theme—the desire to 'recover an ideal, unfallen state through faith and struggle'—and are part of Bede's development of a specifically English island-mythology.[74] While Clarke's fine study thus concentrates on the written manipulation of landscape, it is worth pointing out that places are only partly cultural products and that the interactions of soil, climate, rock, animals, etc. condition their shape as much as does written discourse. That *inventio* narratives for sacred earth should recall an embedded trope such as the *locus amoenus* does not, therefore, render them purely textual products, or negate the physical changes they describe as too deeply inscribed in discourse to be quantified as material in any sense.

*Inventio* episodes, which repeatedly narrate the moment at which the saintliness of a place is recognized, are concerned not only with visible changes in a site's physical characteristics but also with the miracles that occur there. In both cases the role of the observer is crucial as a conduit by which news of the place can be transmitted to the community at large. For example, Bede's first *inventio* account for the death-site of Oswald, like the second, relies on the presence of an especially perceptive passer-by to bring the place out of anonymity and render it legible in religious and cultural terms. When he observes that a sick horse is immediately cured after it rolls onto the spot, this 'uir sagacis ingenii . . . intellexit aliquid mirae sanctitatis huic loco . . . inesse' (intelligent man . . . realized that there must be some special sanctity associated with the place).[75] The rider then puts up a sign so that he may find the site again and, after he spreads the word at a local tavern, a paralysed girl is carried to the spot and cured. In this example, material changes—that is, the hybridizing of saint and place—are observable in their effects on the properties of soil that, in contradistinction to the previous example, is now acting like a saint capable of performing miracles. The overlap between the historical and the geographical

---

[73] Ibid., pp. 25–30.     [74] Ibid., p. 26.
[75] Bede, iii.9.

registers is particularly potent in this example. The holy properties of the place, a geographical location, manifest themselves in an event, the healing, and both place and event become the subject of a textual record, the sign.

Underlying this structure that binds history, place, and text is a further complex relation to events in the past, to which the miracles of the present refer. Saints such as Oswald, who are not definitively credited with any miracles during their life, are predominantly recognized through their facilitation of those miracles performed with the intermediary agency of secondary relics after their deaths. And because place-based secondary relics in one sense materially instantiate the saint, these miracles associated with them can be understood to be performed by the saint. Such miracles are in fact formally very similar to those performed by living saints, which enhances the sense of a correspondence between sacred earth and saintly person. For example, in the second *inventio* account for Maserfelth, the enterprising British passer-by takes some soil from the death-site with him in a bag, which is later miraculously preserved in the midst of a fire in the house where he passes the evening. Since stopping the course of fires was a common miracle performed by living saints, such as Martin and Aidan, this miracle serves again to trouble that boundary between place and man by proving that the earth has all the qualities of a saintly person.[76] At the same time, the miracles that place-based secondary relics perform have a referential quality, in that they are events in the present that gesture back and remind observers of past events in the saint's life. Neither the representational nor the material qualities of place-based post-mortem miracles can be understood to be more important. Rather, both work in tandem to produce a historical structure—that is, the referential element of one set of events referring to another—

[76] Martin throws his body in the course of a fire (p. xiv) that he had actually started himself in order to burn down a pagan shrine, but which then threatened a nearby house. For a convenient translation of Sulpicius Severus's *Life of Martin*, see *Early Christian Lives*, translated and edited by Carolinne White (London: Penguin, 1998), pp. 131–59. Aidan is said to have diverted by prayer a fire, set by Penda, that threatened Bamburgh (*Historia ecclesiastica*, iii.16). A buttress, which Aidan was leaning against when he died, also became miraculously retardant to flame, surviving two fires, and chips of wood from this buttress were used as a healing remedy in water (*Historia ecclesiastica*, iii.17). Slivers of wood from holy relics are commonly used in a way analogous to saintly earth: for example, from the cross at Heavenfield (*Historia ecclesiastica*, iii.2).

which is materially actualized in the interactions of bodies and soil. The infusion of landscape with history is concretely realized in this process.

## Binding Englishness: how saintly soil reaches readers

While the modes by which saintly earth is recognized in *inventio* narratives demonstrate that such soil is both materially and discursively constituted as sacred, I have yet to examine in detail how such soil interacts with the bodies of believers and, by means of such interactions, enmeshes the flesh of believers with history and place. One way in which this process occurs is the potential that *inventio* narratives connected to particular sacred places have to reinscribe the physical environment in general, regardless of documented contact with a saint, and the second is through the touching and consumption of saintly earth.

*Inventio* narratives for sacred places make it clear that they might lay undiscovered for many years, thus implying that the physical world is composed of holy sites waiting to be revealed. Thus the functionality of saintly places is connected to their potential for imaginative extension or co-optation by the reader, with their most transformative effects being on the other and non-holy places. In other words, because anywhere could be holy, not everywhere needs to be. *Inventio* accounts in this way describe and produce not only those specific and isolated places that they are concerned with but also an entire landscape materially infused with history and geography. Perhaps the most powerful component of the material-discursive phenomenon of sacred earth is this ability to reach beyond individual locales to suggest that the entire environment through and in which individuals live is partly composed of history, defined as the lives and actions of previous inhabitants.

Individuals are intimately linked to the geohistorical materiality of saintly earth—in fact, they become part of this network—by means of the dissemination, authorization, and incorporation of soil. Because soil is portable and absorbent, it allows sanctity to be duplicated, transfused, and transported far from those sites originally contacted by the saint. The process is, importantly, constrained by the material properties of the soil itself, which is not anthropomorphized so much as it is rendered more vital, more generative, while it yet remains soil. For this reason saintly earth is created when fluids, blood and wash water, are spilled and soak into the soil, rather than by more superficial forms of contact such as touching, a common method for the production of other kinds of secondary relic. And although the spilling of blood and water has important symbolic dimensions, referencing the wound in the side of Christ and the baptismal ritual, the pouring forth of these fluids at the same time functions as a type of agricultural nurturing of soil, albeit a special one.[77] The hybrid product that is created can be removed and disseminated to ailing persons far distant from the place itself, rather than sick people always having to travel to the site, as occurred with the miracle of the paralysed girl that I described above. As Bede relates, the performance of miracles at Oswald's death-site continue 'usque hodie' (up to the present day), and caused the site to become so popular that the removal of healing earth, used in water as a remedy for illness, left a large hole there. There is no reason to assume that these holes result from eating the earth 'on site', but rather also from the removal of soil to other places, sometimes far distant.

These holes in the ground differentiate those places associated with English saints from the paradigmatic site of Christ's Ascension that underpins them. Whereas the soil at the church of the Ascension is constantly replenished by miraculous means, thus preserving Christ's final footsteps and erasing the worshipful acts of those who have removed the earth, the holes in the ground in England serve as a reminder that both temporality and believers are part of the network that constitutes saintly soil. That is, saintly soil is importantly created in time, since it makes material the miracles of the past and conveys these into the present and even, ultimately, into the bodies of believers. In addition, these holes are a potent indicator of the materiality of soil that, when removed, is somewhere else. No longer at the site, saintly earth is placed next to or is incorporated within the body of those seeking to become *hal*, meaning both *whole* and *healthy*. The void left

---

[77] John 19:34 references the sudden flow of blood and water from the wound in Christ's side made by the soldier's spear during the Crucifixion.

in the ground therefore marks the material transformation of sacred soil into renewed and healed flesh.

The language by which these holes are described emphasizes the slippage between soil and human body, both that of the saint and that of the believer. Bede refers to the hole left by the removal of saintly earth at Maserfelth, the site of Oswald's death, as 'fossam...altam', which the ninth-century Old English translator renders as 'deop seað': 'Ond þæt men to þon gelomlice dydon sticcemælum, þæt heo þa moldan namon, oð þæt þær wæs deop seað adolfen, þætte wæpnedmon meahte oð his sweoran inn stondan.'[78] (And this was done gradually so often, that the clay was removed, till a deep pit was hollowed out, in which a man might stand up to his neck.) The size of the hole is communicated in terms of a male body in the Old English version, where it is described as being so deep that it might accommodate a man up to his neck, in contrast to the more abstract quantification of its depth in the Latin. Holes in the ground, created by pagan persecutors as a method to torture and kill saints, are described in this same way in the *Old English Martyrology*. St Vitalis, for instance, is martyred after he is placed in a 'deopne seað' (deep hole) that is filled with earth and rocks.[79] Similarly, the pagan persecutor of St Marcellus

> het adelfan seaþ oþ gyrdyls deopne, ond he bebead þone Godes wer þæt mon hine bebyrgde in þam seaðe oþ þone gyrdels, þæt him lifiendum were 'þæt to wite' þæt þam forþweardan/ men bið to reste. Ond he þa þurhwunode swa in þam seaðe ðry dagas lifgende in Godes lofsongum, ond þa/ ageaf ðone clænan gast.[80]

> (commanded that a belt-deep hole be dug, and he ordered that the man of God be buried in the hole up to his waist, so that what was a rest to dead men should be a punishment to him while living. And

---

[78] *The Old English Version of Bede's Ecclesiastical History of the English People*, edited and translated by Thomas Miller, Early English Text Society, o.s., 95 (London: N. Trübner, 1890), iii.7. Interestingly, the talking cross of *The Dream of the Rood* also refers to being buried 'on deopan seaþe'.

[79] *Old English Martyrology*, ii.68.3.

[80] *Old English Martyrology*, ii.199.5–12. The similarity in diction between these two episodes, 'deop' and 'seað' being the words chosen in both, encourages the reader to make lateral connections between them. The *Martyrology* includes two saints named Marcellus, the first being Pope Marcellus, whose feast day is celebrated on 16 January. I am discussing the second Marcellus, whose feast day falls on 4 September.

then he survived in the hole for three days alive in praising God, and
then he gave up the pure spirit.)

The situational and verbal play between life and death is very clear here,
with Marcellus being partially buried alive as part of the process by
which he will be born into eternal life through death. That the persecutors miss the point is, as ever, due to their obdurate literalism. But on
one level literalism does condition the description of a hole in the
ground as 'waist-deep', since the practice of digging requires a person
to climb into the hole and, once there, measure its proportions according to those of his own body. However, this particular language of the
body serves to reinforce the way that saintly soil exists in a material and
discursive network with the bodies of those who interact with it: the
saint himself, those who handle the saint's body and pour away wash-
water, those who remove soil to create a hole, and those who consume
it in order to become healed. In other words, the soil is not anthropomorphized by being described as man-shaped in its absence as much as
the reader is reminded by these measurements according to the human
body that sacred earth hybridizes soil and flesh (both the flesh of the
saint and the flesh of those who use such soil in cures) with both history
and geography. This not only works to Anglicize the fabric of the
individual bodies specified in Bede's narrative—that is, the saints and
those healed—but creates a potential by which any soil could be saintly
earth and, by extension, any reader could participate in the experiences
described. In this way saintly earth, by which I mean the discursive-
material network I am delineating, serves to render multiple bodies as
English by creating an environment in which place and history are
materially fused and available for consumption.

While previous scholarship has repeatedly recognized that saints'
lives foster the notion of a larger community, whether that be national
or ethnic, this relationship is usually understood to be symbolic or
representational in nature.[81] Even if we understand the eating of saintly

---

[81] Catherine Clarke's excellent work on literary landscapes is a good example here,
since she understands the *Historia*, and the saints' lives it includes, to have an allegorical
function. For work focusing on the nation and overwriting of the female body, see Sheila
Delany, *Impolitic Bodies: Poetry, Saints, and Society in Fifteenth-Century England*
(Oxford: Oxford University Press, 1998), and Andrea Rossi-Reder, 'Embodying Christ,
Embodying Nation: Ælfric's Accounts of Saints Agatha and Lucy', in *Sex and Sexuality in*

earth in Eucharistic terms, the cannibalistic underpinnings of the process can disappear under the language of trope and metaphor. As Heather Blurton writes, for example, in her excellent study of cannibalism in medieval literature, '[t]he trope of cannibalism is concerned, above all, with the articulation of individual and corporate identity: metaphors of consuming, devouring, incorporating, effacing the boundaries between self and other.'[82] In this model, texts about the ingestion of earth removed from a saintly site would only be imaginary assertions of how boundaries are dissolved and then reconstituted in different forms that limn a new community. They are symbolic expressions of group identity that use material metaphors to represent ideological and psychological framings of self and other, but cannot account for the matter of what is eaten or applied.

And, even though the production and ingestion of saintly earth does occur in a ritualized manner, neither can studies of religious ritual and community fully incorporate the material element involved in sacred soil. For example, contemporary anthropologists of holy places, Angela K. Martin and Sandra Kryst, have studied the post-modern phenomenon of Marian apparition sites, or places where the Virgin Mary has been reported to appear. Martin and Kryst recognize that such places first facilitate a breakdown in normative roles, as governed by heterosexuality and patriarchy, and then reaffirm these communal roles yet more prescriptively. This process is precipitated by the epistemological and spiritual liminality of apparition sites: as Martin and Kryst put it, 'Mary's ability to appear involves a blurring of boundaries between this world and the other world, between sacred and profane places.'[83] The

---

*Anglo-Saxon England: Essays in Memory of Daniel Calder*, edited by Carol Braun Pasternack and Lisa M. C. Weston (Tempe: Arizona Center for Medieval and Renaissance Studies, 2004), pp. 183–202. For scholarship concentrating on the sophisticated linguistic construction of nation in hagiography, see Clare A. Lees, 'In Ælfric's Words: Conversion, Vigilance and the Nation in Ælfric's *Life of Gregory the Great*', in *A Companion to Ælfric*, edited by Hugh Magennis and Mary Swan (Leiden: Brill, 2009), pp. 271–96.

[82] *Cannibalism in High Medieval English Literature* (New York: Palgrave Macmillan, 2007), p. 3.

[83] Angela K. Martin and Sandra Kryst, 'Encountering Mary: Ritualization and Place Contagion in Postmodernity', in *Places through the Body*, edited by Heidi Nast and Steve Pile (London: Routledge, 1998), pp. 153–170, at p. 165.

huge crowds at such sites are involved in a ritualized process of mimesis which 'confuses boundaries between self and environment, allowing one to take on, experience, feel, become, embody certain qualities of place'.[84] While this model allows for the merging of place with the bodies of worshippers, and thus is an interesting analogue for the effect of saintly earth, the process is quite specific to the late capitalist moment and imbricated in postmodern concerns with 'deterritorialization and the breakdown of signifying chains of meaning'.[85] Even though many congregants attend apparition sites in hope of cures, just like those early medieval users of sacred earth, Marian apparition lacks the hands-on aspect of the earlier practice and Martin and Kryst's mimetic model therefore allows for a performative and experiential transformation rather than a material one.

A particular aim of this chapter has been to examine the consumption of sacred earth in early medieval England in such a way as to account for the matter of the soil and of the bodies that were involved in the process, instead of treating it as an entirely ideational, linguistic, or ritualized phenomenon. Combining geobiological and textual research offers an alternative model to explain, without explaining away, how the consumption of saintly earth worked not only to heal bodies but also to infuse them with history and with place. While geobiology can explain in terms we understand why the consumption of soil might be effective against pathogens and bacteria, no medieval soil could have worked without stories—propagated by the great hagiographers of the time like Bede, but probably enjoying a much more vigorous circulation by word of mouth—about the deaths of saints and the miracle-working properties of the places associated with them. Just as clay soils bind pathogens and move them through the intestines, the production and use of saintly soil forms community through a process of material-discursive binding, in which the substance of soil and flesh is successively and mutually transformed by events and by stories about those events. Saintly soil is therefore more properly a process or an assemblage of texts, materials, and actions—including both consumption of soil and consumption of stories about soil—than it is a unitary

---

[84] Ibid., p. 224.
[85] Ibid., p. 226. Martin and Kryst welcome 'a comparative study of premodern, modern, and postmodern apparition events' (p. 226).

substance. This notion of reading (or hearing) as a practice embedded in a broader material-discursive network has significant consequences, in turn, for understanding how the early medieval English formed a connection to the place they occupied and its history, a component that is seen as fundamental to community formation. Rather than understanding these connections to be primarily affective, created by the manipulation of emotional ties to landscape in an elaborate mental play, paying more attention to saintly soil reveals the material dimension of interactions between bodies, narrative, and places in early medieval England.

# | 2 |

# Stones, Books, and the Place of History around AD 900

The previous chapter showed one way in which pre-Conquest texts, as they worked on and with saintly soil, made the past physically available in a tangible and consumable form. The material qualities of soil—its constantly changing nature, porousness, consumability, and transportability—play an active role in this process because they allow for the easy reconstitution and absorption of one property into another. This chapter will examine the position of pre-Conquest historical texts within a material network with very different characteristics, the inscription of memorial texts on stone. As Jeffrey Jerome Cohen has written in his monograph *Stone: An Ecology of the Inhuman*, '[s]tone seems to us a material well suited for memorials and grave markers...its decomposition and constant metamorphoses are, within our native temporality, so unhurried that rock is our shorthand for temporal density.'[1] Although stone is constantly engaged in becoming soil through erosion, the two interact with human bodies and texts in distinctively different ways, with stone appearing to offer a permanent mode of yoking historical narrative to place, rather than a cycle of transformation from one state to another.

---

[1] Jeffrey Jerome Cohen, *Stone: An Ecology of the Inhuman* (Minneapolis: University of Minnesota Press, 2015), p. 35.

*Materializing Englishness in Early Medieval Texts*. Jacqueline Fay, Oxford University Press.
© Jacqueline Fay 2022. DOI: 10.1093/oso/9780198757573.003.0003

This chapter will explore how English texts and artefacts from around the year 900 engage with the material particularity of stone, taking as its evidence a network that includes mortuary inscriptions on stone, stories about inscribed mortuary stones, the circulation of manuscript collections of such inscriptions, and the *Anglo-Saxon Chronicle*, itself an extended record of death dates and places of burial. The decades around the year 900 are of particular interest in this regard, because they witness both the initiation of the *Anglo-Saxon Chronicle* project and also a significant change towards the use of inscribed text on stone for commemorative purposes. The fulcrum to understanding the relationship between textual and lapidary modes of historical record at this time, I will argue, is the word *her* (here), which draws together the network that I describe above and marks the enmeshment of human culture with the materiality of stone. The following sections will trace potential origins and analogues for the term *her*, which is used as the opening word of almost all annals of the *Anglo-Saxon Chronicle*, through Easter tables, and pictorial and diagrammatic conventions, to what I am calling mortuary discourse, or a diverse range of commemorative texts written in books and inscribed on stones. Epitaphs, most of which are in Latin and many of which are recorded from sites in and around Rome, make explicit that location has both a physical and cultural sense: epitaphs are both intensely situated and portable at the same time, serving to invoke the monumentality of Rome in new contexts. Reading the *Chronicle*'s *her* as an echo of the *her* and *hic* of epitaph literature reveals the complex material and textual affiliations of this work, and also allows us to see the ways that the *Chronicle* brings history, location, and reader into alignment. In borrowing the language of mortuary discourse, therefore, the *Chronicle* also borrows its terms of reference, seating its authority not in the speaking and mobile body but in the mute and buried corpse beneath the stone marker.

## Previous historical models

Writing history is, by definition, an act attuned to the potential that different materials have to transcend, and also to authorize, the disappearing field of human interactions, and particularly the ephemeral nature of speech. While the texts and objects that I will focus on in this

chapter richly explore this potential, other historical works written in
early medieval England had already extensively considered this question of how to make tangible the link between the linguistic account in
the reader's hand and the now-absent past events themselves. In narrative histories, in particular, this question emerges as a concern with
sources, provoking what are often lengthy explanatory statements from
the narrator about the origin of the story being told. Perhaps most
famously, Bede observes in the preface to the *Historia Ecclesiastica* that

> [l]ectoremque suppliciter obsecro ut, siqua in his quae scripsimus
> aliter quam se ueritas habet posita reppererit, non hoc nobis inputet,
> qui, quod uera lex historiae est, simpliciter ea quae fama uulgante
> collegiums ad instructionem posteritatis litteris mandare studuimus.[2]

> (Now, in order to remove all occasions of doubt about those things
> I have written, either in your mind or in the minds of any others who
> listen to or read this history, I will make it my business to state briefly
> from what sources I have gained my information ... So I humbly beg
> the reader, if he finds anything other than the truth set down in what
> I have written, not to impute it to me. For, in accordance with the
> principles of true history, I have simply sought to commit to writing
> what I have collected from common report, for the instruction of
> posterity.)

Among the most well-known of medieval statements about sources,
Bede's impulse was common to the project of medieval history more
generally: to insert the text as the final link in a chain of seeing and
hearing bodies stretching from the event itself to the page before the
reader. As time went by, these chains of bodies could become quite
lengthy and confusing, as demonstrated by the opening of Ælfric's Life
of Saint Edmund, a vernacular translation of Abbo of Fleury's Latin *vita*
for the ninth-century saint:

> Sum swyðe gelæred munuc com suþan ofer sæ fram sancta bene-
> dictes stowe on æþelredes cynincges dæge to dunstane ærce-bisceope
> þrim gearum ær he forðferde . and se munuc hatte abbo . þa wurdon
> hi æt spræce oþþæt dunstan rehte be sancta eadmunde . swa swa
> eadmundes swurd-bora hit rehte æþelstane cynincge þa þa dunstan

---

[2] Bede, *Ecclesiastical History of the English People*, edited by Bertram Colgrave and
R. A. B. Mynors (Oxford: Oxford University Press, 1969), pp. 2–7.

iung man wæs . and se swurd-bora wæs forealdod man . Þa gesette se
munuc ealle þa gereccednysse on anre béc . and eft ða þa seo bóc com
to ús binnan feawum gearum þa awende we hit on englisc . swa swa
hit her-æfter stent.[3]

(A certain very learned monk came south over the sea from
St Benedict's place, in the days of King Æthelred, to Archbishop
Dunstan three years before he died. And the monk was called
Abbo. Then they were speaking together until Dunstan told about
St Edmund, just as Edmund's sword-bearer had told it to King
Æthelstan when Dunstan was a young man and the sword-bearer
was a very old man. Then the monk set down the whole story in a
book, and afterwards, when the book came to us within a few years,
then we turned it into English, just as it stands hereafter.)

Ælfric, writing almost 300 years after Bede, felt the same compulsion to
outline the genealogy of his information. As he describes it, the book
comes to Ælfric from Abbo, who spoke to Dunstan, who spoke to the
man who witnessed the death of the saint. As Ælfric reiterates in the
narrative that follows, his account cleaves to the words of the king's
own sword-bearer, the man placed on the spot by God precisely so that
he could testify to Edmund's sanctity:

> Þær wæs sum man gehende gehealden þurh god .
> behyd þam hæþenum . þe þis gehyrde eall .
> and hit eft sæde swa swa we hit secgað her.[4]
> (There was a certain man at hand kept by God
> hidden from the heathen, who heard all this
> and told it afterwards just as we say it here.)

The unnamed sword-bearer is a typical Ælfrician character, since the
homilist is known for removing identifying features such as personal
and place names in his translations. In this case the lack of a name,
along with the fact that he 'belongs' to Edmund—he is 'eadmundes
swurd-bora', Edmund's sword-bearer—doubly emphasizes his arche-
typal position within the chain of narrators.

---

[3] *Ælfric's Lives of Saints*, edited by Walter W. Skeat, Early English Text Society, o.s., 82
(London: Oxford University Press, 1881–5), p. 325. All quotations from the life are taken
from this edition, while translations are my own.
[4] *Ælfric's Lives*, p. 323.

For Bede and Ælfric, the authority of a historical account, or what serves to guarantee the relation between events and their written record, is based on the function of witnessing and, in its connection to seeing and hearing, is founded in the material and bodily realm. The predominance of first person forms and proper names in Bede's preface to the *Historia* are a mark of this respect for the living body of the witness as a guarantor of historical veracity, and what constitutes Bede's 'uera lex historiae' or 'true law of history'. In his seminal investigation of this phrase, Roger Ray demonstrates that it refers to the traditional notion that historiography should be distinguished by relating real events, the truth of which should preferably rest in the figure of the witness but, in cases where there is a reliance only on common report, then the responsibility for truth lies with the sources rather than the historian.[5] While Bede's preface is conventional, as Ray notes, the length of his discussion of sources is idiosyncratic and indicative of a real anxiety about how to guarantee the truth value of texts without a witnessing 'chain'. Similarly, in Ælfric's text, forms of *hieran, secgan,* and *spræcan* proliferate, and mark the degree to which the veracity of the written account is seated in the physical acts of speaking and listening: the text, exactly like the witness, 'says' its story.

A sense of 'authorial persona', while it is a function of the text itself in its grammatical marking of the first person and its deployment of the language of orality, is central to the way that Bede and Ælfric affiliate their written words with the long-past and ephemeral happenings that they are describing. The chain of bodies and texts stretching from the moment of occurrence to the moment of writing is not, it is important to note, a poststructural chain of signifiers endlessly proliferating within language as a self-enclosed system. Rather, Bede and Ælfric are describing and instantiating a transference of the events themselves as they happened and were seen or heard, in which these events pass as a current through the bodies of observers, to the ear of the author, and finally into the words written on the page of the book itself, and to the eye of the reader. The authorial persona is maintained even when Bede's text is translated into Old English in the ninth century. Unlike a number of the Alfredian works, which register the distance between

[5] Roger Ray, 'Bede's Vera Lex Historiae', *Speculum* 55 (1980): pp. 1–21.

the translation and the original by means of tag phrases such as 'cwæð Orosius', the *Old English Bede*, not definitively attached to Alfred's court, makes no such distinction. The Old English 'ic' of the translation therefore silently takes over the place of Bede's Latin first-person forms—for example, 'þæt ðy læs tweoge hwæðer þis soð sy, ic cyðe hwanan me þas spell coman'[6] (that there may be the less doubt whether this be true, I will state the sources of my narrative). This serves as one example of how the authenticity of historical texts in early medieval England was a feature of the materiality of the written book, and its participation in networks of texts and bodies that stretch through and connect widely separated times and places.

However, the majority of historical writing practised in early medieval England, including annals and inscriptions, was non-narrative in nature and included no such self-reflective commentary on sources. The writers/makers and readers of such short texts are nonetheless deeply concerned with the relationship of location to past and present, and highly aware of the participation of different materials within this dynamic relationship. Serving as examples of this concern are the following two entries taken from widely dispersed portions of version A of the *Anglo-Saxon Chronicle*, and a Latin inscription from an English tombstone dating sometime between the ninth and eleventh centuries:

657 Her forþferde Peada, 7 Wulfhere Pending feng to rice...

1066 Her forðferde Eaduuard king, 7 Harold eorl feng to ðam rice.[7]

(Here Peada died, and Wulfhere Pending succeeded to the kingdom; Here King Edward died, and Earl Harold succeeded to the kingdom.)

HIC IN SEPULCRO REQVIESCIT CORPORE HEREBRICHT PRB

(Here in the tomb rests Herebricht the priest in his bodily form.)

---

[6] Quotations in Old English and translation are from *The Old English Version of Bede's Ecclesiastical History of the English People*, edited and translated by Thomas Miller, Early English Text Society, o.s., 95 (London: N. Trübner, 1890), pp. 2–3.

[7] All quotations in the original from the *Chronicle*, unless otherwise stated, are drawn from Janet Bately, ed., *MS A*, Vol. 3 of *The Anglo-Saxon Chronicle: A Collaborative Edition* (Cambridge: D.S. Brewer, 1986). All translations are my own.

Neither text is concerned with the origin of the information that it conveys; the most pressing element in each is the locative opening, *her/ hic,* which makes a different type of authenticating claim than those offered by Bede and Ælfric in their longer narrative works. Such short texts are representative of a large number of such works that link the past—whether that be a body, a name, a life, a transition in kingship— to the present space of reading. In fact, all kinds of early medieval English people, from individual mourners, to stone-cutters, monastic scribes, and even Anglo-Latin poets, were very interested in texts recording when a person died and where that person is buried. However, these works have not previously been recognized to be a group by scholars, and thus the slippages that occur across the different materials used to receive these texts have not been explored. Such an investiga- tion is particularly compelling, because such texts, despite their laconic and formulaic nature, evince much innovation at this time, around 900, when vernacular annals style is essentially being invented and stone grave markers are being used with increasing frequency. Later in the period, and certainly after the Conquest, the resonances that I am tracing between these short texts will no longer be so evident, largely because annals style will become more expansive and narratorial, while grave markers become an accepted phenomenon.

## *Her* in the *Chronicle*

When it was begun around 890–1, the *Anglo-Saxon Chronicle* was characterized by what Cecily Clark has called 'semi-formulaic language' or 'terse, timeless formulas'.[8] The short, declarative sentences and repetitious diction of the ninth-century *Chronicle* was not, she noted, typical of other vernacular texts of the time nor was it somehow inherent to the events themselves. In contrast, Clark found that '[t]he early *Chronicle* style...shows limitations peculiar to itself' and that

---

[8] Clark, 'The Narrative Mode of the Anglo-Saxon Chronicle before the Conquest', in *England before the Conquest,* edited by Peter Clemoes and Kathleen Hughes (Cambridge: Cambridge University Press, 1971), pp. 215–35, at p. 217.

'[w]hether or not the distinction were as yet consciously formulated, "annals" were felt to be a separate genre requiring a style of their own.'[9]

Because the *Chronicle* is so wide ranging both in the number of its manuscript witnesses and in its chronological reach, this new vernacular 'annals style' was disseminated broadly, especially through the Common Stock entries.[10] These annals, up to 890–1, are present in their basic form in all seven manuscripts, with those in version A, or the Parker Chronicle, written in a single late ninth-century hand. Version A is not, however, always the closest to the putative original, with the later manuscripts sometimes preserving better readings.[11] These later manuscripts are variously associated: B is a copy written at one time up to the year 977; C was also copied at one time, in the eleventh century, and contains material apparently copied from B; D is also an eleventh-century production, closely associated with both C and E; E, or the Peterborough Chronicle, is a twelfth-century work, continuing to 1154; F, also twelfth century, is a bilingual and abbreviated version, the compiler of which had access both to A and to the ancestor of E; G, which survives only in a fragmentary state, having been badly burnt in the 1731 Cotton fire, was transcribed from A in the early eleventh century. For my purposes in this chapter, it is the commonalities of these variant versions, the shared material that marks the *Chronicle* as a single venture, that are important.

*Her* is perhaps the most consistent element within this shared material: all but ten of the 232 annals in A that contain entries of the *Chronicle*'s Common Stock begin with *her*, and it is a staple feature of

---

[9]   Ibid., p. 219.

[10]   Janet Bately, however, suggests that the first compilation of material probably ended around 870 and that the following Alfredian annals formed the first continuation ('The Compilation of the Anglo-Saxon Chronicle, 60 BC to AD 890: Vocabulary as Evidence', *Proceedings of the British Academy* 64 [1978]: pp. 93–129). Other seminal examinations of the *Chronicle*'s origins and textual history are Janet Bately, 'The Compilation of the Anglo-Saxon Chronicle Once More', *Leeds Studies in English* 16 (1985): pp. 7–26; 'Manuscript Layout and the Anglo-Saxon Chronicle', *John Rylands University Library Bulletin* 70 (1988): pp. 21–43; *The Anglo-Saxon Chronicle: Texts and Textual Relationships* (Reading: Reading Medieval Studies Monograph, 1991); Audrey L. Meaney, 'St Neots, Æthelweard and the Compilation of the Anglo-Saxon Chronicle: A Survey', in *Studies in Earlier Old English Prose*, edited by Paul E. Szarmach (Albany, NY: State University of New York Press, 1986), pp. 193–243. For a concise summary of the manuscripts and their relations, see Thomas Bredehoft, *Textual Histories: Readings in the* Anglo-Saxon Chronicle (Toronto: University of Toronto Press, 2001), pp. 4–6.

[11]   An eighth manuscript, H, consists of a single leaf.

the account even into the latest continuations in the C, D, and E manuscripts.[12] The presence of *her* within the *Chronicle* thus resonates through many centuries, but the late ninth century will be the time most important to my analysis, since it is then that the Common Stock annalist first uses the term as a consistent opening for his entries, a decision that will determine *Chronicle* form into the twelfth century. Scholars have debated at great length the question of whether the *Chronicle* is an Alfredian production, even though no such connection can be definitively demonstrated, and it is not even clear whether the project emerged from a clerical or secular direction.[13] The link to Alfred has always been attractive, however, because the goals of the project, particularly its vernacular status and broad aim of setting English material within the framework of world and Romano-Christian history, seem to coincide with those of his translation programme more generally. As Thomas Bredehoft has noted, the manuscript context of surviving *Chronicle* versions suggests that the early medieval English themselves felt it to be an Alfredian production, whether it actually was or not.[14] Like other texts associated in some form with Alfred's court, many have read the *Chronicle* as, in R. H. C. Davis's words, 'propaganda' or, in Alice Sheppard's rather more subtle formulation, a set of

---

[12] Within the Common Stock material, the only entries not to open with '*her*' are a handful of the so-called world history annals that begin the text. The opening formula also shows some diversity within the series of entries from 889 to 896, which begin with some variety of 'in this year'. In *MS A*, within this span only 890, 891, and 892 begin with *her*.

[13] Bately ('Compilation') finds no definitive linguistic evidence to link the *Chronicle* with Alfredian texts, although she does not rule out the possibility of the king's involvement, perhaps in a project already under way. For arguments that associate the *Chronicle* with specific places and times, including Alfred's court, Winchester, and the south-west, see R. H. C. Davis, 'Alfred the Great: Propaganda and Truth', *History* 56 (1971): pp. 169–82, and the reply by Dorothy Whitelock, 'The Importance of the Battle of Edington, AD 878', in *Report for 1975, 1976, and 1977 of the Society of Friends of the Priory Church of Edington, Wiltshire*, pp. 6–15; repr. in her *From Bede to Alfred: Studies in Early Anglo-Saxon Literature and History* (London: Variorum Reprints, 1980); Malcolm Parkes, 'The Palaeography of the Parker Manuscript of the Chronicle, Laws and Sedulius, and Historiography at Winchester in the Late Ninth and Tenth Centuries', *Anglo-Saxon England* 5 (1976), pp. 149–71; F. M. Stenton, 'The South-Western Element in the Old English Chronicle', in *Preparatory to Anglo-Saxon England, being the Collected Papers of Frank Merry Stenton*, edited by D. M. Stenton (Oxford: Clarendon Press, 1970), pp. 106–15.

[14] Bredehoft, *Textual Histories*, p. 6.

'constitutive fictions' that serve to instantiate a group identity, either that of the West Saxons or the English.[15]

In contrast, others have seen the *Chronicle*'s repetitive language, of which *her* forms a central part, as disbarring the type of discernment and connection necessary for 'fictions' to be engendered. For these scholars, thinking about the *Chronicle* as establishing English identity goes against the grain of the text's own investment in universality, manifest in its list of AD dates and its deeply standardizing diction, including *her*. As Hayden White famously observed in his classic study 'The Value of Narrativity in the Representation of Reality', annals are seen as a preliminary stage in the shaping of historical accounts because their single principle of arrangement is that of chronology, which cannot allow for the kind of distinction between social and natural happenings nor the connections between events that are essential for the formation of national consciousness.[16] Both Antonia Gransden and Janet Thormann have argued that the *Anglo-Saxon Chronicle* is thus constrained by chronology, focusing their attention on how the act of keeping and compiling the record itself instantiates the group performing these actions.[17]

The scholarly discussion of how the *Chronicle* relates to, performs, instantiates, or constitutes group identity has thus far concentrated on

[15] Davis, 'Alfred the Great'; Sheppard, *Families of the King: Writing Identity in the Anglo-Saxon Chronicle* (Toronto: University of Toronto Press, 2004), p. 4. For another argument that the *Chronicle* constructs national identity, see also Bredehoft, *Textual Histories*, p. 3.

[16] Hayden White, 'The Value of Narrativity in the Representation of Reality', in *On Narrative*, edited by W. J. T. Mitchell (Chicago: University of Chicago Press, 1991), pp. 1–23. For a similar view, see Louis Mink, 'Narrative Form as a Cognitive Instrument', in *The Writing of History: Literary Form and Historical Understanding*, edited by Robert H. Canary and Henry Kozicki (Madison: University of Wisconsin Press, 1978), pp. 129–49. For a critique of White's tropic theory, see Dominick Lacapra, *History and Criticism* (Ithaca: Cornell University Press, 1985). Lacapra argues that White, while representing the historian as 'constrained by codes or structures', ultimately still relies on the notion of an 'inert, neutral documentary record' not so constrained (pp. 34–5).

[17] Antonia Gransden, *Historical Writing in England c.550 to c.1307* (Ithaca: Cornell University Press, 1974), especially p. 29; and Janet Thormann, 'The Anglo-Saxon Chronicle Poems and the Making of the English Nation', in *Anglo-Saxonism and the Construction of Social Identity*, edited by Allen J. Frantzen and John D. Niles (Gainesville: University Press of Florida, 1997), pp. 60–85, at p. 60, and 'The Battle of Brunanburh and the Matter of History', *Mediaevalia* 17 (1994), pp. 5–13.

the question of whether or not the *Chronicle* is a narrative text. Very little attention has been paid, beyond that given to the relationships among the manuscript witnesses, to the *Chronicle* as a material text of history, even though the opening word of almost all its annals, *her*, invites such a focus on the fabric of the page. Taking up this invitation, the following sections will trace a new trajectory of associations for this word when it is used, as it is in the *Chronicle*, to attach something of the past to place—that is, to bind history to multiple geographies, of the page, of the reader, and of locations present and distant. This new trajectory involves a number of different textual forms and genres (including lists, diagrams, inscriptions, and poems) written on both stone and parchment. Of particular interest is how the differing material agencies of these substances shape the connection between place and the past, and thus serve as active co-constitutors of what has previously been conceptualized as the content or ideological message of these texts.

## Picture books: the relationship of paschal annals and other diagrams to the *Chronicle*

To begin with its textual affiliations, where might the use of *her* in the *Chronicle* originate? To what other forms of textual practice is the use of the term connected? Although these issues have been little commented on by scholars, Peter Clemoes, Thomas Bredehoft, and Nicholas Howe represent important exceptions, and their analyses form an important starting point for my own investigations below.[18]

Widely recognized is the link between *her* and the *Chronicle*'s standard layout, in which the historical note is provided adjacent to the year number given on the left-hand side of the page.[19] As Peter Clemoes, Malcolm Parkes, and others have observed, *her* is only absent in any significant way from the Common Stock annals in the account of

[18] Bredehoft, *Textual Histories*, pp. 119–23; Clemoes, 'Language in Context: *Her* in the 890 *Anglo-Saxon Chronicle*', *Leeds Studies in English* 16 (1985): pp. 27–36; and Howe, *Writing the Map*, pp. 102–3 and p. 177.

[19] For discussion of what constitutes the standard layout, since there is a large degree of variation between and within manuscripts, see Bately, *MS A*, xlvi.

Alfred's later wars against the Danes, a section that was apparently composed at one time and copied in the Parker manuscript in what Parkes called a 'history layout' with the annal numbers in the middle of the page.[20] While the entries of this section begin with some variety of the phrase 'In this year', the vast remainder of the Common Stock annals begin with *her* and are formatted in a dual-columnar arrangement. Given this preferred layout, it seems rather obvious that *her*, as a gestural word similar to *this* or *there*, acts as a pointer to the list of dates, and is intended to link the historical account to a representation of time's passage embodied in the year numbers. Clemoes, in his classic short study of the word, certainly read it in this way, observing that '[e]very *Her* statement, referring to an actual event, validated a physical year number' that took its place in 'a chain of eventful years anchored by Christ's birth'.[21] However, as Bredehoft astutely observes, the abbreviated form in which the *Chronicle* records its dates, with *an~* followed by Roman numerals, makes it difficult to know exactly how to read the following use of *her*.[22] The temporal framework of the *Chronicle* is likely taken from the chronological epitome given by Bede at the conclusion of the *Historia ecclesiastica*, and is one route by which the text asserts a relationship to the Latin historiographical tradition.[23] The importation of language associated with this temporal scheme into the vernacular surroundings of the *Chronicle*, however, complicates its interpretation, since it is not clear whether *an~* should be read as *annus* (year) or *anno* (in this year). As Bredehoft notes, the scribe of manuscript E interpreted this abbreviation as *anno*, which he writes out in full several times on the first page of his work, but '[t]he earlier records of the Common Stock...give no such clear indication of the way this word was read.'[24] Clemoes understands it as standing in for the nominative *annus*, which supports his notion of the function of the uninterrupted sequence of annal years.[25] But, as Bredehoft's analysis

---

[20] Parkes, 'The Paleography of the Parker Manuscript', p. 155.

[21] Clemoes, 'Language in Context', p. 31 and p. 32.

[22] Bredehoft, *Textual Histories*, pp. 119–22.

[23] Neither Bede's chronological epitome nor the annals added to the *Historia* probably in eighth-century Northumbria, known as the *Continuatio Bedae*, use locative language in placing their entries.

[24] Bredehoft, *Textual Histories*, p. 120.

[25] Clemoes, 'Language in Context', p. 28.

makes clear, the combination of this Latin chronological system and the vernacular entries is multivalent, and would have elicited different responses from readers with varying degrees of language competency. Those that expanded the abbreviation to *anno* would notice a redundancy of reference: *in this year* being followed by the further marker of *her* (here).

That *her* is integral to *Chronicle* layout—that is, both the use of Latin *an~* and the basic two-column format—would seem to suggest that it is a feature of historical lists in general. As Clemoes puts it, if we understand *her* to refer to the annal numbers, then it forms part of the strategies that make the *Chronicle* a 'declaration of continuity', which in turn indicates that '[t]he compilers of the 890 Chronicle and the genealogist thought alike.'[26] However, related forms of historical record, such as genealogies, regnal lists, calendars, and paschal annals, do not typically utilize deictic language such as *her* to situate their entries. Both calendars and Easter table notices are especially close analogues for the *Chronicle*, which has generally been assumed to grow out of an earlier and simpler annalistic tradition that relied on the ad hoc entry of information in the restricted marginal space of other types of chronological text.[27] But the use of *hic* to introduce chronological information or the names of saints appears to have been rare in English calendars compiled before the eleventh century, normal practice being simply to situate information next to a date. The calendar of St Willibrord, which was probably written shortly after 703, contains only two such entries, reading 'hic bissextus ponitur' (here the bissextile day is placed) and 'hic uenerabilis uirgo susanna migrauit ad christum' (here the worthy virgin Susanna went to Christ), both being early eighth-century additions.[28] Since all but one of the nineteen English calendars edited by

[26] Ibid., p. 31.

[27] For this view, see Reginald L. Poole, *Chronicles and Annals: A Brief Outline of Their Origin and Growth* (Oxford: Clarendon Press, 1926), pp. 41–55.

[28] Fos 35 and 36b. Plates are provided in H. A. Wilson, ed., *The Calendar of St Willibrord from MS. Paris Lat. 10,837: A Facsimile with Transcription, Introduction, and Notes*, Henry Bradshaw Society 55 (1918; repr. London: Boydell Press, 1998); for a diplomatic edition of these pages, see p. 4 and p. 7. The calendar was bound, probably from the first half of the eighth century, with a copy of the Hieronymian Martyrology. Additions to fo. 28b of this text in a later hand recording Willibrord's death and translation also begin with hic: '+hic domnus+/ apostolicus uir/ uuillibrordus/ ep[i]s[copus] migrauit ad /[christus]' (here the apostolic man of the lord,

Francis Wormald are tenth century or later, sporadic entries beginning with *hic* tell us little about earlier calendric vocabulary, although their scarcity does indicate that such locative language was far from normative in this context, even in later practice.[29]

The standard form of paschal annals also seems to mandate that Latin notes about events be positioned in the margin level with the annotation of the appropriate year number, but with no locative introductory term. In fact, a little-studied set of early English paschal annals that pre-date the *Chronicle*, and have recently been brought to the renewed attention of scholars by Joanna Story, suggest that copyists and compilers of paschal annals sometimes revised out any solitary uses of *hic* that they found in their exemplars.[30] The textual history of these annals, known as 'The Frankish Annals of Lindisfarne and Kent', is complex, with seven manuscripts dating from the mid-eighth to the first third of the ninth centuries preserving a related set of material, including annals apparently originally compiled separately in the kingdoms of Northumbria and Kent.[31] As Story notes, although these annals are quite brief, they are of great importance as evidence of the type of source Bede must have used in composing his *Historia* and, in addition, are an indication of the formal models of Latin annalistic writing potentially available in England to the *Chronicle* compilers.[32] Their recognition as important English exemplars have, however, been complicated by the fact that only one of the manuscript witnesses (Story's manuscript M) contains material actually copied in England around the mid-eighth century, shortly after which it was transported to Fulda where it became the progenitor of a manuscript tradition and

---

Bishop Willibrord went to Christ) and '+hic trans+/latio eiusdem/s[anc]ti uvillibrordi (here [is] the translation of the same Saint Willibrord).

[29] *English Kalendars before AD 1100*, Henry Bradshaw Society 72 (1934; repr. London: The Boydell Press, 1988). Additions of chronological notes beginning with *hic* (for example, 'hic mutant anni et concurrentes') in an eleventh- or twelfth-century hand can be found, for instance, on fos 51 and 51b of Cambridge University Library, Ms Kk. V. 32, fos 50–55b (Wormald #6, pp. 74–5).

[30] 'The Frankish Annals of Lindisfarne and Kent', *Anglo-Saxon England* 34 (2005): pp. 59–109.

[31] For Story's meticulous study of the manuscripts and analysis of the likely scenario of composition and transmission, see 'Frankish Annals', p. 60–74.

[32] Ibid., p. 59.

received Frankish continuations.[33] The Easter tables in this Northumbrian manuscript were carefully copied, along with their attendant annals, by a Fuldan scribe towards the end of the eighth century into a manuscript Story designates as F.[34] Story notes that the scribe of F preserved even such eccentricities of his exemplar's layout as could easily have been corrected, such as dotted lines linking ambiguously positioned material to the correct date, and made only two substantive changes: 'Finan meritur' to 'Finan moritur' (Finan died) and 'Colman abiit' (Colman departed) to 'Colman obiit' (Colman died).[35] Such changes, wrought by a highly conservative scribe, provide a good example of the pressure that conventional annalistic subject matter, and the language used to express it, can exert on a copyist. As Story puts it, '[h]is corrections were a reasonable inference given that the other annals refer either to the obits of bishops or accessions of kings, but his corrected reading changed Colman's departure in 664 to a record of his death, which was wrong.' In other words, the annalistic environment suggests to the scribe that *abiit* being a mistake for *obiit* is more probable than Colman having done something else of historical import other than die in this year. Equally interesting, however, is that this scribe also eliminates the *hic* from the entry in M 'hic Finan meritur', with the resulting 'Finan moritur' followed by all subsequent versions of these annals.[36] This elimination of opening *hic* was not an isolated phenomenon. F was itself updated ad hoc at Fulda in the late eighth century with entries, known as the *Annales Fuldenses Antiquissimi*, modelled on those written earlier at Wearmouth-Jarrow. When copied towards the end of the eighth century into Wien, ÖNB Cvp 460, the entry for 786 from F, 'Hic Hartrat et <ceteri comi>tes exil<ati sunt>. Lul obiit' (Here Hartrat and other companions were exiled. Lul died), is

---

[33] Münster in Westfalen, Staatsarchiv MSC. I. 243, fos 1–2 and 11–12. For discussion of this manuscript, see Story, 'Frankish Annals', pp. 61–7.

[34] Tabulae paschales (cycli decemnovennales XXIX–LXVI: a. 5,321,063) cum adnotationibus ('Annales Lindisfarnenses' et Annales Fuldenses antiquissimi)', Bayerische Staatsbibliothek, clm 14,641 32v–46r. For discussion of this manuscript, see Story, 'Frankish Annals', pp. 65–7.

[35] 'Frankish Annals', p. 65.

[36] Ibid., p. 65 and pp. 108–9, and plates 1a and 1b.

changed to 'Lul obiit. Ha.trat et ceteri exiliati <sunt>' (Lul died. Hatrat and others were exiled), again eliminating the introductory *hic*.[37]

These examples work in two ways, of course. On one hand, they provide evidence for a very early tradition of Latin annal-writing in England in which the use of an occasional *hic* to locate an entry was permissible. On the other hand, they also indicate that such an opening was somewhat rare and, because it was so often eliminated from subsequent versions, that Latin annalists felt such locative language to be unnecessary and extraneous. Thus within paschal annals the normalizing force of standard diction seems to work in a precisely opposite direction to that in the *Chronicle*, where the vernacular equivalent of *hic, her*, is privileged as a mandatory element. Paschal annals are not therefore a source for the *Chronicle*'s use of *her*, a fact that lends authority to recent scholarly work insisting on a more complex understanding of the relationship between paschal and national annals than has been traditionally conceived. Whereas earlier scholars represented the two in terms of a developmental model, with paschal annals the primitive archetype of the more sophisticated national annals, the recent detailed work of Story, Richard Corradini, and Rosamund McKitterick has suggested that both forms were practised coincidentally in medieval scriptoria because they fulfilled differing functions. Story observes of the Continental annal tradition stemming from the Frankish annals of Lindisfarne and Kent that

> [t]he Easter tables provided a rigid structure that linked the Frankish present to the whole of the Christian past, and provided systematic chronological stepping-stones back via the emperors of old to the birth (and death) of Christ himself. Uniquely, as a form of historical expression, the tables also provided a route to the future, since they contained not only the ghosts of Easters past but also those of Easters-yet-to-come.[38]

---

[37] Richard Corradini, 'The Rhetoric of Crisis: *Computus* and *Liber annalis* in Early Ninth-Century Fulda', in *The Construction of Communities in the Early Middle Ages: Texts, Resources and Artefacts*, edited by Richard Corradini, Max Diesenberger, and Helmut Reimitz (Leiden: Brill, 2003), pp. 269–321, at p. 288 and pl. 3.

[38] Story, 'Frankish Annals', p. 74. For the relationship of paschal and national annals, see Story, pp. 72–4. See also Corradini, 'Rhetoric of Crisis', for the fascinating argument that paschal annals respond to a crisis in monastic memoria in ninth-century Carolingia (in particular, pp. 295–303 for comments on the special function of Easter table annals).

Such a revised understanding of the relationship between paschal and full annals has several important consequences for the *Chronicle*, because, while its form recalls that of paschal annals, the idiosyncrasies of that form should no longer be perceived as derived from or constrained by an earlier, more primitive model. In particular, the fact that the *Chronicle* shares a familial resemblance to paschal annals allows for its historical material to be situated in relation to Rome and Latin traditions of record-keeping: to borrow, in other words, part of the uniqueness of historical expression that Story describes as characteristic of Easter table annals. However, at the same time, the *Chronicle*'s stylistic departures from paschal annals offer a new set of possibilities for historical writing, possibilities achieved through its distinctive vernacular idiom.

That paschal annals do not share the *Chronicle*'s choice of language is significant to understanding the different way that each approaches the question of historical representation. Annals, of any kind, convert the temporal register of events into the spatial dimension of the page by means of their list of years, which provides a visual analogue to time's passage. Clemoes commented therefore that 'the 890 *Chronicle* was a sort of diagram', in which the year numbers functioned as a form of chronological picture and the entries as captions. Supporting Clemoes's point are the distinctive similarities between the *Chronicle*'s use of *her* and terminology used to situate inscriptions to pictures. As he noted, the preference for *hic* plus a preterite verb in the titles of the Bayeux Tapestry—for example, 'Hic Harold mare navigavit' (Here Harold crossed the sea)—is a particularly close analogue for *her* in the *Chronicle*.[39] That such a device might be an English invention is confirmed for Clemoes by its use in eleventh-century English translations of Latin

---

See also Rosamund McKitterick, who examines the role of annals in forming a sense of the past in Francia (*History and Memory in the Carolingian World* [Cambridge: Cambridge University Press, 2004], p. 8), and Nicholas Howe, *Writing the Map*, p. 177, for comments on the role of Easter tables in relation to the *Chronicle* and vernacular senses of time and place. For the earlier notion of paschal annals as the primitive progenitor of annals proper, see Poole, *Chronicle and Annals*.

[39] Clemoes, 'Language in Context', pp. 28–9. The majority of the Bayeux Tapestry inscriptions are structured in this way; for the precise statistics, see Clemoes, n. 9. For the Bayeux Tapestry itself, see Martin K. Foys, ed., *The Bayeux Tapestry* (Leicester: Scholarly Digital Editions, 2003), or http://www.bayeuxtapestry.org.uk.

titles in native manuscripts of the *Psychomachia*. As he observes, whereas ninth- and tenth-century French manuscripts provide Latin titles that simply state or describe the action of the accompanying illustration, avoiding any vocabulary such as *here, there* or *this*, two-thirds of the 120 Old English inscriptions add the word *her*.[40] Clemoes adds two further examples in which *hic* or *her* are employed to link script to pictures: the Franks casket and an eleventh-century stone slab from St Nicholas's parish church, Suffolk.[41] For Clemoes, *here* in these pictorial examples serves to 'perform the double function of referring to picture and previous event in conjunction' and thus bridges the past of the event and the present of the account, a function analogous to that he argues is served by the word *her* in the *Chronicle*.[42]

These pictorial examples are compelling evidence that the practice of writing the *Chronicle* was understood to be coterminous in some sense with that of illustrated texts. However, as a special type of visual text, in which words are manipulated in space rather than in relation to any graphic representation, the *Chronicle* is ultimately more akin to diagrams than to pictorial texts in general. Although 'diagram' is in fact the word Clemoes used to describe the *Chronicle*, he did not compare its locative language to that used within diagrams and to introduce diagrams into a written text. Drawing such a comparison is compelling, however, because it would place the *Chronicle* within a lengthy tradition of thinking about chronological concepts in spatial terms. *Computus*, the monastic practice of time-keeping directed in particular toward calculating the dates of liturgical feasts, produced its own specialist literature in early medieval England, in the form of collections

[40] Clemoes, 'Language in Context', pp. 29–30. For the precise statistics, see n. 14. For the text of the Latin and English inscriptions, see Julius Zupitza, 'Englisches aus Prudentiushandschriften', *Zeitschrift für Deutsches Alterthum* 20 (1876), pp. 36–45.

[41] The relevant inscriptions on the Franks casket read: 'Her Hos sitiþ on harmberga agl[.] drgiþ swa hiræ Ertae gisgraf sarden sorga and sefa torna' (Here Hos sits on the sorrow-mound; she suffers distress as Ertae had imposed it on her, a wretched den of sorrows and of torments of mind); 'her fegtaþ titus end giuþeasu' (Here Titus and a Jew fight); and 'HIC FUGIANT HIERUSALEM' (Here its inhabitants flee from Jerusalem). Text and translation from R. I. Page, *An Introduction to English Runes* (London: Methuen, 1973), pp. 174–82. The stone slab (Okasha #58) reads, '[:]HER : SCE [M] IHA[E]L : FEHT þIÐ ÐANE : DRACA :' (Here St Michael fights [fought] against the dragon). As transcribed by Elisabeth Okasha, *Hand-List of Anglo-Saxon Non-Runic Inscriptions* (Cambridge: Cambridge University Press, 1971).

[42] Clemoes, 'Language in Context', p. 30.

of diverse material related to the reckoning of time.[43] Easter tables, and the paschal annals they housed, formed an important component of such collections, which were rich in diagrams that, in Philippa Semper's words, 'operate as visual "texts", organizing and displaying the "order of the world"'.[44] Computistical and chronological works were therefore closely related in medieval textual culture. Bede, for instance, chose to conclude his great *computus* work, *De Temporum Ratione*, with a world chronicle. These twin interests in historiography and *computus* suggest—as does Corradini's detailed study of the use of such chronological texts in the context of ninth-century Carolingia—that both functioned within overlapping and complex monastic strategies of *memoria*. Both, in other words, served to investigate the ways that written words can be employed to represent and structure notions of 'past, presence and future'.[45] Because the *Chronicle* shares a fundamental similarity of approach with the *computus* as a whole, such texts form a natural comparative when considering how the *Chronicle* might have worked as a diagram.

Byrhtferth's *Enchiridion*, a bilingual treatise on the *computus* apparently intended for the instruction of monks and clerics, and probably composed between 1010 and 1012, represents one such important *computus* text.[46] Clemoes, in his analysis of the *Chronicle* as diagram, noticed a connection between the *Chronicle*'s use of *her* to 'validate' a physical year number and Byrhtferth's 'use of language to validate numbers visually', although he did not explore this suggestion any further.[47] Although the *Enchiridion* was written slightly over a century

---

[43] For a discussion of the broad scope of medieval *computus*, see Evelyn Edson, *Mapping Time and Space: How Medieval Mapmakers Viewed their World* (London: British Library, 1997), p. 96.

[44] Philippa Semper, 'Doctrine and Diagrams: Maintaining the Order of the World in Byrhtferth's Enchiridion', in *The Christian Tradition in Anglo-Saxon England: Approaches to Current Scholarship and Teaching*, edited by Paul Cavill (Cambridge: D.S. Brewer, 2004), pp. 121–37, at p. 126.

[45] Corradini, 'Rhetoric of Crisis', especially p. 303.

[46] *Byrhtferth's Enchiridion*, edited by Peter S. Baker and Michael Lapidge, Early English Text Society, s.s., 15 (Oxford: Oxford University Press, 1995), pp. xxvii–xxviii. This is the standard edition of the text, and Baker and Lapidge include modern representations of the diagrams, whereas an earlier edition, *Byrhtferth's Manual*, edited and translated by S. J. Crawford, Early English Text Society, 177 (London: Oxford University Press, 1929), contains plates of many of the diagrams.

[47] Clemoes, 'Language in Context', pp. 31–2.

after the *Chronicle* was initiated, it nonetheless provides a valuable store of information about vernacular diagram culture, since Byrhtferth was no slavish copier of inherited schematics, but an active composer of diagrams in his own right. He was, as Peter Baker puts it, 'an enthusiastic draftsman—one who believed fervently that seeing concepts laid out spatially was the best way to achieve an understanding of them'.[48] In addition, Byrhtferth had probably read the *Chronicle*, since he very likely had access to a version of it when he composed a set of Latin annals, now lost, for the years 958–92. Cyril Hart even proposed that Byrhtferth wrote the B text of the *Chronicle*, although this has not been accepted by scholars working on either text.[49] Most agree, though, that the certain presence of various sets of annals at pre-Conquest Ramsey indicates that it must have been a historiographical centre of some importance, which suggests that Byrhtferth would have had ample opportunity to consult and consider annalistic layout.

The diagrams of Byrhtferth's collection can be understood as fulfilling various mediating functions within a text that, in its bilingual format and its consideration of audience, is deeply invested overall in issues of translation and pedagogy.[50] As Semper argues, they are one important method of integrating information drawn from different ideological contexts, and of instructing the reader in the pre-eminence of Christian models for understanding the world.[51] Locative markers, as mediators between the visual and the textual, serve a central role in these functions. For instance, *her* is frequently used in the *Enchiridion* as the point of relation between a written text and an accompanying

[48] Peter S. Baker, 'More Diagrams by Byrhtferth of Ramsey', in *Latin Learning and English Lore: Studies in Anglo-Saxon Literature for Michael Lapidge*, edited by Katherine O'Brien O'Keeffe and Andy Orchard (Toronto: University of Toronto Press, 2005), pp. 53–73, at p. 54.

[49] Cyril Hart, 'The B text of the Anglo-Saxon Chronicle', *Journal of Medieval History* 8 (1982), pp. 241–99. Hart provides an edition of Byrhtferth's annals at pp. 295–6. For opposition to Hart, see Alfred Smyth, *King Alfred the Great* (Oxford: Oxford University Press, 1995), esp. pp. 456–60. For late tenth-century Ramsey as a historiographical centre, see Smyth, and Baker and Lapidge, *Byrhtferth's Enchiridion*, p. xxxiii. For overall discussion of the relationship between these annals, see Janet Bately, *Texts and Textual Relationships*, pp. 55–9.

[50] For discussion of the *Enchiridion* in relation to its audience, see Rebecca Stephenson, 'Scapegoating the Secular Clergy: The Hermeneutic Style as a Form of Monastic Self-Definition', *Anglo-Saxon England* 38 (2009): pp. 101–35.

[51] Semper, 'Doctrine and Diagrams.'

diagram: the figure of the zodiac, to cite one example, is followed by the statement, 'Nu her ys gemearcod se circul þe ys zodiacus gehaten' (Now the circle that is called the zodiac has been recorded here), which simultaneously calls the reader's attention to what has been depicted and allows for a transition back to a continuous prose portion.[52] The second figure of the zodiac, which includes the length of time that the sun spends in each sign, is both introduced and followed by such a *her* formula: 'swa we hyt her amearcod habbaðu... Her ys zodiacus syne-wealt amearcod' (as we have marked it here... Here is the circular zodiac drawn).[53] A similar function is served by the term *her* in Byrhtferth's tables of the names of the months in different languages. These tables are little more than vocabulary lists extending over half a page and separated from the main text by lines that form arcaded columns. Each list begins with a descriptive word that seems intended as a title, although it is not visually distinguished (either by script, size, or position) from the words that compose the lists themselves—*Hebrei* (Hebrew), *Aegiptisc* (Egyptian), and *Grecisce* (Greek).[54] In contrast, the list of the English months is given in a box delineated by double ink-lines and extending across the full horizontal writing space. This box is bisected by the 'title' statement, which is separated from the list itself by vertical lines: 'On Englisc her synt þæra .xii. monða naman' (Here are the names of the twelve months in English).[55] Because this phrase is within the diagram while it is also separate from the words of this diagram and the main text, it serves to mediate the various types of writing included on the page: it is both part of the diagram, a 'title', and part of Byrthferth's continuous prose explanation, where it acts as a transitional phrase akin to those surrounding the figures of the zodiac.

---

[52] Baker and Lapidge, *Enchiridion*, p. 6, fig. 1. Crawford, *Byrhtferth's Manual*, p. 8.

[53] Baker and Lapidge, *Enchiridion*, pp. 106–9, fig. 16; Crawford, *Byrhtferth's Manual*, p. 116.

[54] Baker and Lapidge's figs 5–8, 'The Months' (pp. 24–5), bear little resemblance to the layout of these diagrams in the primary manuscript witness for the *Enchiridion*, the mid-eleventh-century copy in Oxford, Bodleian Library, Ashmole 328 (S.C. 6882, 7420) (for date and discussion of the manuscript, see Baker and Lapidge, *Enchiridion*, pp. cxv–cxxi). While the editors present these figures within one cohesive table, and in the same format on both pages of their facing-page edition and translation (although they translate the terms of the table into modern English), they note that in Ashmole 328, figures 5–6 appear on one page and 7–8 on the following.

[55] Baker and Lapidge, *Enchiridion*.

The inclusion of *her* serves to direct the reader in how to manage the different types of texts that Byrhtferth brings together, and to understand the ways in which they are intended to exemplify each other. As Semper comments, Byrhtferth's diagrams 'exist in dynamic interrelationship with the text that introduces or follows them, and they are specifically presented as a better means of understanding what is to be learnt'.[56]

Bede's *De Locis Sanctis*, a treatise composed around 702–3 on the major sites of the Holy Land and substantially based on Adamnan's earlier work of the same name, provides another example of a diagram in which *here* is used internally. *De Locis Sanctis*, substantial portions of which Bede also included in the fifth book of his *Historia ecclesiastica*, provides an interesting comparative to the *Chronicle*, because it is a work fundamentally about the relation of history and geography, and the role of reading in allowing access to both. The genre of writing dedicated to describing the Holy Land ranged widely through its historical, topographical, and toponymical dimensions, and was directed more toward virtual than real travellers. Diagrammatic representations of places in such works can serve to collapse the temporal dimension of events into the spatial register of place; they are a method, in other words, of taking events out of time and organizing them by means of the space in which they occurred.[57] Bede's diagram of the basilica on Mount Sion is a good example. Within a simple outline of the shape of the church, statements of *what happened* are linked by means of *hic* to the precise locations *where they happened*: 'Hic sancta Maria obiit' (here Saint Mary died), 'Hic columna stat marmorea petra cui adherens dominus flagellatus est' (here stands the marble column

[56] Semper, 'Doctrine and Diagrams', p. 126.

[57] The original text has been edited by J. Fraipont, *Bedae uenerabilis de locis sanctis*, *Corpus christianorum series Latina* 175 (Turnhout: Brepols, 1965), pp. 249–80, with a line drawing of the diagram at p. 258. For a translation of Bede's text, see *Bede: A Biblical Miscellany*, translated by W. Trent Foley and Arthur G. Holder (Liverpool: Liverpool University Press, 1999), with a representation of the relevant diagram at p. 10. For a plate of this diagram in Adamnan's *De Locis Sanctis*, see *Adamnan's De Locis Sanctis*, edited by Denis Meehan, Scriptores Latini Hiberniae 3 (Dublin, 1958; repr. 1983), 62. That no manuscripts of *De locis sanctis* survive from early medieval England does not mean, of course, that none existed at the time. The text is quite widely attested in post-Conquest Continental and English manuscripts (see M. L. W. Laistner, *A Hand-List of Bede Manuscripts* [Ithaca: Cornell University Press, 1943], pp. 83–6).

on which the lord clung as he was whipped), 'Hic sp*iritus* s*anctus* super
apostolos descendit' (the Holy Spirit came down on the apostles here).
In terms of modern understandings of the relation between diagrams
and surrounding prose text, such uses of *here* within a diagram would
probably be conceived of as separate from its function in introducing
titles, as in the examples from the *Enchiridion*. However, the division
between language constitutive of a diagram and that used to name or
label this diagram is less clear-cut in early medieval textual culture,
which does not map this distinction in terms of an inside–outside
model. In other words, whereas a titular phrase will likely appear
above or below a modern diagram—and be clearly separated from it
both by page space and by marks of punctuation—a phrase with an
equivalent function can, in an early medieval text, appear within the
bounds of the diagram itself. The use of both *her* and *hic* within and
around the diagrams I have discussed therefore suggests that such
locative language is part of pre-Conquest writers experimenting with
the visual dimensions of the written medium to recreate the spatial and
temporal registers of lived experience. As Semper argues, Byrhtferth's
diagrams 'require active reading processes—in some cases the physical
turning of the manuscript in order to read labels that are upside
down—which in turn facilitate the learning of the material they contain'.[58] Diagrams, whether they aim to recreate history and geography
for their reader or to teach the thorny principles of *computus*, share this
experiential component: they are intended actively to involve the reader
and thus to mediate him or her with the text itself.

Having established that *her* and *hic* work within diagrams specifically to facilitate this mediation, by drawing attention to the page itself
and to the activity of reading, it is worth bringing this insight to bear on
the contrast between paschal annals and the *Chronicle*. While both
Easter table annals and the *Chronicle* use page layout to communicate
the connection between time and events (and thus to make the account
temporal), paschal annals can be seen as naturalizing this link, whereas
the *Chronicle*'s use of *her* draws attention to it as a product of the
architecture of the page itself. Paschal annals, by not including situational adverbs, more concisely achieve the aim of connecting a textual

[58] 'Doctrine and Diagrams', p. 126. As Semper notes, this does not mean that diagrams
are 'open-ended' and allow for any possible interpretation, however (p. 126, esp. n. 19).

statement of *what happened* to a date that indicates *when it happened*, and without emphasizing the structure that expresses this connection. So, if the defining characteristic of a diagram is its ability to communicate relationships between concepts briefly and elegantly by means of the extra-verbal element of spatial arrangement, paschal annal-writers seem to have been correct in finding *her* extraneous, since placing historical information against a year number allows the format of the page to communicate in an obvious way that this event occurred in this year. What we might describe as the double redundancy of *her* within the economy of the *Chronicle* page—where year number and entry are already linked not only by the layout but also very likely by the *an~* abbreviation for *anno* (in this year)—serves radically to foreground the fact that the relation between time's passage and events narrated, what is in other words specifically historical in the text, is a relation tied to the book and the page.

In this respect, *her* in the *Chronicle* has much in common with the vernacular formulas *her onginneð* for Latin *incipit*, and *her endað*, for *explicit*, in which *her* makes obvious that a beginning or an ending is simultaneously experienced and spatially embodied on the page. Such formulas are commonly used in vernacular texts, appearing in the *Old English Bede*, the Old English translation of Gregory's *Dialogues*, the Old English Orosius, and Ælfric's *Lives of Saints*, among other places. Within the list of chapter headings of the *Old English Bede*, for instance, the beginning and ending points of the five books are punctuated by means of formulas such as 'Her endað seo forme bóc. Her onginneð seo oðer bóc' (Here ends the first book. Here begins the second book).[59] The beginnings and endings of the books themselves in the main text are more diversely marked: the close of the first book and beginning of the second is indicated by a formula very close to that in the table of contents; the conclusion of the second book is marked by a vernacular formula, whereas the beginning and end of the third book, as well as the beginning of the fourth and fifth, are all marked by Latin formulas; and the close of the fourth and fifth books goes unmarked. Byrhtferth begins the *Enchiridion* not only with statements of beginning in both

---

[59] Miller, *Old English Bede*, pp. 10–11.

Latin and English but also, characteristically for him, with a discussion of the meaning of beginning:

> Incipit compotus Latinorum ac Grecorum Hebreorumque et Egiptiorum, necnon et Anglorum. Incipit, id est inchoat uel initium sumit siue exordium accipit... Her onginð gerimcræft æfter Ledenwarum and æfter Grecum and Iudeiscum and Egiptiscum ad Engliscum þeodum and ma oðra.[60]

> (Here begins the *computus* of the Romans and the Greeks and the Hebrews and Egyptians, as well as of the English. *Incipit*: that is, 'starts' or 'takes its inception' or 'receives its send-off'... Here begins the *computus* according to the Romans, and according to the Greek, Jewish, Egyptian and English peoples, and others as well.)

Because 'here begins' is a standard expression for beginning in Modern English also, Baker and Lapidge's translation necessarily obscures the difference in the two languages in Byrhtferth's original. Unlike Latin *incipit*, though, which D. Vance Smith, in his study of beginnings in the fourteenth century, glosses as '[i]t begins, from *capio*, take or seize, a purposive action, an "arbitrary" beginning, the beginning of a text', the vernacular *her onginneð* inextricably yokes the fact of beginning to the local environment of the book, and is more particular than it is arbitrary or abstract.[61] What the addition of this locative language emphasizes, in other words, is that the reader or audience's experience of the fact of beginning or ending a text is inseparable from its written notation, which converts the temporal qualities of starting and finishing into the spatial logic of the book.

When such language is added to an annalistic text like the *Chronicle*, it offers a quite radically different notion of the connection between time and events than that more abstract relation produced by paschal annals. Since it is not, strictly speaking, necessary to the account, *her* becomes available to serve a surplus function that is connected to its deictic properties: it links the historical account to the local context of the reader. As Nicholas Howe observes, *her* is capable of referring both to '"here in the record of history" and here in "the larger location of

---

[60] Baker and Lapidge, *Enchiridion*, pp. 2–3.

[61] *The Book of the Incipit: Beginnings in the Fourteenth Century* (Minneapolis: Minnesota University Press, 2001), p. 1.

England", and should be taken to mean something like "here and now" or "here in this time and place"'.[62] The use of *her*, then, not only fuses the geographical with the historical but also complicates the distinction between the occurrence and the reception of events, as it refers both to the past of the account and the present of its reading.

## *Here lies*: mortuary formulas on stones

While I have thus far emphasized the innovative nature of *her* in the *Chronicle*, its valence within this work is not entirely without precedent in other types of historical texts. This section will argue that the use of *hic* or *her* at the opening of epitaphs would have provided readers with a model for understanding the new (to the late ninth century) function of locative language within vernacular annals. Reading the *Chronicle* in the context of mortuary literature in this way might at first sound improbable, but the two are likely closely related in origin, purpose, and subject matter. In fact, virtually every annal of the *Chronicle* mentions the death of notable figures, and in many cases such notices are the sole content of the annal: counting instances only of the most common formulaic expression used for reporting deaths (personal name plus *gefor* or *forðferde*) yields eighty instances in the Common Stock alone. However, epitaph literature has never been suggested as a formal analogue for the use of *her* at the opening of annals in the *Chronicle*, although Joanna Story has made a compelling argument for the probable relation between epitaphs and paschal annals as methods for recording names, and dates of death and burial. In her study of the Frankish annals of Lindisfarne and Kent, she observes that the Kentish annals may have preserved information initially recorded as inscriptions on royal and archiepiscopal tombs, most likely within SS Peter and Paul at Canterbury.[63] In addition to acting as a source for annalistic content, however, I am suggesting that mortuary discourse may have conditioned the characteristic idiom of the *Chronicle*, especially its use of opening *her*, and certainly could have influenced how users of the annals received that idiom. In particular, the demonstration of such a

---

[62] Howe, *Writing Home*, 177.
[63] Story, 'The Frankish Annals', pp. 92–7.

formal link to epitaph literature allows us to understand in more specific terms how the *Chronicle* functioned within a network of practices of memorial archiving involving stones and books.

Recent archaeological studies have concentrated on the social semiotics of burial practices in early medieval England; like a text, as Martin Carver eloquently observed, 'burials have a language'.[64] As Howard Williams and others argue, the associated complex of activities that clusters around the death of an individual (preparation for burial, disposal of the body, ceremony, and commemoration) are deeply social, concerned with 'both group inclusion and exclusion'.[65] In general, English 'Christianity brought with it...a commemorative emphasis upon topography and monumentality at the expense of portable artifacts', or in other words, a movement away from burial with grave goods and a more global approach to situating burial-places in the landscape.[66] Recent archaeological interpretation, however, has argued that 'mortuary practices', in Williams's terms, are implicated in complex ways in the supersession of one governing ideological paradigm by another, such as paganism by Christianity, since they can be employed to register residual or relapsed loyalty to an older system, or to assert the existence of minority identity in the midst of a more dominant culture. Although the role of pagan and Christian within pre-Conquest burial practices, and the transition from one to the other, is thus often presented as occurring in an uncomplex and unilateral fashion in the early period, more recent work has emphasized that this process was far from finished by the ninth century, when the *Chronicle* was copied. Since internment customs were not controlled by the

---

[64] Carver writes that '[a] grave is...a text with an attitude, a text inflated with emotion...it is a palimpsest of allusions' ('Burial as Poetry: The Context of Treasure in Anglo-Saxon Graves', in *Treasure in the Medieval West*, edited by Elizabeth M. Tyler [York: York Medieval Press, 2000], pp. 25–48, at p. 37).

[65] *Death and Memory in Early Medieval Britain* (Cambridge: Cambridge University Press, 2006), p. 12; see also p. 88. For additional discussion of the role that burial practices play in construction of social memory, see Howard Williams, 'Introduction: The Archaeology of Death, Memory and Material Culture', in *Archaeologies of Remembrance: Death and Memory in Past Societies*, edited by Howard Williams (New York: Kluwer Academic/Plenum Publishers, 2003), pp. 1–24. The essays collected in this volume, which examine mortuary rituals ranging in date from the Bronze Age to the present, exemplify the new interdisciplinary and constructivist approach to burial archaeology that Howard describes in his introduction.

[66] Williams, *Death and Memory*, p. 45.

Christian church, the practice of burying grave goods was not eradicated in the centuries following the conversion; objects have been found in graves from the seventh through to the eleventh century, and especially in the ninth century.[67]

Although, as Thompson emphasizes, no pre-Conquest period is characterized by complete uniformity in burial practices, the decades surrounding 900 have been seen to register distinctive changes in the 'landscape, practice and ideology of burial'.[68] In particular, the concept of 'Christian burial', and its association with a specific kind of bounded cemetery space, begins to emerge at this time, although it takes centuries to become fully normative. Increased numbers of grave markers and sculpture form part of these changes, which involve a broad movement in the symbolic economy of burial from a primarily below-ground syntax of grave goods to an above-ground use of markers and inscriptions.[69] Even those few elaborately furnished burials around 900 are related, Dawn Hadley argues, to this broader political and religious shift, rather than being mutely reflective of ethnic difference between the Christian English and the pagan Vikings, as was traditionally thought. These graves do not mark 'innate ethnic differences but a society undergoing major transitions in political authority, lordship and ecclesiastical organization'.[70] In other words, the brief return to below-ground display is a nostalgic symptom of radical change occurring in the late ninth century within the field of burial practices,

[67] Ibid., p. 45. More detail on Scandinavian burials within England can be found in Dawn Hadley, *Death in Medieval England* (Stroud: Tempus, 2001), pp. 33–4; pp. 109–11; and pp. 140–2. For the chronology of burial practices, see Andrew Reynolds, *Later Anglo-Saxon England: Life and Landscape* (Stroud: Tempus, 1999), p. 24; Victoria Thompson, *Dying and Death in Later Anglo-Saxon England* (Woodbridge: Boydell Press, 2004), esp. pp. 27–30.

[68] Thompson, *Dying and Death*, p. 31. This roughly coincides with the shift from a Middle to Late period around 850, divisions commonly employed by archaeologists (for these divisions, see Reynolds, *Later Anglo-Saxon England*, p. 23). See Martin Carver, 'Burial as Poetry', pp. 26–7, for bibliography supporting the argument that a similarly radical change occurred in mortuary practices around 650, after which point burial goods for the majority were converted into taxation paid to the church. Burial goods are thereafter placed only in the graves of monarchs and members of the ruling classes, because these receive the full symbolic investment of community identity.

[69] Thompson, *Dying and Death*, p. 126. See also, Hadley, *Death in Medieval England*, p. 111 and p. 126.

[70] Hadley, *Death in Medieval England*, p. 111.

associated with an increased preference for visible surface marking on stone.

Memorial formulas comprise one of the five types of inscription, as classified by Elisabeth Okasha in her invaluable hand-lists of non-runic inscriptions found on early medieval English stonework.[71] Although it is true of the lapidary evidence that, as R. I. Page observed, the 'here lies' formula is unusual before the Conquest but common enough after it, a number of pre-Conquest grave markers inscribed with this phrase do survive.[72] And since it is widely recognized that surviving grave furniture from early medieval England represents only a small proportion of the original corpus, it is reasonable to assume that such inscriptions were more prevalent than their somewhat scanty numbers suggest.[73] Okasha conservatively counted only three occurrences of this latter formula in her initial *Handbook*, but this number is increased to eight by the additional evidence from her supplemental lists and also by including those inscriptions that are incomplete, but which clearly display the locative language *her* or *hic*.[74] Although about three-quarters of all carved stonework is found in the north of England

---

[71] While many of these markers are miscellaneous, others are inscribed with regularly occurring dedicatory phrases, following the *beacen*, *ora pro*, or *here lies* models. See the following works by Elisabeth Okasha: *Hand-List of Anglo-Saxon Non-Runic Inscriptions*; 'A Supplement to Hand-List of Anglo-Saxon Non-Runic Inscriptions', *Anglo-Saxon England* 11 (1983): pp. 83–118; 'A Second Supplement to Hand-List of Anglo-Saxon Non-Runic Inscriptions', *Anglo-Saxon England* 21 (1992): pp. 37–85; 'A Third Supplement to Hand-List of Anglo-Saxon Non-Runic Inscriptions', *Anglo-Saxon England* 33 (2004): pp. 225–81. For the *beacen* stones, which include a two-line alliterative verse formula commemorating their recipient, see also Elisabeth Okasha, 'The Commissioners, Makers and Owners of Anglo-Saxon Inscriptions', *Anglo-Saxon Studies in Archaeology and History* 7 (1994): pp. 71–7, at p. 74 and pp. 75–6.

[72] 'How Long Did the Scandinavian Language Survive in England? The Epigraphical Evidence', in *England before the Conquest: Studies in Primary Sources presented to Dorothy Whitelock*, edited by Peter Clemoes and Kathleen Hughes (Cambridge: Cambridge University Press, 1971), pp. 165–81, at p. 180. For an excellent introduction to the range and function of memorial objects in medieval England, see Hadley, *Death in Medieval England*, pp. 125–73.

[73] Williams, *Death and Memory*, 150.

[74] To Okasha's Monkwearmouth II, Whitchurch and Winchester I, can thus be added Canterbury VII, Lincoln II, Whitby III, Winchester VIII, and York VIII. Okasha transcribes Hartlepool O, lost and with fragments preserved only in the form of a modern rubbing, as '—[Q]VIESC[I]T [...] CO—', which she speculates 'may have been of the form, HIC IN SEPULCRO REQUIESCIT CORPORE, but it is too fragmentary to be certain' (Hand-List, #44).

during this period, these eight examples are more widely dispersed, with half located in the north and half in the south. Their dates are also wide ranging, spanning from the eighth to the eleventh or possibly twelfth centuries.[75]

Like the *Chronicle*, very few particulars are known about the composition practices underlying pre-Conquest inscriptions or their function within a textual community. As Okasha puts it,

> [w]ork remains to be done on the composers of the stone texts of Anglo-Saxon England. We should like to know who these men were, their level of education, their status in society. We should like to know if they were the same men who actually engraved the stones. We should like to know if, when both Old English and Latin texts occur on a stone, the same man composed both. We should like to know more about the reading public: whom did the composers think would read these stones? Who actually did read their stones?[76]

Only two of these markers name their dedicatees as priests, suggesting that grave markers could have functioned as a record, perhaps in the absence of other historiographic outlets, for the relationships and lives

[75] Okasha dates Hartlepool O to the eighth century; Whitby III (Okasha #124), which bears the clear inscription 'HIC RE[...] [P]V—', is dated as eighth to ninth century. Monkwearmouth II (Okasha #92) is dated as ninth to eleventh century and possibly even pre-875. It is particularly well preserved, having been found face down below ground, and reads 'HIC IN SEPULCRO REQVIESCIT CORPORE HEREBRICHT PRB:' (Here in the tomb rests Herebericht the priest in his bodily form). Whitchurch (Okasha #135) dates from a similar period, the ninth to eleventh century, and carries its inscription across the thickness of its rounded top, reading '+HIC CORPVS FRI[Đ]BVRGAE REQVIESCIT IN [PA]CE[M] SEPVLTVM' (+Here lies the body of Fri[ð]bvrg, buried in peace). Although the date of York VIII (Okasha #153) is uncertain, its inscription is similar to that of Whitchurch: Okasha gives it as '+HIC [...]CES[...] ITEM [...R]A[...] VVLFHER[E RE]QVIESC[VN]T __' (+Here [...] rest Vvlfher[e]...). Lincoln II (Okasha # 226) is a lead cross, found in the vicinity of a stone coffin, and dates from the eleventh or twelfth century; its inscription reads, 'CORPVS : SIFORDI : PRESBITERI : SC̄E ELENE : 7 SC̄E MARGARETE TITVLATVS HIC IACET' (Here lies named the body of Siford, priest of St Helen and St Margaret).

[76] 'Vernacular or Latin? The Languages of Insular Inscriptions, AD 500–1100', in *Epigraphik 1988: Fachtagung für mittelalterliche und neuzeutliche epigraphic. Graz, 10–14 Mai 1988*, edited by Walter Koch (Wien: Verlag der österreichischen Akademie der Wissenschaften, 1990), pp. 139–62, at p. 145. For specific discussion of the possible functions of inscribed memorial stones in particular, see Okasha, 'Memorial Stones or Grave-Stones?' in *The Christian Tradition in Anglo-Saxon England: Approaches to Current Scholarship and Teaching*, edited by Paul Cavill (Cambridge: D.S. Brewer, 2004), pp. 91–101.

of wealthy secular persons.[77] Certainly the lengthy inscription of one
such artefact, Canterbury VII (Okasha #161), is indicative of the ways
that stone markers acted as historical texts in their own right, reading
'CONDITVS: HIC EST EDZIE [QV.:] GE[R . R]ALD [:] FILIVS
EDWARDI...QVI OBIIT IN XPO [:] IN XIII KL IVNII [:] SEP
DICITO ANIME REQVIESCAT IN [:] PACE HERIVVALD ME
FECIT' (Here is interred Edzie or Ge[r. r.]ald, son of Edward..., who
died in Christ on 19 May. Say always to his soul 'May he rest in peace'.
Herivvald made me.) Although this stone is probably late—the form of
the names and script leads Okasha to assign a tentative date in the late
tenth or eleventh century—it gives the same type of information about
name, kin relationships, and date of death (albeit by day rather than by
year) that would be given in an annal account, strengthening the notion
of an underlying affinity between the two forms. While much uncer-
tainty surrounds the origin and production of the *Chronicle* and of such
grave markers, both thus seem to adopt similar formal strategies in
fulfilling what is presumably a related function of record.

The examples of lapidary inscriptions discussed thus far are in Latin,
but all the memorial formulae identified by Okasha occur in the
vernacular also, with no reason immediately obvious for the choice of
one language above the other. Okasha has investigated what motivates
the choice of language for pre-Conquest stone inscriptions in 'Vernacular or Latin?' and finds that neither type of monument, date,
literacy level, nor content seems materially to impact the choice,
although script and language are somewhat correlated with Old English
inscriptions mostly being written in Roman script and sometimes also
in runes. When the same script is used for both languages, Okasha finds
little distinction in letter forms.[78] She notes that, although we might
expect works with an ecclesiastical content to be written in Latin,
inscriptions in pre-Conquest England are not distinguished in this
way by content or audience.[79] Since it has often been compared to
other forms of writing in Latin, especially the Continental annalistic

---

[77] These two are Monkwearmouth II and Lincoln II. For discussion of the secular use
of grave markers, see Hadley, *Death in Medieval England*, p. 126.

[78] Okasha, 'The Non-Runic Scripts of Anglo-Saxon Inscriptions', *Transactions of the
Cambridge Bibliographical Society* 4 (1968): pp. 321–8, at p. 337.

[79] Bately, 'Vernacular or Latin?' pp. 143–4.

tradition, the fact that many of the *here lies* markers are in Latin thus does not mitigate their relevance as potential analogues for the *Chronicle*. Epitaph literature and the *Chronicle* can instead be thought of as related forms of historical discourse.

The vernacular form of Latin *hic requiescit*, *her liþ*, appears in a number of annals of the *Chronicle*, even as early as the Common Stock. As Bately noted, the *lic liþ* collocation is used ten times in the 890 Chronicle (in annals 716, twice in 755, 784, 855, twice in 860, 867, 871, 874, and 888), and is normative for this section, with *lic resteþ* appearing only in a stretch of early eighth-century annals (and, more precisely, in 716) that Bately finds distinctive.[80] Although, as Bately comments, the preference for *resteþ* instead of *liþ* in certain annals 'could reflect the Latin verb *requiescere*', both usages suggest, if not that grave markers are a direct source for these annals (which, given the partial nature of lapidary evidence, would be hard to prove), that they certainly exerted a stylistic influence on *Chronicle* phraseology.[81] *Lic liþ* is definitely the more productive formula of the two, being used into the tenth- and eleventh- century annals of the continuing versions. Although the annal opening *her* and the phrase *lic liþ* are typically separated by intervening historical information (whereas, on a grave marker this order would be reversed with *her lic liþ* beginning the account), the collocation of these particular words in the *Chronicle*, by recalling their use within epitaphs, complicates the referential function of *her* and makes far more specific the claims for its geographical valence. For example, annal 860 reads 'AN. .dccclx. Her Eþelbald cyng forþferde, 7 his lic liþ æt Scireburnan' (860. Here King Ethelbald died and his body lies at Sherborne). The *her* in this annal not only gestures to the location on the manuscript page that serves to represent time past but also serves to construct the idea of a place common to the book, the reader, and Ethelbald's body: 'Her…his lic liþ æt Scireburnan.'

Since almost all commentators agree that the *Chronicle* project was initiated in the late ninth century, within those decades around 900

---

[80] Bately, 'Compilation', p. 105 and p. 105, n. 2. Bately also lists this formula as appearing in 738, although here the reading is distinctive for not including the word 'lic': 'hie restaþ begen on Eoforwicceastre on anum portice'.

[81] Ibid., p. 105, n. 2.

significant to the change in burial practices from below- to above-ground marking, it is compelling to read its use of opening *her* as participating in these wider attempts to preserve and mark events. Within such a context, the ways in which the *Chronicle* may be described as a social text emerge more clearly, precisely because its innovative historiographic idiom need no longer be seen as anomalous but as participating in a wider cultural focus on the intersections between text, space, and history. The decision to begin annals with *her*, when read against this background, is revealed as lending a specific type of historical authority to the account, one not based in the living body of the witness but in the fecund dead body marked by the gravestone.

## *Here lies*: mortuary formulas in books

What I have been calling thus far mortuary discourse, or epitaph literature, is produced from the interactions between words and the material that these words are written or incised on. The stone grave markers that become increasingly evident around 900 harness the resistant matter of stone to lend permanence to the record—to trans-late, as it were, the perishable materiality of the human body and the transience of its actions into a more durable form embedded in the landscape. As Jerome Cohen has written, '[i]ncised, painted, dressed, arranged, stone is that with which we form alliance to transmit endur-ing meaning.'[82] Of course, as the partial nature of many of the inscrip-tions described above indicate, stone is also changing and perishing, albeit much more slowly than the fabric of human bodies. In the meantime, while stone's activity and movement are imperceptible to us, the permanence and fixity of stone markers bring the past into the present through the medium of place.

In its use of *her*, the *Chronicle* invokes this meeting between textua-lized history and its material component, a boundary that the grave-stone works to mark by simultaneously hiding the corpse and registering its presence in the form of an inscription. Gravestone

---

[82] Cohen, *Stone*, p. 103.

inscriptions thus offer the possibility of a fully materialized sign system at the same time that they make concrete the referential structure of language: texts written on stones literally sit atop, but also conceal, their referents. Like the hagiographical texts that I discussed in the last chapter, epitaph literature is thus especially concerned with the question of presence and absence, because, in a way analogous to saints themselves, epitaphs are at once inherently localized—since they are connected to a body buried in a particular place—and are also movable, amenable to copying and circulation in collections within manuscript books. Peter Brown noted this intersection in *The Cult of the Saints*, writing that 'in the cult of relics also, late-antique and early-medieval piety...gloried in particularity. Hic locus est: "Here is the place", or simply *hic*, is a refrain that runs through the inscriptions on the early martyrs' shrines of North Africa.'[83] Mortuary inscriptions themselves developed in tandem with the practice of venerating saints. The fourth-century epigrammatical program of Pope Damasus was central to the emergence of written collections, known as *syllogae*, of Latin verse epitaphs, transcribed from their locations on memorial stones and widely circulated within Europe as composition models.[84] If the *Chronicle* is citing epitaph literature in its use of opening *her*, it is thus against a background in which the border between lapidary inscriptions and written text is already quite fluid, in the early part of the pre-Conquest period in England as on the Continent.

In fact, a *syllogae* collection was put together at Worcester in the late eighth century, either by or at the behest of Milred, bishop from 743–5 to 774–5.[85] Although no contemporary manuscript witness to this

---

[83] *The Cult of the Saints*, p. 86.

[84] For the Damasian inscriptions and the many examples therein of epitaphs using hic formulae, see *Epigrammata Damasiana*, edited by Antonius Ferrua (Rome: Pontifico Istituto di Archeologia Cristiana, 1942).

[85] Patrick Sims-Williams, 'Milred of Worcester's Collection of Latin Epigrams and Its Continental Counterparts', *Anglo-Saxon England* 10 (1982): pp. 21–38; 'William of Malmesbury and La Silloge Epigrafica di Cambridge', *Archivum Historiae Pontificiae* 21 (1983), pp. 9–33; *Religion and Literature in Western England 600–800* (Cambridge: Cambridge University Press, 1990), pp. 328–59; and Michael Lapidge, 'Some Remnants of Bede's Lost Liber Epigrammatum', *English Historical Review* 90 (1975): pp. 798–820. For the relation of Milred's codex to the Continental tradition of syllogae, see also Richard Sharpe, 'King Ceadwalla's Roman Epitaph', in *Latin Learning and English Lore: Studies in Anglo-Saxon Literature for Michael Lapidge*, edited by Katherine O'Brien O'Keeffe and Andy Orchard (Toronto: University of Toronto Press, 2005), pp. 171–93, at pp. 173–5.

collection survives, the careful work largely of Patrick Sims-Williams and Michael Lapidge has allowed much of its content to be reconstructed through its appearance in three later sources: a mid-tenth-century copy of the original collection, consisting now only of one bifolium preserved in the library of the University of Illinois, Urbana-Champaign; John Leland's incorporation of twenty-nine verses from the collection, which he examined in full at Malmesbury in the sixteenth century, into his *Commentarii* and *Collectanea*; and the papal inscriptions and epitaphs included in William of Malmesbury's *Liber Pontificalis*.[86] Luitpold Wallach describes the original collection as consisting of dedication inscriptions, or tituli, from churches and altars, and tombstone epitaphs from England, Gaul, and Italy, along with epigrams from manuscripts, contents that testify to the active circulation of pilgrims between England and Rome as early as the eighth century.[87] Given this pilgrim traffic, Lapidge notes that Milred's codex, while providing definite evidence that *syllogae* were composed in England by the eighth century, is only one example of what was likely an enthusiastic interest of early English churchmen. As both Lapidge and Sims-Williams observe, in its inclusion of Roman material and stylistic indebtedness to Christian Latin poetry, Milred's codex is an example of Rome's influence on early English epigraphic and epigrammatic verse.[88] However, it was also innovative both in containing a large portion of Latin poems composed in England and in expanding the gambit of a *syllogae* collection, providing models for epitaphs and for church and manuscript dedication, among other topics: as Lapidge puts it, it is a 'specifically English *sylloga* with English models and English terms of reference'.[89]

The existence of Milred's codex thus not only supports the idea that epitaph literature would be widely enough known within early

---

[86] For a reproduction and edition, widely critiqued, of the University of Illinois manuscript, see Luitpold Wallach, 'The Urbana Anglo-Saxon Sylloge of Latin Inscriptions', in *Poetry and Poetics from Ancient Greece to the Renaissance: Studies in Honor of James Hutton*, edited by G. M. Kirkwood (Ithaca: Cornell University Press, 1975), pp. 134–51. For an edition of the poems in Leland's manuscript, see Lapidge, 'Bede's Lost', pp. 802–20.

[87] Wallach, 'Urbana Anglo-Saxon', p. 137.

[88] Sims-Williams, 'Milred of Worcester's Collection', p. 27 and p. 38.

[89] Lapidge, 'Bede's Lost', p. 801.

medieval England to serve as a potential model for other historiograph-ical genres, such as annals, but also testifies to the complex interactions between the textual and the material dimensions of such writing, as well as to its functionality in particularizing English material. Like other *syllogae*, the inscriptions of which were initially transcribed from their material contexts on stones, Milred's collection served to mediate the textual and the architectural, in the form of writing in books and writing on stones and, at the site of this mediation, propagated new forms of cultural identity by disseminating authorized epitaph models into new environments. Although, as Lapidge observes, 'these *syllogae* were to the medieval world what the stone-cutters' manuals had been in Roman times', they certainly served functions supplementary to the practical one of providing inscription models, with their contents often at several stages of remove from the material context of the grave-site.[90] The same parallel between *syllogae* and stone-cutters' manuals is made by Luitpold Wallach, whose examination of Carolingian inscriptions suggests that writers often used *syllogae* as models.[91] Although it is hard to determine whether such collections resulted from a first-hand encounter with memorial stones or from re-copying texts already in existence, it is clear that *syllogae* generate new meanings that both transport and transcend the particulars of the local context of the epitaphs they contain. Inscriptions on stones and in books formally interact with and refer to each other, then, with even the memorial inscriptions themselves serving, as Okasha has argued, not primarily to mark a body, but as a type of lapidary *liber vitae*.[92]

Milred's collection was not alone in disseminating *hic* models for situational poetry. Along with an epitaph for Monica, the mother of Augustine, which opens with the *hic posuit* formula, and one for Bede beginning *hic requiescit*, the codex also included a *hic iacet* epitaph for Bugga, the seventh-century founder of the double monastery at With-ington, Gloucestershire.[93] As Lapidge notes, the choice to include Bugga's epitaph is revealing of the particularly English orientation of

[90] Ibid., p. 359.

[91] 'Alcuin's Epitaph of Hadrian I', *American Journal of Philology* 72 (1951): pp. 128–44, at p. 144.

[92] 'Memorial Stones or Grave-Stones?'

[93] For Monica's epitaph, see Wallach, 'Urbana Anglo-Saxon', p. 141; for Bede and Bugga's epitaphs, see Lapidge, 'Bede's Lost', p. 815 and p. 819.

the collection, since it was probably at least partially motivated by land-rights issues: Bugga was central to a complex settlement dispute over the monastery, which was ultimately decided in favour of the see of Worcester.[94] Whoever wrote Bugga's epitaph also had access to Aldhelm's poem celebrating the foundation of her church at Withington, one of a number of his dedication inscriptions for churches and altars (a poetic form known as *tituli*) based on late Antique models and collectively labelled the *Carmina ecclesiastica*.[95] Aldhelm's familiarity with Damasian inscriptions and the Continental *syllogae* tradition has even led scholars to speculate that he was the author of the English collection that served as the model for Milred's codex, although, as Andy Orchard notes, 'it is impossible to prove'.[96] Closely related to epitaph literature, dedication *tituli* also frequently open with a *hic* formula and serve to record the historical details of a church's founding, as well as to invoke the dedicatory saints. As John Higgitt comments, their primary function 'would seem to have been to furnish a proof that the church had been consecrated and a record of the details and date, so that the anniversary might be kept as a feast'.[97] The five examples composed by Aldhelm, which, although they did not circulate as a single collection, were widely read and imitated in England during the eighth and ninth centuries, show how situational language (such as *hic*) had become characteristic of the genre even when divorced from a material context. As Lapidge observes of Aldhelm's *tituli*, 'some, but not all, may have been composed for actual dedications'; certainly the eighty-five-line poem dedicating Bugga's church would seem to have been too long for such a purpose.[98] Although it describes the surroundings of the church as *hic*, which perhaps suggests that it was kept there in textual form, the primary function of this *titulus* seem to have been artistic and historical, since it records the battles and kinship relations

[94] Lapidge, 'Bede's Lost', pp. 815–16.

[95] For discussion and translation of the *Carmina Ecclesiastica*, see Aldhelm's *The Poetic Works*, translated by Michael Lapidge (Cambridge: D.S. Brewer, 1985), p. 10, pp. 35–58.

[96] *The Poetic Art of Aldhelm* (Cambridge: Cambridge University Press, 1994), p. 212. For Aldhelm's knowledge of the syllogae tradition, see pp. 203–12.

[97] 'The Dedication Inscription at Jarrow and its Context', *Antiquaries Journal* 59 (1979): pp. 343–74, at p. 346.

[98] Aldhelm, *The Poetic Works*, p. 10.

of Bugga's father, King Centwine of Wessex. As such, Aldhelm's *Carmina ecclesiastica* are a measure of the reciprocities between lapidary inscriptions and written texts, and the historiographic impulse underlying both.

The popularity of such texts in the early part of the period in particular is appropriate because, like Damasus, English churchmen were engaged in a project of reinterpreting and reassigning value to place. Locative language in this context, although deeply formulaic, played a specific role in yoking history, geography, and the reader. Alcuin's self-composed epitaph, for instance, opens 'Hic rogo, pauxillum veniens subsiste viator' (Here, I beg thee, pause for a while traveller) and exploits the theme of 'quod tu es, ego fui; quod ego sum, tu eris' (what you are, I was; what I am, you will be)'. A prose legend beginning 'Hic requiescit beatae memoriae domnus Alchuinus, abba, qui obiit in pace XIV Kal[endas] Iun[ias]' (Here rests the lord Alcuin of blessed memory, the abbot, who died in peace on 19 May) was added after Alcuin's death.[99] The repeated *hic*, at the beginning and end of the epitaph, serves to connect the historical details (name, status, date of death) with place and, by emphasizing the theme of substitution, encourages the reader to meditate on his or her own subjection to temporal processes of change and decay. Alcuin's work, like Aldhelm's, became a model for epigram composition: his epitaph for Pope Hadrian I can still be seen in the Portico of St Peter's at Rome, and begins 'Hic pater ecclesiae . . . requiem . . . habet' (Here rests the father of the church).[100]

In composing these epitaphs, Alcuin had access not only to a version of Milred's collection but also to the poetic epitaphs that Bede had included in the *Historia ecclesiastica* for Gregory, Cædwalla, Theodore, and Wilfrid.[101] Bede was evidently quite interested in the *syllogae* form,

---

[99] For the text, which survives only in manuscript form, and translation of the epitaph, see Wallach, 'The Epitaph of Alcuin: A Model of Carolingian Epigraphy', *Speculum* 30 (1955): pp. 367–73.

[100] Luitpold Wallach established Alcuin's authorship of the Hadrian epitaph based on numerous textual parallels with his poetry ('Alcuin's Epitaph'). Wallach gives the full text of the epitaph at p. 131. As Lapidge observes, Hadrian's epitaph (consisting of thirty-eight lines of verse plus one prose sentence) provides a sense of the material constraints that inscription placed upon the length of a poem, since this stone measures 7 feet, 3 inches by 3 feet 10 inches (*The Poetic Works*, p. 229, n. 18).

[101] These epitaphs are be found in ii.1; v.7; v.8; v.19.

because he notes in the bibliographic coda to the *Historia* that he composed 'librum epigrammatum heroico metro siue elegaico' (a book of epigrams in hexameters and in elegiac couplets).[102] Although this book has unfortunately been lost, Lapidge has reconstructed its probable contents by reference to Milred's codex and other surviving texts, and finds that 'Bede was modelling himself on his fourth-century predecessor, Pope Damasus' in his composition of *tituli* and epigraphs for books.[103] As a historian, Bede was no doubt interested in the way that epitaph literature served to digest the pertinent facts and dates of a person's life. Augustine's prose epitaph, which Bede also includes in the *Historia*, is a good example, reading:

> Hic requiescit domnus Augustinus Doruuernensis archiepiscopus primus, qui olim huc a beato Gregorio Romanae urbis pontifice directus, et a Deo operatione miraculorum suffultus, Aedilberctum regem ac gentem illius ab idolorum cultu ad Christi fidem perduxit, et conpletis in pace diebus officii sui defunctus est septima kalendas Iunias eodem rege regnante.[104]

> (Here lies the most reverend Augustine, first archbishop of Canterbury, who was formerly sent hither by St Gregory, bishop of Rome; being supported by God in the working of miracles, he led King Æthelberht and his nation from the worship of idols to faith in Christ, and ended the days of his office in peace; he died on 26 May during the reign of the same king.)

As Story notes, the form of the date of death resembles that used in the Frankish annals of Lindisfarne and Kent, while the brevity of its account of Augustine's achievements recalls annalistic writing more generally.[105] This similarity is particularly clearly demonstrated by those epitaphs, like Alcuin's, that close with a prose summary. Cædwalla—the seventh-century king of Wessex who gave up his kingdom, travelled to Rome, and died there only days later—was another

---

[102] For discussion of this lost book, see Lapidge, 'Bede's Lost', and *Anglo-Latin Literature 600–899* (London: Hambledon Press, 1996), pp. 314–20.

[103] *Anglo-Latin Literature*, 317.

[104] Bede, ii.3.

[105] Story, 'Frankish Annals', p. 94. Story also notes that excavations at Canterbury revealed two lead coffin plates inscribed with epitaphs for early Kentish kings that begin *Hic requiescit*.

recipient of such an epitaph, with twenty-four lines of poetry followed by a summative prose conclusion:

> Hic depositus est Caedual, qui et Petrus, rex Saxonum, sub die XII kalendarum Mairaum, indictione secunda, qui uixit / annos plus minus xxx, imperante domno Iustiniano piissimo Auğ. ān. secundo.[106]

> (Here was buried Cædwalla, otherwise Peter, king of the Saxons, on 20 April, in the second indiction, being thirty years of age more or less, in the reign of the most religious ruler the Emperor Justinian, in the fourth year of his consulship; and in the second year of the papacy of the apostolic ruler, Pope Sergius.)

As Richard Sharpe observes in his detailed study of the epitaph's transmission, Bede's is the only version to preserve this prose coda, which suggests that he was using another *sylloge* that circulated in early medieval England but has not survived.[107] In Bede's rendition of it, however, Cædwalla's epitaph is representative of a tradition in which the aesthetic flights of the poetic tribute succumb to a prosaic urge for historical detail linked to the grave-site by the adverbial opening *hic*.

Cædwalla's is an interesting epitaph to bear in mind while moving this discussion away from the presence of *hic/her*-formula epitaphs in early medieval England, and toward a consideration of what function such language in this context might share with its use in the *Chronicle*. Demonstrating the extent of engagement with epitaph literature in eighth- and ninth-century England is, however, not intended only as a simple proof of the availability of sources and analogues for such language. The evident interest in the form—demonstrated by the fact that all the major authors of the early pre-Conquest period make some contribution to it—is deeply connected to its locative properties, which are rendered explicit in those inscriptions that begin with a deictic term like *hic*. Cædwalla serves in this respect as a figure for the complex relations between authority and place that the epitaph—and as I am arguing, the *Chronicle*, too—serves to refract. As an English king buried

---

[106] Bede, v.7. For the transmission history and a reconstruction of this epitaph, see Sharpe, 'King Ceadwalla's Roman Epitaph'.

[107] Sharpe, 'King Ceadwalla', p. 179. Sharpe notes that '[t]he most exact text has reached us, not through any of the syllogae, but through Bede. Whether he obtained a copy directly from Rome or from somewhere in England, we do not know' (p. 185).

in the heart of Rome with an inscription that preserves both his Old English and his new Christian name, Cædwalla's epitaph epitomizes the synchronous presence of Rome in the making of English identity. While his epitaph situates his death within Roman Imperial and Christian time, the text is brought back to England to survive in its most accurate form within the pages of an iconic work of English history. Perhaps more clearly than any other example of the form, Cædwalla's epitaph makes clear that pinpointing what the introductory *here* of an epitaph might refer to is complex indeed. Those pre-Conquest authors who experimented with such situational inscriptions, in writing as new Damasians, intended such locative language not only to refer in a simple way to the surroundings in which their words were inscribed, but literally to remake their native environment into a monumental site akin to Rome, and to assert an authority for their own writing equivalent to that of the founders of Roman Christian culture.

Textuality works here in tandem with the reuse of Roman stonework for pre-Conquest grave markers, a practice especially associated with York: both the inscription and the stone are borrowed and appropriated.[108] Such literature is thus inscriptive in more than one sense, productive of a certain identity for early medieval English culture as it is written. The overt reference to the local that is a characteristic of epitaph literature, most signally represented by a *hic* formula, plays an important role in this function because, while seeming to fix a stable connection between text and place, it actually radicalizes these relations. *Hic* refers not only to physical space nearby (England) but also to physical space far distant (the Roman setting of the archetype), as well as to a textual tradition, the authority of which is being invoked. In this sense the locative language of epitaph literature serves to complicate the boundaries between material monument and text, and between history and geography.

---

[108] Hadley, *Death in Medieval England*, p. 134. See also, Thompson, *Dying and Death*, esp. pp. 156–63. Consider also Wilfrid's use of Roman architectural models, particularly of relic crypts, in building churches at Ripon and Hexham in the seventh century (Éamonn Ó Carragáin, 'The City of Rome and the World of Bede', Jarrow Lecture [St Paul's Parish Church Council, 1994], p. 7).

# Conclusion

The *Old English Martyrology* entry for the discovery of the body of St Stephen tells how a mass-priest named Lucianus, having been told the location of Stephen's body in a dream, is sent with other holy men to the site:

> þa dulfon hi in þęre ylcan stowe. Ða gemetton hi stán mid eorðan bewrigenne; þa wæs on þam awriten: Her ys se Godes Stehpanus. Þa segdon hi þæt ðam bisceope; ða com he ðider mid oþrum halgum bisceopum. Þa ontyndon hi þa þruh; ða com þær út micelre wyn-sumnysse ste`n'c, ond monige/ untrume men þær wæron sona hale gewordene. Ða gelæddon hi ðone lichoman in Hierusalem. Hit węs ær þær singal druwung, ond sona æfter þam com geþuhtsum rén on eorþan.[109]

> (When they dug in that same place, they found a stone covered with earth on which was written: here is Stephanus of God. When they had told this to the bishop, then he came there with other holy bishops; when they opened the coffin, then there came forth a very pleasant smell, and many sick people there were immediately cured. Then they brought the body to Jerusalem; before this there had been a continual drought, and directly after that plentiful rain fell on earth.)

In this episode, inscription forms part of a battery of conventional signs of the body's authenticity: the sweet smells marking the saint's co-presence in the grave and in paradise, the performance of miraculous cures at the burial site, and the ushering in of a period of agricultural productivity that accompanies the arrival of the saint's body in the city. As much as they make the saint's body the site of a complex meeting between past and present, in marking the ways in which the past of the saint's holy life impacts the present of the narrative, all of these hagiographical commonplaces are not only explicitly historical but advance a notion of history itself as essentially spatial. The function of *her* in the label, 'her is se godes Stephanus', is thus to unite what is left behind—textual history, in the form of the inscription, and matter, in the form of the corpse—and to insist that the one is embodied in the

---

[109] Günter Kotzor, ed., *Das altenglische martyrologium* (Munich: Bayerische Akademie der Wissenschaften, 1981), ii.170.11–18 to ii.171.1–3.

other. As this episode makes clear, the truth of the historical statement on a tombstone is thus not the living and speaking body of the witness, but the matter of the decaying body beneath the marker.

Tombstone inscription, as I have been arguing, is a form of historiography that, at least in England, is practised in a regular way on stone from the decades around 900, but which exists as a textual genre far earlier. Since the *Chronicle* project itself emerges at the close of the ninth century, its innovative and insistent use of *her* as an annal opening can be understood as part of a larger movement that uses writing to mark the material remnant of history and to position it within contemporary systems of meaning. In invoking the form of mortuary discourse, then, the *Chronicle* can be seen also to borrow the epitaph's particular claim to transcendence of the gap between the matter and the text of history, a transcendence that does not rely on the figure of the witness that undergirds much medieval historiography. It seems compelling to think of the *Chronicle* borrowing from epitaph's bodily logic, not least because the both liminal and unifying potential of the dead body happens to coincide with the *Chronicle*'s own interests in the boundary between past and present, and in community. *Her* in the *Chronicle* serves a function as dual as that of the corpse, both marking and bridging the distance between the past of events and the present of reading, as well as working to unify the disparate material of the *Chronicle*'s account. When read against the background of epitaph literature, *her* is thus revealed both as likening the architecture and unity of the book to that of the stone marker and the dead body, and as substituting the one for the other. What is being created by the formal interconnection of these texts, which effects a specific and complex set of material and discursive relations between the stone marker above the corpse and the page of a book, is the notion of history as a shared body disconnected from any individual observer or participant.

As James Campbell observes, Gaimar, who in the twelfth century translated significant portions of the *Chronicle* in his own *L'Estoire des Engles*, made the following comments about how that text was used during the reign of Alfred:

> Chronicles it is called, a big book.
> The English went about collecting it.
> Now it is thus authenticated;

> So that at Winchester, in the cathedral,
> There is the true history of the kings,
> And their lives and their memorials.
> King Alfred had it in his possession,
> And had it bound with a chain.
> Who wished to read it might well see it,
> But not remove it from its place.[110]

Although Dorothy Whitelock was sceptical of Gaimar's story, which seems to conflate treatment of the *Chronicle* with that of Alfred's translation of the *Pastoral Care*, Campbell is less suspicious, and suggests that it 'is not at all implausible. It could be that the *Chronicle* lay in major churches for clerics and literate aristocrats to read, the locale reinforcing the content.'[111] Although much about both the *Chronicle*'s origins and its function in the late ninth century remains mysterious, the *Pastoral Care* represents one of the few well-documented cases of broad and deliberate dissemination of texts to ecclesiastical centres throughout Alfred's kingdom, and it is not unreasonable to imagine that distribution of the *Chronicle* was conducted in a similar way. If, as Gaimar claimed, the book found a place within such ecclesiastical centres, the *her* that opens each annal would indeed point beyond or through the page to the church or minster environs, locating the *Chronicle* within overlapping and complementary strategies of record, architectural, material, and textual. To read the *Chronicle* in this way is thus to argue that its formal properties are both drawn from and function within a continuum of ecclesiastical and communal techniques of record, practised inside and outside the pages of books.

---

[110] James Campbell, 'What Is Not Known about the Reign of Edward the Elder', in *Edward the Elder, 899–924*, edited by N. J. Higham and D. H. Hill (London and New York: Routledge, 2001), pp. 12–24, at p. 15. *Lestorie des Engles solum la translacion Maistre Geffrei Gaimar*, edited by Thomas Duffus Hardy and Charles Trice Martin, Vol. 2 (London: Rolls Series, 1899), p. 76. For original, see Gaimar, Vol. 1 (London: Rolls Series, 1888), p. 93. For discussion of Gaimar's access to the *Chronicle*, see *L'Estoire des Engleis*, edited by Alexander Bell (Oxford: Anglo-Norman Text Society, 1960), pp. liii–lv. I owe direction to these editions to Campbell's essay.

[111] Campbell, 'What Is Not Known', p. 16.

# | 3 |

# The Trans-Planted Politics of Eleventh-Century England

A single tombstone survives from the entire pre-Conquest period with the inscription 'Here Lies' written in Old English rather than Latin. Dating to the eleventh century and located in Winchester, the marker reads, '+HER L[I]Ð G[VN]N[I:] EORLES FEOLAGA' (Here lies G[vn]n[i], Eorl's companion).[1] As the sole vernacular example of the formula, this stone is a good reminder that eleventh-century England was not monolithic. While the primary language used for this inscription is English, the name *Gunni* and the terms *eorl* and *feolaga* are all markers of Scandinavian influence, extending in this case into the centre of Wessex, far distant from the areas of densest Scandinavian settlement in the north-east. Even if, as R. I. Page suggests, this stone dates from after Cnut's accession in 1016, and it might well be earlier, its hybrid nature indicates the degree to which eleventh-century English culture was the product of Scandinavian invasions and settlements

---

[1] Winchester I (Okasha #138). As Okasha notes, 'Eorl' would be a rare form if it were a personal name, and the text could also mean 'the Earl's companion' or 'an earl's companion' (p. 138). See also the original publication notice for the stone: Martin Biddle, 'Excavations at Winchester 1965: Fourth Interim Report', *Antiquaries Journal* 46 (1966): pp. 308–32, at p. 325.

*Materializing Englishness in Early Medieval Texts*. Jacqueline Fay, Oxford University Press.
© Jacqueline Fay 2022. DOI: 10.1093/oso/9780198757573.003.0004

that started well before the date of 900 that formed the focus of my last chapter.[2]

Not many texts of the period, however, address the effects of Scandinavian invasion on what we might understand as everyday matters, such as language encounters, trading, fashion, marriage, or living arrangements: how, in short, the English got along with, lived, and died alongside Scandinavian settlers, and what they recognized or understood about each other's differences. The *Anglo-Saxon Chronicle*, for example, includes many entries describing the movements and actions of the *here*, the invading Scandinavian army, against the English *fyrd*, but does not dwell on the long process of acculturation that must have happened after the *here* began to settle. Homiletic texts, such as Ælfric's life of Saint Edmund, portray Scandinavians as bloodthirsty and evil; in the *Battle of Maldon* they are presented as guileful and cunning. In contrast to these purposeful, rhetorically exaggerated portraits of Scandinavians, historians suggest that in fact the Scandinavian conquest of England, which preceded the Norman by fifty years, was a less dramatic usurpation than that of 1066, less focused on conquest than continuity. It was, as Ann Williams puts it, 'accompanied by much upheaval and destruction', but 'its effects seem...to have been temporary...and one may suspect that the country as a whole was no more "Scandinavian" after the conquest of Cnut than it had been before'.[3] Elaine Treharne's study of vernacular textual production after 1020, a topic much neglected by scholars, poses similar challenges to the idea that the 1016 conquest profoundly transformed or damaged English culture.[4] Swegn Forkbeard's, and ultimately his son Cnut's, successful takeover of the country in 1016 was the culmination in some sense of thirty years of sustained Scandinavian attacks on Æthelred's England, attacks that brought northmen to the country not only as aggressors but also as mercenaries and settlers. A century earlier still, during the reign of Æthelred's great grandfather Alfred the Great,

---

[2] 'How Long Did the Scandinavian Language Survive in England?', p. 180. Okasha also dates Winchester I as late tenth to eleventh century.

[3] Ann Williams, '"Cockles amongst the Wheat": Danes and English in the Western Midlands in the First Half of the Eleventh Century', *Midland History* 11 (1986), pp. 1–22, at pp. 15–16.

[4] Elaine Treharne, *Living through Conquest: The Politics of Early English, 1020–1220* (Oxford: Oxford University Press, 2012).

similarly virulent waves of Viking attacks had led to the partition of the country between English and Danes, and the subsequent entrenchment of a significant Scandinavian presence in the north of England. That England appears to have been no more 'Scandinavian' after the conquest of 1016 is arguably because it was fairly 'Scandinavian' before Cnut's accession, but in ways that are little addressed in texts of the time.

In the absence of robust textual evidence, this chapter will take up the question of how ethnic difference might have been both understood and lived in the early eleventh-century context specifically by reconstructing the larger network within which surviving textual accounts would have functioned. My particular focus is Æthelred's injunction in 1002 that all the Danish men in England be killed on St Brice's Day, an order that makes little sense against the backdrop of decades of migration and settlement by Scandinavians in England, because it seems to rely on a notion of Scandinavians being easily distinguishable from the English. Although what exactly happened on St Brice's Day remains opaque, the recent discovery of two mass graves of Scandinavians at Oxford and Ridgeway Hill provides material evidence that such massacres really did happen during this period. However, only one surviving textual justification for the massacre exists, a charter issued by Æthelred that references the parable of the cockles among the wheat from Matthew 13:24–30 in order to characterize the Scandinavians' relationship to the English. Interrogating what it means to represent the Scandinavians and the English as plants, and these plants in particular, this chapter will trace this reference to cockles and wheat through texts and into fields both represented and real. The primarily agrarian context of early medieval England would have conditioned its audience to respond in very particular ways to texts featuring plants. The reaction of the early medieval audience of these texts would have been informed, permeated even, by experiences with plants, just as, conversely, experiences with plants would potentially be informed, enriched, or in some way affected by common discursive notions about these same plants. Although the charter has been examined from many vantage points—such as its language and form—the modes by which the borrowed biblical parable resonates with its audience's lived experience with plants have not yet been explored. This material context for the charter adds significant dimensions to our understanding of how it would have been received and the role it played in reinforcing the embodied nature of Scandinavian and English identity. Encounters with weeds, reading about weeds, and encounters with people represented as weeds, I will argue, make intermingled contributions to the experience of being English in the early eleventh century.

# Historical background to the St Brice's Day massacre and the St Frideswide charter

Much scholarship has already been written on the St Brice's Day massacre, most of it concentrating on what the massacre indicates about the state of Æthelred's rule. Despite his later reputation for ineptitude, the massacre seems not to have been what it might seem—namely, an erratic act of desperation by a regime that felt itself fundamentally threatened by a foreign power—since England by many accounts flourished during the years leading up to 1002.[5] J. Campbell even interprets the massacre itself 'as an indication of English administrative efficiency', asking 'what other king of the time could have organised simultaneous massacres in several places on the same day?'[6] Simon Keynes observes that 'the internal and cultural affairs of the kingdom were able to prosper' at this time, as centralized production of diplomas was not affected by Viking attacks and a reformed coinage system, which mandated a state-supervised recoinage every six years, also continued to operate smoothly.[7] In fact, as Keynes notes, 'it is important to appreciate just how well it fared at this time under apparently adverse political circumstances', with coinage exhibiting a strikingly uniform quality.[8] Detailed analyses of the coinage and mints

---

[5] The classic study of the origin of Æthelred's reputation as a bad king, which is largely promulgated in writing that post-dates his reign, is Simon Keynes, 'The Declining Reputation of King Æthelred the Unready', in *Ethelred the Unready: Papers from the Millenary Conference*, edited by David Hill (Oxford: British Archaeological Series, 1978), pp. 227–54.

[6] 'England, France, Flanders and Germany: Some Comparisons and Connections', in *Ethelred the Unready*, pp. 255–70, at p. 260.

[7] *The Diplomas of King Æþelred*, p. 208, p. 115, and p. 193.

[8] Keynes, 'Declining Reputation', pp. 193–4.

of Æthelred's reign by Michael Dolley and D. M. Metcalf support this conclusion.[9] In addition, the reign was a high point for legislation, so much so that Patrick Wormald concludes that '[n]o government which participated in this remarkable process can easily be dismissed as inept.'[10] James W. Earl notes that a 'high clerical culture' flourished during this period, and that 'many of our surviving manuscripts and much Latin and Old English literature date from this highly productive decade...framed by the disastrous Battle of Maldon in 991 and Æþelred's attempt to exterminate Danes in England'.[11] Against this background of successful English governance comes both the St Brice's Day massacre and discourse about Scandinavians that is generated *by* and *for* the English: as Julian Richards notes, 'the Vikings in England failed to produce their own historian; their deeds are known solely through the eyes of West Saxon chroniclers'.[12] And these accounts are often highly condemnatory of the English for both their moral worth and their strategies of opposition, despite the ostensible success of Æthelred's government.

Given the dearth of contemporary sources that reference the massacre, what actually happened on St Brice's Day, or what the exact intent of Æthelred's order was, is fairly opaque.[13] As the C, D and E versions of the *Anglo-Saxon Chronicle* note, Æthelred

> het ofslean ealle þa deniscan men þe on Angelcynne wæron; ðis wæs gedon on Britius mæssedæig, forðam þam cyninge wæs gecyd þæt hi woldan hine besyrwan æt his life 7 siððan ealle his witan 7 habban siþþan his rice.[14]

---

[9] Michael Dolley, 'An Introduction to the Coinage of Æthelræd II', in *Ethelred the Unready*, pp. 115–33; and D. M. Metcalf, 'The Ranking of the Boroughs: Numismatic Evidence from the Reign of Æthelred II', in *Ethelred the Unready*, pp. 159–201.

[10] 'Æþelred the Lawmaker', in *Ethelred the Unready*, pp. 47–80. Keynes also notes the superior nature of legislation produced at this time, *The Diplomas of King Æþelred*, p. 196.

[11] 'Violence and Non-Violence in Anglo-Saxon England: Ælfric's "Passion of St Edmund"', *Philological Quarterly* 78 (1999), pp. 125–49, at p. 125.

[12] *Viking Age England* (Stroud: Tempus, 2004), p. 12.

[13] Useful discussions of the massacre include Hadley, '"Cockle amongst the Wheat"'; Keynes, *The Diplomas of King Æþelred*, pp. 202–5; and Jonathan Wilcox, 'The St Brice's Day Massacre and Archbishop Wulfstan', in *Peace and Negotiation: Strategies for Coexistence in the Middle Ages and Renaissance*, edited by D. Wolfthal (Turnhout: Brepols, 2000), pp. 79–91.

[14] See vols. 5, 6, and 7 of *The Anglo-Saxon Chronicle: A Collaborative Edition: MS C*, edited by Katherine O'Brien O'Keeffe; *MS D*, vol. 6, edited by G. P. Cubbin (Cambridge:

commanded to be slain all the Danish men who were among the
English people; this was done on Brice's mass-day, because the king
was told that they would plot against his life and afterwards all of his
councillors, and then have his kingdom.

How the order was carried out, by whom, and toward whom, are all
questions that cannot be definitively answered on the basis of written
evidence. As Stephen Harris notes, although later historians, such as
William of Malmesbury, give vivid and emotional accounts of the
killing that emphasize the ways in which it pitted the English against
the Danes, such accounts are not reliable.[15] Harris himself refers to the
massacre as an 'extirpation of Anglo-Danes in this ancient act of ethnic
cleansing', which implies that it was directed toward all Anglo-
Scandinavians resident in the country, but the majority of scholars
suggest that it probably involved only new immigrants, brought to
the country as mercenaries, merchants, or settlers.[16] The exact numbers
involved are difficult to determine also. Ian Howard estimates that, in
the last decade of the tenth century, Scandinavian mercenary forces
settled in the south-west on what he calls 'peace land', or land on which
they were billeted when not on campaign, may have numbered between
2,000 and 4,000, or 0.1–0.2 per cent of the total population.[17] Although
Howard believes that these mercenaries were the primary target of the
massacre, he agrees that merchants were also involved and that the
overall number targeted would have been higher. The only other close
source for this event is a charter for St Frideswide's Oxford, issued by
Æthelred in 1004 to renew the monastery's privileges after the burning

---

D.S. Brewer, 1996); and *MS E*, vol. 7, edited by Susan Irvine (Cambridge: D.S. Brewer,
2004). Original quoted from *MS C*, edited by Katherine O'Brien O'Keeffe. Translations
are my own.

[15] Harris, *Race and Ethnicity*, p. 107. Simon Keynes makes the same observation and
provides detail of later historians' lurid tales of the massacre (*The Diplomas of King
Æþelred*, p. 204).

[16] Harris, *Race and Ethnicity*, p. 108; Ian Howard, *Swein Forkbeard's Invasions and the
Danish Conquest of England 991–1017* (Woodbridge: Boydell Press, 2003), p. 61; Hadley,
'Cockle amongst the Wheat', p. 117; Keynes, *The Diplomas of King Æþelred*, 204); Pauline
Stafford, 'The Reign of Æthelred II, A Study in the Limitations on Royal Policy and
Action', in *Ethelred the Unready*, pp. 15–46, at p. 31.

[17] *Swein Forkbeard's Invasions*, 22.

of its church during the St Brice's Day massacre.[18] As Keynes and Hadley both argue, given that the only place for which there is evidence of the massacre being carried out is thus far-distant from the regions of Danish settlement, it seems likely that those killed were members of itinerant groups rather than long-term settlers—that is, 'people who had come recently from Denmark and who might be going back there'.[19]

While close attention to the historical context for the massacre thus suggests that it was not genocidal in its aims, such reinterpretation of the source material should not, as it often does, collapse the very distinction that brought it into being: the distance between the written staging of the event and its enactment. In other words, it is important to recognize the difference between the historical effect of the massacre, which we cannot access (the details of who was affected and how it was carried out) and the rhetorical positioning of the massacre in contemporary textual sources. These sources, and particularly the 1002 CDE annal of the *Chronicle*, do represent the order as based on the assumption of an immediately apprehensible difference between the English and the Scandinavians, or, in other words, as genocidal in its aspirations. If it might be unclear, to us and presumably also to contemporaries, exactly whom Æthelred's order is directed against (Anglo-Scandinavians, Danish aggressors, or recently settled Danes), this ambiguity does not derive from the phrasing of the order itself, which makes no such fine distinctions, but draws on a holistic language of entire peoples, 'ealle ða Deniscan men' (all the Danish men). The order thus describes an action, the killing of all the Danes among the English people, which would have been impossible to enact according to the letter, and which *was not*, according to scholars, enacted in this way. This raises the question: why issue an order that assumes and asserts an ahistorical difference between English and Danes—a difference that

---

[18] Sawyer number 909. An online and revised version of Sawyer's catalogue can now be found at http://www.esawyer.org.uk/about/index.html. For the original, see Spencer Robert Wigram, ed., *The Cartulary of the Monastery of St Frideswide at Oxford*, 2 vols., Oxford Historical Society 28, 31 (Oxford: Clarendon Press, 1895–96), 1: 2–3. All quotations in the original from the charter are drawn from this edition; all translations follow Dorothy Whitelock, ed., *English Historical Documents 500–1041*, vol. 1 (New York: Routledge, 1996), #127, p. 545.

[19] *The Diplomas of King Æþelred*, 204; 'Cockle amongst the Wheat', p. 117.

could only be meaningful in this context if it presented itself uncomplicatedly in physical terms—in an environment in which such a difference was clearly untenable? A closer reading of the texts suggests that the fuel for the massacre is not simply Æthelred's 'increasingly tenuous hold on power' (which, as I have shown, has been widely disputed by historians, such as Keynes and Howard, who point to the healthy economic condition of the eleventh-century English state under Æthelred's rule), but is instead to be found in the unique strains that Scandinavian settlement had placed on identificatory structures.[20] The significance of the massacre would not therefore have been entirely available to the participants of the time. In other words, conceptualizing the massacre only in terms of intent or in relation to the king's personality, as many scholars do, misses the way that on a structural level the massacre simultaneously suggests, and then undermines, the notion that ethnicity can be known through the body. That such a claim enacts a certain violent simplification within the discursive field exactly mirrors the material violence inscribed on the individual bodies of Danes.

Like the 1002 annal, the 1004 St Frideswide charter issued by Æthelred offers an account of the massacre that epitomizes Brian Stock's definition of the too-coherent historical picture as 'a police state', in which 'the weapons have merely been concealed'.[21] Underlying the cold cartulary style is an equally chilling narrative, in which a group of Danes, resident in the country but not necessarily mercenaries, seek shelter in their local church only to be burned to death by their neighbours:

---

[20] Harris, *Race and Ethnicity*, p. 107. I am suggesting here that the significance of the massacre would not have been entirely available to the participants of the time. In other words, it is not satisfactory to conceptualize it only in terms of intent, as James Earl does, for instance, when he suggests that it 'made a certain kind of sense...as revenge for decades of Viking atrocities' ('Violence and Non-Violence', p. 126). Nor is it sufficient solely to rationalize the events of Æthelred's reign in terms of the king's own personality: to ask, as Pauline Stafford puts it, '[w]ere the problems which Æthelred faced unique, and are they to be blamed primarily on the character of the king and the exceptionally self-seeking nature of his great nobles?' ('The Reign of Æthelred II', in *Ethelred the Unready*, at p. 15).

[21] Brian Stock, *Listening to the Text: On the Uses of the Past* (Philadelphia: University of Pennsylvania Press, 1996), p. 88; Originally published by Johns Hopkins University Press in 1990.

cunctis que hanc paginulam intuentibus qua racione id actum sit paucis verborum signis retexam. Omnibus etiam in hac patria degentibus satis constat fore notissimum quoniam dum a me decretum cum consilio optimatum satrapum que meorum exiuit ut cuncti Dani, qui in hac insula velut lollium inter triticum pululando emerserant, iustissima examinacione necarantur, hoc que decretum morte tenus ad effectum perduceretur, ipsi qui in prefata vrbe morabantur Dani, mortem euadere nitentes, hoc Xpi sacrarium, fractis per vim valuis ac pessulis, intrantes asylum sibi repugnaculum que contra vrbanos suburbanos que inibi fieri decreuerunt, set cum populus omnis insequens, necessitate compulsus, eos eiicere niteretur nec valeret, igne tabulis iniecto, hanc Ecclesiam, vt liquet, cum ornamentis ac libris combusserunt.

(I will relate in a few words to all who look upon this document for what reason it was done. For it is fully agreed that to all dwelling in this country it will be well known that, since a decree was sent out by me with the counsel of my leading men and magnates, to the effect that all the Danes who have sprung up in this island, sprouting like cockle amongst the wheat, were to be destroyed by a most just extermination, and this decree was to be put into effect even as far as death, those Danes who dwelt in the afore-mentioned town, striving to escape death, entered this sanctuary of Christ, having broken by force the doors and the bolts, and resolved to make a refuge and defence for themselves therein against the people of the town and the suburbs; but when all the people in pursuit strove, forced by necessity, to drive them out, and could not, they set fire to the planks and burnt, as it seems, this church with its ornaments and its books.)

That such a lengthy account of events is provided in the context of a charter is itself an innovation of the latter part of Æthelred's reign, the documentary production of which, as Keynes observes, is 'dominated by a type of diploma incorporating in the dispositive section an account of the circumstances leading up to the transaction that in some cases amounts to a description of the recent history of the estate, and that considerably augments the length of the text'.[22] This formal change enhances the ways in which charters can be seen to function as historical texts, since the additional section both narrativizes and

---

[22] *Diplomas of King Æþelred*, p. 95.

contextualizes events. The 1004 charter calmly justifies the massacre of two years previously, describing it as a 'iustissima exinanitione' (a most just extermination), and represents the English as 'necessitate compulsus' (compelled by necessity), in their actions. The relationship between the English and the Danes is dramatically polarized here, with the newly settled Scandinavians being depicted as cockles among the wheat of the English, an image which echoes Matthew 13:24–30. In this parable a lord sows good seed in a field only to find that his crop is riddled with weeds, which have been secretly strewn by his enemy at night. To pull up the weeds would also be to pull up the wheat, so the lord allows both to grow concurrently until harvest time, at which point the weeds are burned and the wheat stored in the barn. The interpretation of the parable, given in the same chapter, reveals its apocalyptic bent, with the good seed representing good men, and the cockles evil men sown among mankind by the devil, and then reaped and burned on Judgement Day.

In invoking the parable, Æthelred is able to map moral worth by means of a shorthand familiar to medieval audiences from homiletics and scriptural texts that use plants to represent ideal human characteristics. Examples of such parables abound in biblical discourse, and many feature a limited selection of agricultural plants. For example, the parable of the sower—in which the seed that finds good soil yields a large crop, whereas the seed that falls on rocky ground or shallow soil withers—illustrates how the differing degree of human receptivity affects the productivity of the Christian message (Matthew 13:1–9; Mark 4:1–9; Luke 8:4–8). Such accounts suggest that plants are given to human society as a representational device at the same time that they are given as food: as Genesis 1:29–30 reads,

> [t]hen God said, 'Behold, I have given you every plant yielding seed that is on the surface of all the earth, and every tree which has fruit yielding seed; it shall be food for you; and to every beast of the earth and to every bird of the sky and to every thing that moves on the earth which has life, I have given every green plant for food.

More profoundly, the Genesis account makes it clear that plants only exist because of a collaboration between God and man, which creates the environmental conditions for vegetation to thrive: 'Now no shrub of the field was yet in the earth, and no plant of the field had yet sprouted, for the Lord God had not sent rain upon the earth, and there was no man to cultivate the ground' (2:4–5).

This mode of understanding plants as both subservient to and symbolic of human culture forms the broader context for Æthelred's translation of the massacre into religious terms in the St Frideswide charter, where he makes what was most likely an action motivated by political concerns into a universal competition between good and evil, pagan and Christian. In addition, the parable's binary between the cockles and the wheat, when used as an image for the difference between the English and recently arrived Scandinavians, allows Æthelred to assert that ethnicity exists as a visible material difference and thus occludes the very real complications of drawing a fast distinction between English and Danes. Like the 1002 annal, then, the St Frideswide charter explicitly uses the language of ethnicity—this is a massacre targeted toward *Dani*—but it also provides an ideological justification that at once re-presents these ethnic terms as moral in nature and, at the same time, maintains that ethnicity is easily accessible as a visual category of knowledge.

While Æthelred's original audience would have been deeply attuned to this tradition of reading plants as morally symbolic, any translator of biblical texts involving flora or fauna must also contend with a potential conflict between the specificity of the examples given, which might have particular resonances in the local context, and the universalizing intent of giving them in the first place. The register of botanical experience is seldom if ever brought into the discussion of religious texts featuring plants, even though the rhetorical effectiveness of such texts is based on the probability that the audience knows something about the plants that are referenced. Parables deliberately do not present fanciful or exotic plants that the audience would find hard to imagine, but homely plants that common people would have much experience with and knowledge about, and with which they could easily identify. The material context thus contributes significantly to the way that the parable makes and conveys meaning across groups with differing levels of education and in variant geographic contexts. At the same time, the specific botanical context could potentially intrude experiences that conflict with or complicate the purpose to which the parable is being put, since the behaviours, appearance, reactions, and effects of actual plants may or may not confirm what texts assert about these plants.

How would Æthelred's deployment of this parable, and these plant references in particular, have worked for the early medieval English audience, particularly when we take into account the material context of their experiences with plants?

# Words and weeds

Although the St Frideswide charter is entirely in Latin except, as is the norm for charter production at the time, for the vernacular description of the bounds of the land being granted, the parable of the cockles and wheat had been translated into English as part of the Old English Gospels and was also referenced elsewhere in Old English texts, which provide evidence of the various plant-word equivalents in the two languages and the cultivars they might have recalled.

As David Gledhill observes in *The Name of Plants*, the vernacular names of plants 'present few problems until communication becomes multilingual and the number of plants named becomes excessive'.[23] Because multiple plants may share the same common name or, conversely, multiple names may be used for a single plant, identifying what exact species is intended when a writer uses a vernacular name can be difficult. In addition, when names are translated from one language to another, it is possible that a species substitution also occurs, with the writer choosing to name a plant that is familiar from his or her local context in order to convey the sense, rather than the letter, of the original. In the case of the parable of the cockles and the wheat, it seems likely that species substitution occurred as the Gospel text moved north and was translated from Latin into the vernacular, since the purpose of the text is in the contrast between the desirable domesticated cultivar and the noxious interloper, rather than the specific plants originally referenced. For this reason, understanding the acquired and particular resonances of the parable in the English context necessitates

---

[23] David Gledhill, *The Names of Plants* (Cambridge: Cambridge University Press, 2002), p. 1. For a discussion of some of the particular problems with Old English plant names, see Antonette DiPaulo Healey, 'Perplexities about Plant Names in the Dictionary of Old English', in *Old Names, New Growth*, edited by Peter Bierbaumer and Helmut W. Klug (Frankfurt am Main: Peter Lang, 2009), pp. 99–120.

tracing which plants the text might have suggested to the local audience.

The Latin word *triticum*, used in the charter to designate the cereal crop, is the term adopted in modern classificatory systems for the wheat genus in general, but during the pre-Conquest period this term could have suggested bread wheat (*Triticum aestivum*), club wheat (*Triticum aestivum* var. *compactum*) or possibly even barley (*Hordeum vulgare*).[24] Whereas barley was the grain most commonly grown at the start of the period, by the Norman Conquest bread wheat had taken over this position, probably because of climatic changes and developments in ploughing technology and techniques that assisted the less hardy *Triticum aestivum* to survive in more waterlogged areas of heavier soil.[25] Although the change to bread wheat occurred in tandem with the period of Scandinavian migrations, the new farming technology and practices were unlikely to have been brought to England from Scandinavia; recent settlers most certainly shared English appetites for bread wheat, however.[26] Since wheat is, as Banham puts it, 'a fussy crop, requiring a relatively long growing season and a fertile but well-drained soil, whereas other cereals are far less demanding', certain areas of the country would have experienced a far slower change from barley to wheat, and barley remained the second most cultivated grain throughout the period due to its use in other foodstuffs and in beer.[27] Nevertheless, the general shift from barley to bread wheat indicates that the English 'certainly preferred wheaten to barley bread' and, moreover,

---

[24] See Debby Banham, 'The Staff of Life: Cereals, Bread and Beer', in her *Food and Drink in Anglo-Saxon England* (Stroud: Tempus Publishing, 2004), pp. 13–28.

[25] See Tom Williamson, *Shaping Medieval Landscapes: Settlement, Society, Environment* (Macclesfield: Windgather Press, 2003); Debby Banham, ' "In the Sweat of Thy Brow Shalt Thou Eat Bread": Cereals and Cereal Production in the Anglo-Saxon Landscape', in *The Landscape Archaeology of Anglo-Saxon England*, edited by Nicholas J. Higham and Martin J. Ryan (Woodbridge: Boydell Press, 2010); Debby Banham and Rosamond Faith, *Anglo-Saxon Farms and Farming* (Oxford: Oxford University Press, 2014); and Jacqueline Fay, 'The Farmacy: Wild and Cultivated Plants in Anglo-Saxon England', *Interdisciplinary Studies in Literature and the Environment* 28.1 (2021), pp. 186–206.

[26] Debby Banham, 'Race and Tillage: Scandinavian Influence on Anglo-Saxon Agriculture?' in *Anglo-Saxons and the North*, edited by Matti Kilpio, Leena Kahlas-Tarkka, Jane Roberts, and Olga Timofeeva (Tempe: Arizona Center for Medieval and Renaissance Studies, 2009), pp. 165–91.

[27] Banham, *Food and Drink*, pp. 14–15.

that bread was massively important in their lives, forming the staple of every meal and the core of their social relationships (preserved in the terms *hlaford*, the loaf-guardian, and *hlafdige*, the bread-kneader).[28]

Rituals such as prayers and charms accompanied every stage of bread production, from ploughing the field to serving at table, indicating the importance assigned to a successful outcome of each task.[29] The early medieval English were sustained by bread, and thus the reference to *Triticum* in the St Frideswide charter would inevitably have recalled specific grain plants of absolutely central importance to the audience. After the introduction of the potato, and certainly given the ease with which mass-produced bread can now be purchased, the importance of cereal grains to daily life in Britain has been much diminished. For an early medieval audience, however, the significance of the cereal plants mentioned in the charter would have been very clear. 'The burgeoning fashion for growing wheat', as Banham puts it, the new agricultural techniques and equipment involved in growing it, and its central role in food rents would have ensured that bread was on the mind of every person regardless of social class.[30]

The St Frideswide charter refers to the arable weeds by the term *lollium*, generally used in the Latin tradition to translate the Greek *zizanion*, a *hapax legomenon* that most scholars have assumed refers to *Lolium temulentum* L. (family: Poaceae), a highly invasive annual grass that originated in the Mediterranean, but which is now widespread everywhere that grain is cultivated.[31] Both *lollium* and *zizania* are associated with Old English *coccel* in the glossary tradition and will

[28] Ibid., p. 14 and p. 17.

[29] These rituals are explored by Debby Banham in 'The Staff of Life: Cross and Blessings in Anglo-Saxon Cereal Production', in *Cross and Cruciform in the Anglo-Saxon World*, edited by Sarah Larratt Keefer, Karen Louise Jolly, and Catherine E. Karkov (Morgantown: West Virginia Press, 2010), pp. 279–318.

[30] 'In the Sweat of Thy Brow', p. 187.

[31] John Lytton Musselman, 'Zawan and Tares in the Bible', *Economic Botany* 54 (2000): pp. 537–42, at p. 537. Musselman undertakes a botanical investigation to determine the question of what plant would have been intended by the word *zizania* in the original context of the Holy Land. As he points out, its frequent translation by 'cockle' represents a substitution of a prevalent European plant species for whatever the original intended, since *Agrostemma githago* is uncommon in this geographical area of the Holy Land. For beautiful hand-drawn illustrations of the plants discussed here, and others from the Bible, see Winifred Walker, *All the Plants of the Bible* (New York: Doubleday, 1975), in particular p. 52, p. 190, and p. 208.

not until the fourteenth century be rendered as *tares* or *darnel*, still the common name for *Lolium temulentum* in Modern English. While *Lolium temulentum* is now prevalent in Britain, it is difficult to know exactly when the varietal arrived in Britain or when it became well established. The Archaeobotanical Computer Database provides scant examples dating from before or during the early medieval period in Britain, suggesting that the terms *lolium* and *zizania*, along with *coccel* in English, could call to the mind of an early medieval audience other varietals of arable weeds that populated their cornfields more heavily at the time.[32]

In particular, common corncockle or *Agrostemma githago* L. (family: Caryophyllaceae) is much better attested throughout England during the early medieval period than is *Lolium temulentum*.[33] John Hall notes that, along with bran in medieval cess pit deposits, corncockle is the most notable of the arable weeds preserved, appearing at almost every site where plant deposits have been found.[34] Although corncockle is not in the same family as the cereal grasses, like *Lolium temulentum*, and the mature specimens look very different to wheat because they have pinkish-purple flowers, the 'growing plants are surprisingly similar to growing cereals, being of comparable size and colour with leaves held nearly vertically in crowded conditions'.[35] Like darnel, corncockle is alien to the British Isles, being a plant brought by humans, intentionally or unintentionally, to an area; native plants, in contrast, are those that arrive in an area without human intervention, by dispersal of seed via wind, sea, or animals. More particularly, corncockle is classified as an

---

[32] P. Tomlinson and A. R. Hall, 'A Review of the Archaeological Evidence for Food Plants from the British Isles: An Example of the Use of the Archaeobotanical Computer Database (ABCD)', *Internet Archaeology* 1 (1996), http://intarch.ac.uk/journal/issue1/tomlinson/toc.html. Accessed 30 October 2018. According to the *Dictionary of Old English Plant Names*, the terms *lolium* and *zizania*, along with *giþrife* and *lasur*, are used for a variety of arable weeds during the period (*Dictionary of Old English Plant Names*, edited by Peter Bierbaumer and Hans Sauer with Helmut W. Klug and Ulrike Krischke, 2007–9, http://oldenglish-plantnames.org, s.v. 'Giþrife'. Accessed 18 November 2018.

[33] Musselman. See also Banham, *Food and Drink*, p. 23.

[34] 'The Fossil Evidence', p. 264.

[35] L. G. Firbank, '*Agrostemma githago* L. (*Lychnis githago* (L.) Scop.)', *Journal of Ecology* 76 (1988), pp. 1232–46, at p. 1237.

archaeophyte, or an alien plant that became established before 1500.[36] In practice, the distinction between native and alien plants is not absolute, because of cross-breeding, reinforcement of native plants with introduced seed, and the fact that introduced plant species often 'escaped' from gardens. *Agrostemma githago* likely originated in the eastern Mediterranean and was introduced to Britain by 500 BC, probably alongside changes in farming and increases in trade and population movement that facilitated its spread.[37] In particular it spread throughout Britain during the Roman occupation, when more land was claimed for farming, grain was imported from the Mediterranean along with the associated seeds of arable weeds, and both were transported by road.[38] Increased farming during the early medieval period, when ox-teams and heavier ploughs were able to turn previously unworked areas to cultivated use, accelerated this spread yet further. Evidence from cess pits and rubbish tips show densities of between 10 and 100 corncockle seeds per 1,000 grain seeds, which means that 2–4 seeds of the weed would have been sown for every square metre of grain.[39] As a plant found more or less exclusively in cultivated situations, corncockle thus relied on human activity for its success. As Matthew Battle perceptively puts it, 'the denomination "weed"... sticks to species sharing a set of habits and characteristics that tie them to human forms of life'.[40] In fact, *Agrostemma githago* is one of a group of plants without a natural environment anywhere, called by some 'homeless' or '*heimatlos*' plants.

Like *Lolium temulentum*, corncockle seed was present in cereal crops because the weed grew so readily in turned fields, and the similar size, shape, and weight of the grain and the seed made removal very difficult before milling.[41] Only with the onset of herbicides and clean seed corn, achieved by the development of sorting technology, were darnel and

---

[36] Christopher D. Preston, David A. Pearman, and Allan R. Hall, 'Archaeophytes in Britain', *Botanical Journal of the Linnean Society* 145 (2004), pp. 257–94, at p. 257.

[37] Ibid., pp. 257–94.

[38] Peter Vincent, *The Biogeography of the British Isles: An Introduction* (London: Routledge, 1990), p. 217.

[39] Firbank, '*Agrostemma githago*', p. 1243.

[40] Matthew Battles, *Tree* (New York: Bloomsbury, 2017), p. 19.

[41] Allan Hall, 'The Fossil Evidence for Plants in Mediaeval Towns', *Biologist* 33 (1986), pp. 262–7, at p. 264.

corncockle largely eliminated from English fields in the twentieth century. Corncockle, in particular, was completely eradicated from all cereal crops except rye by 1952, and by the 1970s was even considered endangered, although it is experiencing a recent resurgence as a garden plant.[42] Although this type of homogenizing of the fieldscape is frequently seen as negatively impacting biodiversity, leading to greater support for local farms and the reintroduction of arable weeds, accidentally ingesting either darnel or corncockle seed is problematic, since both have harmful effects on humans. *Lolium temulentum*, like many grasses of the family Poaceae, is host to a variety of fungal endophytes of the *Neotyphodium* genus and Flavicipitaceae family that produce ergot alkaloids toxic to mammals, including livestock and humans.[43] Endophytes, plants that live on or inside other plants, develop a symbiotic relationship with their hosts that can be deleterious in nature but that frequently has beneficial effects for those host plants, including the production of substances that deter grazers and insects and thus preserve the endophyte's habitat.[44] Since the Poaceae, or grass, family includes not only the *Lolium* genus but also the cultivated grain grasses such as wheat, rye, and barley, these latter can also serve as hosts to ergot fungi of the Clavicipitaceae family. However, the presence of fungal spores in cereal crops is reduced by husbandry techniques such as crop rotation and deep ploughing, which buries and neutralizes the schlerotium, or ergot, a mass or growth that allows for overwintering by preserving a dormant form of the fungus until conditions become compatible for regrowth.[45] Wild grass varietals like *Lolium temulentum* work counter to these eradication techniques, spreading

[42] Firbank, '*Agrostemma githago*', p. 1244.
[43] Takuya Shiba, Koya Sugawara, and Akira Arakawa, 'Evaluating the Fungal Endophyte *Neophytodium occultans* for Resistance to the Rice Leaf Bug, *Trigonotylus caelestialium*, in Italian Ryegrass, *Lolium multiflorum*', *Entomologia experimentalis at applicata* 141.1 (2011), pp. 45–51. https://doi.org/10.1111/j.1570-7458.2011.01162.x
[44] Christopher L. Schardl, et al., 'Loline Alkaloids: Currencies of Mutualism', *Phytochemistry* 68 (2007), pp. 980–96.
[45] G. L. Schumann and S. Uppala, 'Ergot of Rye', *The Plant Health Instructor* (2000, updated 2017); H. Walker Kirby, 'Ergot of Cereals and Grasses', *Report on Plant Diseases* 107 (1998), pp. 1–4.

the fungus back into the field by seeding themselves from the unculti-vated margins where the endophyte remains undisturbed.

A percentage of the ergots, visible as black growths that replace the plant ovaries, are swept up with the harvest and make their way through the threshing and grinding process and into flour. Since the ergots contain toxic alkaloids, which are not harmed by heat, bread made from affected flour could produce either gangrenous or convul-sive symptoms of varying severity depending on the particular toxin and its concentration. Called St Anthony's fire in the Middle Ages, symptoms could include hallucinations, paralysis, tremors, mania, and the feeling of burning or crawling on the skin; the condition could result in gangrene, the loss of limbs, or death.

Unlike *Lolium temulentum*, corncockle is toxic not because of the presence of an endophyte but because its seeds contain a colloidal glycoside with the properties of a sapotoxin, known as githagenin, comprising about 5 to 7 per cent of their overall weight.[46] Scientists disagree as to whether the toxicity of corncockle is connected to features that make its close proximity to wheat beneficial, like *Lolium temulentum*, or detrimental for the cereal plant. Like saponins, toxic compounds used in soap and fire extinguishers, githagenin imparts foaming or frothing properties to water. A bioactive molecule with high heat resistance and low water solubility, the toxic properties of githa-genin are not affected by grinding or cooking, although flour contain-ing corncockle seed has a demonstrably greyish colour, a bitter taste, and a distinctive smell. Grinding the seed in fact enhances its toxicity by removing the hard coat that retards absorption of the toxin when the seed is consumed whole. Consumed whole or in bread, githagenin causes a breakdown in red blood cells, marked in humans by symptoms of tiredness, weight loss, indigestion, diarrhoea, and, when consumed in large enough amounts, progressive weakening and death. As John Hall observes, '[i]t is likely that small amounts consumed with the daily bread caused at least mild indigestion or nausea; larger amounts

---

[46] For information on the toxic properties of *Agrostemma githago*, see John M. Kingsbury, *Poisonous Plants of the United States and Canada* (Englewood Cliffs: Prentice Hall, 1964), pp. 245–6; Marion Cooper and Anthony W. Johnson, *Poisonous Plants in Britain and their Effects on Animals and Man* (London: Her Majesty's Stationery Office, 1984), pp. 77–8.

(perhaps in years of poor harvest, when the correspondingly more abundant weed seeds were less zealously picked out of the crop) would undoubtedly have caused serious illness and even death.'[47] Evidence for a climatic dip in the early eleventh century suggests that poor harvests were prevalent during this time, including the 'great hunger throughout the English people ... such that no one ever remembered one so grim before', recorded for 1005 in the *Anglo-Saxon Chronicle*.[48] The early medieval English audience of the parable, then, would all have experienced the effects of *Agrostemma githago* to some degree.

## How plants change the story

Knowing more about the appearance and behaviours of the arable weeds that were likely recalled to the mind of the early medieval English audience by the parable—that is, *Lolium temulentum* and *Agrostemma githago*—makes us aware of the narrative's material interactions and the meanings and effects that open from these. The toxicity of these weeds when processed and consumed in bread on one hand materializes the charter's use of the parable to demonstrate the inherently poisonous nature of Scandinavians within England. Within the discursive register, the parable's vegetal imagery functions as a metaphorical means of representing and constructing human difference and assigning negative characteristics to Scandinavians. Within the material register, the effect of the plants themselves can be felt by the parable's audience within their own bodies in the form of physical illness. The intention of Æthelred's political repurposing of the parable is very clear: Scandinavians are aggressive interlopers within the English population who threaten the health of the body politic and thus deserve to be

[47] 'The Fossil Evidence', pp. 264–5. For a study of twentieth-century instances of bread poisoning, mostly caused by *senecio* varietals, see D. G. Steyn, 'Poisoning of Human Beings by Weeds Contained in Cereals (Bread Poisoning) and Senecio Poisoning in Stock', *Journal of the Royal Sanitary Institute* 56 (1935), pp. 760–8. As Steyn observes, during years of insufficient rainfall, wheat does not grow to its normal height and is cut close to the ground, increasing the chance of contamination with the seeds of arable weeds (p. 766).
[48] *MS C*, edited by Katherine O'Brien O'Keeffe, p. 91.

violently eradicated. The nausea, or worse, experienced by those who had eaten bread made with grain mixed either with corncockle or darnel seed interacts with the words of the parable to materialize this message within the individual bodies of English readers. These physical interactions, then, become part of the overall reaction to the text and a constitutive element in the process of ethnic identification that it undertakes.

But just as the poisonous matter of the plant works with the grain of the charter's overt message, plant behaviour at the same time undermines it. Particularly problematic is Æthelred's attempt to use plants to assert that ethnic difference is self-evident and easy to perceive and, thus, the massacre of Scandinavians is justifiable. Even while striving to purify the concept of ethnicity by representing it as an immediately and uncomplicatedly apprehensible plant difference, the imbrication of Scandinavian and English identity irrepressibly returns in the St Frideswide charter through this very same image. The particular choice of wheat and arable weeds in the parable is made to exploit the confusing formal similarity of these plants in the field, especially when both are in the early stages of growth. Because the survival of arable weeds depends upon their ability to grow to maturity unnoticed within the cornfield and, likewise, the presence of arable weeds improves the insect resistance and growth of wheat, similarities between the two species would have been evolutionarily enhanced over time since their growing side by side is of mutual benefit. As mutualists, wheat and arable weeds cannot easily be separated in the field, as the parable itself makes very clear. When the servants ask the lord whether they should root out the weeds in his field, he responds:

> Þa cwæð he nese þe læs ge þone hwæte awurtwalion. þonne ge þone coccel gadriað; Lætaþ ægþer weaxan oð riptiman. and on þam riptiman ic secge þam riperum gadriaþ ærest þone coccel and bindaþ sceafmælum to forbærnenne. and gadriaþ ðone hwæte into minum berne.[49]

> (Then he said no, lest you root out the wheat when you gather the cockle. Let both grow until harvest and in the harvest I will say to the

[49] Original quoted from R. M. Liuzza, ed., *The Old English Version of the Gospels*, Early English Text Society, o.s., 504 (Oxford: Oxford University Press, 1994), p. 28. Translation is my own.

> reapers: gather first the cockle and bind it into sheaves to be burned, and gather then the wheat into my barn.)

While the Gospel text concludes with an apocalyptic image of the burning of the cockles and the harvesting of the wheat, it simultaneously emphasizes that the two are, in some senses, mutually reliant, and that no hasty judgements should be made as to the identity of either.

Such is certainly the message derived from the parable in the commentary tradition, which profoundly discouraged thinking about the weeds and wheat as types of people, but emphasized instead an abstract equation to good and bad thoughts or words.[50] Commentators asserted that the parable was about giving the benefit of the doubt to sinners in this world, while leaving judgement as to absolute moral worth to the divine. Augustine, for instance, highlighted the difference between vegetal and anthropomorphic categories, writing that

> [t]here is this real difference between people and real grain and real weeds, for what was grain in the field is grain and what were weeds are weeds. But in the Lord's field, which is the church, at times what was grain turns into weeds and at times what were weeds turn into grain; and no one knows what they will be tomorrow.[51]

Jerome similarly cautioned against making quick judgements about which people might be cockle and which wheat, noting that, '[b]etween wheat and weeds there is something called darnel, when the plant is in its early growth and there is no stalk yet. It looks like an ear of corn, and the difference between them is hardly noticeable.'[52] In his homily for the twenty-first Sunday after Pentecost, Ælfric similarly uses the cockles and wheat episode to emphasize that good and bad people are mingled in the world, and cannot be separated except by divine judgement:

> On þyssere andwerdan gelaðunge sind gemengde yfele 7 gode: swa swa clæne corn mid fulum coccele: ac on ende þyssere worulde se soða dema hæt his englas gadrian þone coccel byrþenmælum 7 awurpan into ðam unadwæscendlicum fyre; Byrþenmælum hi

---

[50] For a range of responses, see *Ancient Christian Commentary on Scripture: New Testament Ia, Matthew 1–13*, edited by Manlio Simonetti (Downers Grove, IL: Intervarsity Press, 2001), pp. 276–9.

[51] Ibid., p. 277.     [52] Ibid., p. 278.

gadriað þa synfullan fram þam rihtwisum. þonne ða manslagan beoð
togædere getigede innon þam hellicum fyre. 7 sceaþan mid sceaþum,
gytseras mid gytserum. forliras mid forlirum. 7 swa gehwylce mán-
fulle geferan on þam ecum tintregum samod gewriþene cwylmiað:
and se clæna hwæte bið gebroht on Godes berne þ[æt] is þ[æt] ða
rihtwisan beoð gebrohte to þam ecan life: þær ne cymð storm ne nan
unweder þæt ðam corne derie.[53]

(In this present church are mingled evil and good, just as clean corn
with foul cockle: but at the end of this world the true Judge will
command his angels to gather the cockle into large bundles, and
throw it into the unquenchable fire. Into large bundles they will
gather the sinful from the righteous: then will murderers be tied
together within the hellish fire, and robbers with robbers, the misers
with the misers, adulterers with adulterers; and so all evil companions, bound together, will suffer in eternal torments; and the clean
wheat will be brought into God's barn: that is, the righteous will be
brought to eternal life, where neither storm nor any bad weather
comes that may harm the corn.)

Turning to the vegetal realm in order to borrow examples that could be
used to stabilize categories of difference between people, or bolster
arguments about what constitutes human being in particular, has a
long and complex philosophical and theological history; and this scene
of weeds and wheat, particularly as it is reused in the St Frideswide
charter, brings together many of the recurring and most problematic
elements of this history. Michael Marder, founding scholar in the field
of critical plant studies, explains that, beginning with Aristotle, wheat
was central to the discussion of being, particularly the development of
the concept of actualization.[54] In the *Metaphysics*, the notion that a
growing stalk *is* wheat 'goes to illustrate the strongest sense of being in
the copula', more powerful than that provided by the sense that a
sculpture is in the stone or a half-line is in a line.[55] For Aristotle, a
grain of wheat has the same kind of potentiality, in terms of its
capability to generate another stalk of wheat, as does the material for

[53] *Ælfric's Catholic Homilies: The First Series*, edited by Peter Clemoes, EETS s.s. 17
(Oxford: Oxford University Press, 1997), p. 480.

[54] See Michael Marder, 'Aristotle's Wheat', ch. 7 in his *The Philosopher's Plant: An
Intellectual Herbarium* (Columbia: Columbia University Press, 2014), pp. 21–37.

[55] Ibid., p. 22.

a man or an animal, but plants themselves are differentiated from humans in their incapacity for self-reflective, abstract thought. Plants, Marder explains, pose a threat to Aristotle's vision of an orderly universe in which each being should actualize its particular and inherent potential, with 'multiple instances of plants confounding differences and oppositions'—with plants behaving, in other words, in ways that they should not according to the Aristotelian schema.[56] Drawing most of the apparatus for his thinking from animal life, Aristotle did not account for the much higher degree of genetic plasticity in the plant world where, for example, apple seeds generate a new form with every planting. The potentialities of a plant are too diverse ever to be fully actualized or anticipated, a fact that cannot help but trouble the ontological framework Aristotle is, in part, using them to develop.

Following Aristotle, ancient botanical authors classified plants, as they did other living beings, according to their gene (genos in the singular) and eide (eidos), terms that are roughly equivalent to genus and species in that the latter is a subset of the former, but which are not used systematically beyond that. Gavin Hardy and Laurence Totelin, in their work *Ancient Botany*, thus suggest they be more properly translated by the more generic English terms '"type", "kind" or "variety"'.[57] Ancient botanical authors believed that genos and eidos were not fixed and, in particular, that certain plants could change into others, including wheat into darnel. Galen, in *The Properties of Foodstuffs*, describes how his father conducted an experiment to determine whether darnel was in fact a transformed version of wheat and barley.[58] After carefully removing any alien seed, his father sowed wheat and barley separately, and then observed how much darnel grew in each plot. Since almost none grew amongst the barley, while a moderate amount grew amongst the wheat, the results confirmed the idea that darnel was wheat in another incarnation: the two plants share an origin in the same seed, and one simply changes into the other. Although modern plant geneticists have disproved this proposition, these early perceptions of species malleability form part of the original context of the parable and travel with it as the narrative moves to new linguistic, cultural, and climatological contexts. These assumptions make perfect sense in

[56] Ibid., p. 37.     [57] (London: Routledge, 2016), p. 70.
[58] Ibid., p. 74.

observational terms, terms that would have been shared, even if the exact intellectual tradition of Greek and Roman plant lore was shared only in a diffuse way, with pre-Conquest farmers.

Aligning the exegetical commentary on Matthew 13 with the writings of classical agronomists and botanists shows Jerome to be more attuned to the latter than Augustine, when he wrote that 'between wheat and weeds there is something called darnel'. Augustine's statement, on the other hand, that 'what was grain in the field is grain and what were weeds are weeds [b]ut in the Lord's field, which is the church, at times what was grain turns into weeds and at times what were weeds turn into grain', does not really reflect contemporary ideas about vegetal being, and instead uses plants to maintain an anthropocentric fiction of a 'real difference between people and real grain and real weeds'. Given that the cornfield, towards which the parable seems to look for a more stable ontological register for the expression of human characteristics, turns out rather to be a botanical minefield of vegetal instability and transformative potentiality, it is not surprising that the exegetical tradition defers to the greater insight of the heavenly judge, asserting that no earthly figure has access to the type of spiritual sight required to distinguish between the cockles and the wheat. The coevolution of wheat and arable weeds, which had led to their formal similarity and their mutually beneficial properties and behaviours, materializes this point for the diverse audiences of the parable, reinforcing that a good exegete—or more broadly, a good Christian—is also a prudent farmer, and vice versa.

## Mutuality and ethnicity

The interconnections between the discursive and material contexts of the cockles and wheat story are complex and contradictory; returning to the St Frideswide charter with renewed attention to both yields a fuller sense of the text's meanings and effects. To use Karen Barad's term for this type of dynamic and mutually constituted agency, the charter intra-acts not only with other texts but also with human bodies and with plants. Certain of these intra-actions involve meanings and effects that would very likely have been appealing to Æthelred in his self-justifying aim in issuing the charter, as I discussed above. In other ways those material vegetal agencies resist co-optation by the discursive frame of scripture or law, returning other, perhaps unanticipated, interpretive possibilities. Because of the plants, what appears to be, and is used by Æthelred as, an assertion that both ethnic and moral difference is a straightforward matter, is also a complex illustration of the mutability of such identificatory categories and a cautionary tale about mistaking wheat for weeds, English for Danes, or Danes for the damned. The demonstrable ways in which arable weeds and wheat are mutualists—their formal similarity, symbiotic interactions, and even the belief that they are the same plant at different stages of development—intra-actively produce both English and Scandinavians in a way that runs directly counter to the surface intent of the charter to distinguish them. In particular, the material dimensions of the narrative reinforce the ways that the English and the Scandinavians are similar, making it very difficult to choose between or categorize them.

Much about the political situation in England at the turn of the eleventh century resonates with this counternarrative, and highlights the malleability of the categories that Æthelred is attempting rhetorically to control. Such malleability is obvious even in the brief 1002 annal from the CDE versions of the *Chronicle*, which I discussed earlier as one of the two sources, along with the St Frideswide charter, closest in time to the massacre itself. The annal observes that Æthelred ordered the Danes to be killed because of their treachery, a fault that was not limited to Scandinavians: 'forþon þam cynge wæs gecydd þæt hi woldon hine besyrewian æt his life. 7 syððan ealle his witan. 7 habban syþðan his rice' (because the king was told that they would plot against his life and afterwards all of his councillors, and then have his kingdom). Æthelred may have been thinking here of the unreliable mercenary armies that he had taken on following a treaty made in 993/4, but which they had broken in 997–9 and 1001, with the betrayal of the Scandinavian leader Pallig being particularly galling to the king. Pallig was Swein Forkbeard's brother-in-law and apparently contracted with Æthelred before 1001, when the *Anglo-Saxon Chronicle* notes that he deserted.[59] Additional payments of £24,000 were, however, made in 1001–2, presumably for similar mercenary services.[60] Recuperating hostile Danish

[59] Keynes, *The Diplomas of King Æþelred*, p. 205.
[60] Howard, *Swein Forkbeard's Invasions*, p. 61.

armies as mercenary troops in this way was a tactic of long lineage, and not a sign of particular desperation as it has often been interpreted. Alfred had used it during the ninth-century Viking incursions and Æthelred was to continue the policy later in his reign: for example, in 1012 Swein Forkbeard's primary commander, Thorkell the Tall, transferred his allegiance to Æthelred.[61]

Rather than being specifically Danish characteristics, treachery and betrayal were endemic to the latter part of Æthelred's reign, at least if we believe the account given in the *Anglo-Saxon Chronicle*.[62] As Pauline Stafford notes, the years 1002 to 1006 saw the exile of ealdorman Leofsige of Essex, the killing of Ælfhelm of York at the King's order, the blinding of his two sons, and the exile of the thegn Wulfgeat. Ealdorman Ælfric is the object of particular scorn in the *Chronicle* account, where he is accused of warning the Danes of an impending English attack in 992 and of faking illness in order to avoid leading the *fyrd*, the English army, in 1003. In an elegant interpretation of the *Chronicle*'s condemnatory narrative, Stafford suggests that the events of the St Brice's Day massacre were imbricated in the complex domestic politics of Æthelred's reign, and in particular his policy toward rule of the north, which seemed destined to create treachery and the perception of treachery. As she notes, because the king had few land-rights with which to reward ealdormen appointed to the north, such leaders had to cement their position with the local nobility, an act which could easily be interpreted as disloyalty toward the king, as happened in 1006 with ealdorman Ælfhelm of York.[63] The political environment of the late tenth and early eleventh centuries, therefore, does not suggest that, as the 1002 order for the massacre presents it, treachery was associated only with the Danes, nor could it be eliminated from the kingdom along with a portion of its population. The historical evidence suggests that the order maps a desired alignment of ethnic and ethical concepts at a time at which the capaciousness and fluctuation of such categories was more than evident.

---

[61] Keynes, *The Diplomas of King Æþelred*, p. 202 and p. 221.

[62] For a summary of the major betrayals detailed in this text, see Keynes, *The Diplomas of King Æþelred*, pp. 205–6; and Stafford, 'The Reign of Æthelred II', pp. 30–1.

[63] Stafford, 'The Reign of Æthelred II', p. 31. For the creation of these large ealdormanries, see pp. 17–19, and for Æthelred's policy of dissolving them, at least in southern areas, see p. 29.

The particular problems experienced by those ealdormen located in the north, and especially the link that Stafford identifies between the charge of treachery and the specific challenges of northern rule, indicate the extent to which ethnicity is also admixed with regionalism during this period. For instance, Keynes's examination of the charter evidence for the tenth and eleventh centuries indicates that the king and his *witenagemot* met far more frequently in places south of North-ampton, with Shrewsbury, Penkridge, Nottingham, Lincoln, and York representing the only northern sites at which councils were held.[64] As Stafford observes, '[g]eography was a real circumscription on late Saxon royal power ... it is ... apparent that although faced with the problems of being kings of all England, tenth-century rulers were still most securely based in Wessex and south-west Mercia, and the Thames was still a dividing line of significance.'[65] Presumably this fact explains why, during the period from 978 to 1009, when it was normal practice for all ealdormen currently serving to appear at meetings of the *witenagemot* and sign witness lists, 'the only ealdormen who do not appear consistently during their periods of office are some of northern origin'.[66] One late tenth-century document, affirming the will of Æþelric of Bocking, is particularly interesting for the way that it collapses regional into ethnic vocabulary, by recording that the document is attested not only by the signatories but also by 'ealle ða ðegnas ðe þær widan gegæderode wæron ægðer. ge of Westsexan. ge of Myrcean. ge of Denan. ge. of Englon' (all those thanes who were gathered there from far and wide, both from Wessex and from Mercia, from among the Danes and the English).[67] Keynes suggests that 'Danes' here is

---

[64] See map in *The Diplomas of King Æþelred*, p. 36; and also the maps on p. 18 and p. 20 of Stafford, 'The Reign of Æthelred II'.

[65] Stafford, 'The Reign of Æthelred II', pp. 19–21.

[66] Ibid., pp. 157–8.

[67] Sawyer number 939. Text from *Regesta regum anglorum: A Searchable Edition of the Corpus of Anglo-Saxon Royal Diplomas 670–1066* at http://www.trin.cam.ac.uk/char twww/NewRegReg.html. The translation here is my own, and I should note that Old English people-names are difficult to render in modern English because it is unclear whether they are intended to refer in the plural to groups of people or, in the singular, to the land inhabited by these people. The grammatical endings are ambiguous: they could represent a corruption of dative plural –um resulting from the levelling of vowels in unstressed syllables that occurred in late Old English, or they could be read as –an endings (if we assume that the nouns are being declined as weak). It seems likely, in any case, that such words had a flexibility in Old English that they do not retain in Modern English, and

'presumably a generic term for the inhabitants of the Danelaw', and notes that, because only two of Æthelred's diplomas include substantial numbers of witnesses with Scandinavian names, we have no way of knowing whether this meeting at Cookham to affirm Æþelric's will was unusual. At the least, however, the phraseology of this charter, 'ge of Westsexan. ge of Myrcean. ge of Denan. ge. of Englon', suggests that the writer understands the regional categories to be in some sense involved in the ethnic; in fact, the latter pair acts almost like a gloss on the former. Such wording indicates an apprehension of or striving for a type of comprehensiveness that contains, and is defined by, an internal difference. That is to say, the tag phrase referring to the diverse origin of additional witnesses stands in for the totality of Æthelred's kingdom and identifies its mixed composition. This document, in defining an English community specifically as comprised of parts within a whole, runs entirely counter to the surface intent of the St Frideswide charter.

Although much about the production of charters remains obscure, it seems likely that, as Keynes suggests, the king travelled with some sort of official group of scribes charged with generating such documents.[68] It is important to note, therefore, that such language specifying the internal composition of the country as 'ge of Westsexan. ge of Myrcean. ge of Denan. ge. of Englon' is almost certainly being generated by southern scribes who were central to Æthelred's peripatetic court. The project of Æthelred's government is not, therefore, rhetorically to downplay the differences among his subjects, but to acknowledge and incorporate them. In fact, if we understand such difference partly as a discursive product of textual culture, then we have to admit the ways in which such difference is actually produced by Æthelred's court. His provision of dual legal codes, for instance, seems 'part of an overall attempt to define procedural aspects of the distinction in legal terms

---

could refer to both people and land in conjunction. For more on this topic, see my 'The Interests of Compounding: Angelcynn to Englaland in the Anglo-Saxon Chronicle', in *Anglo-Saxon Texts and Their Transmission: Essays in Honour of Donald G. Scragg [on the occasion of his seventieth birthday]*, edited by Hugh Magennis and Jonathan Wilcox (Morgantown: West Virginia University Press, 2006), pp. 337–67.

[68] Keynes, *The Diplomas of King Æþelred*, p. 229.

between English and "Danish" areas of the kingdom'.[69] Wormald suggests that these two codes—Woodstock and Wantage, traditionally known as I and III Æthelred—were actually the second and third promulgated by the king, produced in close temporal succession with Wantage in 997 and Woodstock a little before.[70] Despite being chronologically close, Wantage is distinct for the degree to which it reveals Scandinavian influence; Wormald has suggested that such influence could only have come about had delegates from the Danelaw met the king at Wantage and been given guidelines that they then expanded independently. The resulting product seems deliberately intended to incorporate Scandinavians within the official fabric of the kingdom: as Wormald puts it, '[t]he Wantage Code . . . reflected royal policy, and it was ostensibly issued in Wessex. But no West Saxon king or council could have produced a code so thoroughly Scandinavian in form and content.'[71]

When reconsidered against this background, it becomes evident that Æthelred's government was disseminating contradictory messages about ethnic diversity in ways that seem all too familiar from the modern context. On the one hand, the presence of Scandinavians and Anglo-Scandinavians is being acknowledged and their legal customs and regional identity recognized and incorporated; on the other, they are positioned as a menace, over-running the country and threatening its integrity. Within this context, St Brice's Day, like massacres in general, can be seen to be about the body, both of individuals and of groups, since its efficacy is based on an assumption and assertion of palpable material difference between constituencies, whether that difference be understood as marked by skin colour, hair colour or style, dress, or language. While, in practice, the bounds of such fields are discursively established and changeable, the rhetoric and act of massacre asserts their essential nature while claiming that the excision of one group will cement the unity of that remaining. The compulsion of such a claim at the turn of the eleventh century is the opposite side of

[69] Ibid., p. 197. For Æthelred's legal policy, see Wormald, 'Æþelred the Lawmaker'; for Æthelred I and III in particular, see pp. 61–2.

[70] Wormald, 'Æþelred the Lawmaker', p. 63.

[71] Ibid., pp. 61–2. In his summary Wormald describes the two codes in this way: 'Woodstock concerned with surety and witness, and aimed at "English" England; Wantage seeking the same objectives, and others, in the Danelaw' (p. 63).

the highly composite nature of English identity—whether defined in political, territorial, historical, or legal terms—at this time and the high tolerance for, in fact encouragement of, such hybridity on the part of Æthelred's government. The fact that Scandinavians were simultaneously settlers, attackers, and mercenaries in the English army, while English supporters of Æthelred frequently changed sides or practised treachery, made for confusing and changeable alliances between concepts of ethnicity and loyalty, alliances that eluded easy comprehension in somatic terms.

If we concentrate only on the level of the text itself, its interactions with and repurposing of ideological narratives, then we miss not only how these narratives are reinforced and challenged by the matter of plants but also how plants serve an intra-active role in the constitution of ethnic and other types of human categorical difference in Æthelred's England. As members of an agricultural society, the majority of the population would have both contemplated and practised plant cultivation a good deal, because plants were overwhelmingly important in their daily lives as a source of food, medicine, and, in the form of timber, of building material.[72] As Banham puts it, even though the experiences of the early medieval English must have differed quite a bit depending on social status and education, 'for all of them, whatever the outer reaches of their universe, much of its core will have been concerned with food production'.[73] When translating or otherwise appropriating a biblical text about weeds, then, the pre-Conquest writer could anticipate a level of specialized knowledge in an audience familiar with real cornfield weeds, their growth habits, and the controlled dangers of ingesting them. Homiletic and biblical texts comparing people to plants, which emphasize their analogous and symbolic relationship, are thus not always clearly separable from the everyday intermingling of the early medieval English with the plants they cultivated and that

[72] For the many and varied uses of plants in early medieval England, see C. P. Biggam, 'The True Staff of Life: The Multiple Roles of Plants', in *The Material Culture of Daily Living in the Anglo-Saxon World*, edited by Maren Clegg Hyer and Gale R. Owen-Crocker (Exeter: University of Exeter Press, 2011), pp. 23–48.

[73] '*Lectun* and *Orceard*: A Preliminary Survey of the Evidence for Horticulture in Anglo-Saxon England', in *The Anglo-Saxons: The World through Their Eyes*, edited by Gale R. Owen-Crocker and Brian W. Schneider (Oxford: BAR British Series, 2014), pp. 33–48, at p. 33.

sustained them in various ways. The comparison being drawn between invasive plants and people is not just figural in the St Frideswide charter, then, but part of a material continuum including actual encounters with weeds. By necessity these encounters would have involved paying close attention to the physical characteristics of weeds, in order to identify their differences from crop plants, and may also have involved bodily illness caused by accidentally eating them. When these botanical interactions are given equal weight as the intellectual, theological, and political contexts of the charter, it becomes clear that the material realm does not simply serve to confirm or bolster the discursive content of the charter. Instead the observation and ingestion—the practices of living alongside, in other words—arable weeds combine with the words of the charter to produce a multilayered Englishness, the blended historical, geographical, and political content of which is both thought and felt. Encounters with weeds, reading about weeds, and encounters with people represented as weeds thus mingle together on a continuum involving both discursive and material modes of being English.

# | 4 |

# *Beowulf* and Ethnic Matters

The previous chapter investigated how ethnic difference was understood and lived in the early eleventh century by expanding the
interpretive frame to account for the material intra-actions of texts,
bodies, and plants. This chapter will take a slightly different approach
in order to consider how another text committed to writing during this
time period, *Beowulf*, also explores questions of difference and the body
in ways that relate to and condition the lived experience of its audiences. *Beowulf*, a poem set in sixth-century Scandinavia, which presents
its characters in a highly positive light, has seemed an unusual fit in the
eleventh-century context of its single manuscript witness, copied during a time when Scandinavians were attacking England. As a heroic
poem, it functions to idealize certain forms of behaviour and values that
can be identified as Germanic, but it does not engage with Englishness
or England in any specific way. And as a poem, with the necessity to
adhere to alliterative, metrical, and stylistic norms, it would seem the
form most distant from the type of material engagement that previous
chapters have aimed to open up for other types of texts. And yet,
notwithstanding its distant setting and fantastical plot, no reader of
*Beowulf* could fail to notice the degree to which it is concerned with
bodies human and other-than-human, as heads melt on funeral pyres,
arms are ripped off, and hands grasp and break swords.

   As violent dismemberment is central to the narrative, particularly in
the first two monster fights, *Beowulf* seems to invite a reading situating

*Materializing Englishness in Early Medieval Texts*. Jacqueline Fay, Oxford University Press.
© Jacqueline Fay 2022. DOI: 10.1093/oso/9780198757573.003.0005

it in relation to those violent matters of embodied ethnic identity discussed in the previous chapter. However, very real difficulties are attendant on developing such an interpretation, obvious and enticing though the connections are. The impossibility of securely dating the poem poses problems in reconstructing any material-discursive network for it and, perhaps more profoundly, the severed body parts under consideration seem resolutely located within the representational realm of aestheticized violence, where bodies have been considered symbolic rather than material entities.[1] As Stacy Klein puts it in her own study of queens in Old English literature, the '[d]ifficulties of securely locating Old English poetry, either temporally or geographically, have deterred all but a very few scholars from reading the poetic corpus through the lens of cultural criticism.'[2] For the materialist scholar, the dislocation of *Beowulf* from any particular geo-historical context is similarly problematic, since it makes the project of tracing its material intra-actions complicated.

While certain of these problems are particular to Old English poetry, especially the issue of dating, others are associated with the broader question of literature's relation to materiality in general. Within the fields of new materialism and ecomaterialism, various models are emerging that attempt to account for this relationship, but many rely on fundamentally immaterial, symbolic tropes such as haunting or allegory, in which literary elements such as plot and character are understood to be representative of material interactions, or they

---

[1] The only relatively fast date attached to the poem is that of its copying in the unique manuscript exemplar London, British Library, Cotton Vitellius A.xv. Most scholars have followed Ker and Dumville in dating the manuscript to around the year 1000 (David Dumville, '*Beowulf* Come Lately: Some Notes on the Palaeography of the Nowell Codex', *Archiv für das Studium der Neueren Sprachen und Literaturen* 225.1 [1988], pp. 49–63). However, a significant alternative argument, originated by Kevin Kiernan (*Beowulf and the Beowulf Manuscript* [Ann Arbor: University of Michigan Press, 1981; rev. ed. 1996]), places the manuscript around 1010–20, during the reign of Cnut. As Robert E. Bjork and Anita Obermeier point out in their excellent summary of the issues surrounding dating the poem, 'Date, Provenance, Author, Audiences', current thinking about the poem's date of composition has moved toward a late date close to the moment of copying (*A Beowulf Handbook*, edited by Robert E. Bjork and John D. Niles [Exeter: University of Exeter Press, 1996], pp. 13–34). Michael Lapidge, in contrast, has argued that the errors of the manuscript reveal the presence of an underlying eighth-century archetype ('The Archetype of *Beowulf*', *Anglo-Saxon England* 29 [2000], pp. 5–41). For a thorough discussion of the dating question, see the essays in *The Dating of* Beowulf, edited by Colin Chase (Toronto: University of Toronto Press, 1981).
[2] Stacy Klein, *Ruling Women: Queenship and Gender in Anglo-Saxon Literature* (Notre Dame: University of Notre Dame Press, 2006), p. 6.

position literary texts as didactic, capable of changing their audiences' minds about materiality. Valuable as these approaches are, in certain respects they preserve a distance between literature and matter, which this chapter aims to trouble by restoring the dismembered and displayed body parts of *Beowulf* to the broader material and discursive context of stories told by and about embodied identity in early eleventh-century England. In particular, I will use Wendy Wheeler's notion of literature as an 'aesthetic organism' to analyse how *Beowulf*— in a series of scenes focused on bodily dismemberment, display, exchange, and interpretation—encourages a type of play with and around the meanings of matter. Far from being confined within the poem as a linguistic artefact, this type of play evolves the stories told about and by bodies in early eleventh-century England.

# Bodies, things, and biosemiotics

*Beowulf* has long been read and understood in relation to the material culture of early medieval England, but recent work in this area has taken a new turn in its focus on the agency of things in the poem. Rather than focusing on the illustrative or contextual role of objects, work like that by Aaron Hostetter recognizes that the poem is full of disruptive things that interrupt and confound not only the characters but also the audience: as he describes it, '[w]e might want to read a story about ideals and motivations, yet the poem insists that we apprehend these by way of the objects that surround and permeate the institution it celebrates.'[3] Hostetter is one of a number of recent scholars who have explored how 'things' in *Beowulf* disturb and draw attention to the human systems of interpretation by which power relations are organized according to that which is legible. As both Hostetter and James Paz observe, *Beowulf* is characterized by moments where things—swords, helmets, torques, but also body parts and other beings such as Grendel's Mother—exceed and disarm the careful modes of human communication that the poem at the same time celebrates and showcases.[4] By

---

[3] Aaron Hostetter, 'Disruptive Things in *Beowulf*, *New Medieval Literatures* 17 (2017): pp. 34–61, at p. 34.

[4] James Paz, 'Æschere's Head, Grendel's Mother, and the Sword that Isn't a Sword: Unreadable Things in *Beowulf*, *Exemplaria* 25 (2013): pp. 231–51.

tracing the ways that non-human things repeatedly unsettle and affect the human community in *Beowulf*, Hostetter and Paz recognize that '[p]owerful things are not inert and static, rather they are fictional occasions...continuous moments of material being that often seem to stand in the way of the story and its actors.'[5] An important insight of this recent work is thus that affect in *Beowulf*, rather than being solely a human propensity, is distributed across human and non-human actors: humans are capable of making and interpreting things, but they are also affected, changed, and voiced by them.

This chapter will build upon this recent work on resistant and unreadable things in *Beowulf*, concentrating on many of the same episodes in the poem while extending the analysis to include the poem itself as a type of organism, or thing, producing 'para-subjective effects' spanning also its audience.[6] For this notion of poetry as an 'aesthetic organism', I rely on the work of Wendy Wheeler, who aims to capture the potentiality that emerges in a dynamic and unfolding process of reception implicating and changing both work and audience.[7] Rooted in biosemiotics, Wheeler's work positions the development of literary meanings in relation to the playful and interpretive structures conditioning evolution in general. During the 1980s and 1990s, scientists realized that the overwhelmingly semiotic nature of their vocabulary for a range of biological functions—'codes, transcriptions, messengers, reinscription, translation, transduction, genetic information, chemical signals, cell signaling'—was not metaphorical, but indicated a profound and systematic homology between systems usually seen as decisively different due to the nature/culture divide.[8] Biosemiotics, the field emerging from this realization, explores how biological processes function according to a type of play, or an open-ended exploration of relationships among system elements and between systems themselves. Biological play as the predominant mode by which evolutionary change happens, as opposed to the principle of selection which dominated theoretical biology post-Darwin,

---

[5] Hostetter, 'Disruptive Things', p. 35.    [6] Ibid.

[7] Wendy Wheeler, 'Natural Play, Natural Metaphor, and Natural Stories: Biosemiotic Realism', in *Material Ecocriticism*, edited by Serenella Iovino and Serpil Oppermann (Bloomington: Indiana University Press, 2014), pp. 67–79, at p. 77. See also, Wendy Wheeler, *The Whole Creature: Complexity, Biosemiotics and the Evolution of Culture* (London: Lawrence and Wishart, 2006).

[8] Wheeler, 'Natural Play', p. 71.

has much in common with the type of interactive meaning generation in literature, in which audiences continually reassess and integrate elements into an interpretation that shifts over time and in response to systems and elements *infra* and *extra* to the text itself.

While this description of meaning creation could apply to any text, it is particularly true of literature specifically because of the artful and deliberate nature of its construction and, in particular, the high degree of substitutive forms it contains. Wheeler is decisive on this point:

> metaphor and metonymy, the means by which meanings grow in the meeting of reader and aesthetic text, are not simply interesting but unimportant literary devices, but are the real means by which both natural and cultural semiosis drives natural and cultural evolution and development ... [t]he recognition of similarity in difference (metaphor) is a real causal factor in both natural and cultural development.[9]

From this vantage point, literature is not a special case of anything, but typifies the relations and interactions of organic systems in general. However, the special features of certain types of literature, more specifically Old English poetry, can potentially distil a higher concentration of moments or forms of 'recognition of similarity in difference' than do others. For example, the density of compound words in Old English poetry continually brings semantic components into new wholes and, in the case of kennings, specifically provokes the recognition of a metaphoric relationship between word and referent. At the level of the line, Old English poetry employs alliteration to join two metrically self-contained units, while the technique of formulaic composition generates huge networks of interchangeable components. And in formal and structural terms, Old English poetry is characterized by elaborate patterns, such as the 'envelope structure' or 'ring composition', created by the careful arrangement of similar and different elements.[10] Careful arrangement, moreover, that cannot really be said to be overseen by the agency of any single human consciousness, given

[9] Ibid., p. 70.
[10] Classic studies of *Beowulf*'s reciprocal style include Fred C. Robinson, Beowulf *and the Appositive Style* (Knoxville: University of Tennessee Press, 1985); John D. Niles, Beowulf: *The Poem and Its Tradition* (Cambridge, MA: Harvard University Press, 1983), esp. pp. 152–62. The notion of interlace, which places less emphasis on duality,

the processual and collaborative work over a long period of time that most likely produced *Beowulf* in particular. As Elizabeth Tyler puts it, '[i]f accretive texts challenge modern ways of reading, with their expectations of author, date, provenance and stylistic coherence, *Beowulf* presents the ultimate challenge.'[11] Although not all of these features are unique to Old English poetry, being characteristic of other poetic traditions with roots in oral composition, the particular combination of these features is distinctive, and effectively saturates this form of literature in modes that require 'recognition of similarity in difference' from its audience.

The continual recognition and organization of relations among literary and linguistic elements by a work's audiences is part of an aesthetic organism like *Beowulf* and, as Wheeler argues, is also part of the play by which culture itself evolves. Wheeler's approach is similar, in this respect, to that of many scholars who have considered the ways that literature, in particular heroic poetry, socializes its audiences. Peter Richardson, for example, in an essay on imaginative literature and state formation, aptly describes how Old English poems affect their audiences, writing that

> even the most sophisticated...poems script, and do not merely reflect, far-reaching social processes...This scripting is more imaginative and oblique, though no less assiduous, than what we see in the overtly political material. It is also more interesting, largely because so much of it occurs below the horizon of consciousness. While many...poems exhort directly, their most powerful effects often derive from richly implicated patterns of audience identification, which are themselves invited by the adroit manipulation of narrative perspective.[12]

---

is also commonly adduced as a structural model for the poem, following John Leyerle, 'The Interlace Structure of *Beowulf*' *University of Toronto Quarterly* 37 (1967), pp. 1–17.

[11] *Old English Poetics: The Aesthetics of the Familiar in Anglo-Saxon England* (York: York Medieval Press, 2006), p. 149.

[12] Peter R. Richardson, 'Making Thanes: Literature, Rhetoric and State Formation in Anglo-Saxon England', *Philological Quarterly* 78 (1999), pp. 215–32, at p. 216. For related comments, see also Stephen Harris, *Race and Ethnicity in Anglo-Saxon Literature* (New York: Routledge, 2003), p. 5.

Richardson is but one step away here, it seems to me, from Wheeler's notion of literature's role in cultural evolutionary play, albeit that his notion of scripting assumes the intentionality of an 'adroit manipulation', or a director. Absent this type of wilful agency, and Richardson is describing a system of patterns in interaction with which the audience is changed in ways that they are not aware of and that exceed the level of intellect or 'consciousness'. As Klein has thoughtfully put it, '[i]n this, *Beowulf* is typical of Old English poetry, whose great power resides in its ability to suggest things without really saying them.'[13] Such suggestions or effects are part of what Daniel Donoghue, in his study of *How the Anglo-Saxons Read Their Poems*, calls the 'dark-matter energy of oral poetry', those sets of conventions and expectations that the pre-Conquest audience would have internalized from their ongoing experiences with poetry.[14] Analogous to the dark matter that makes up about 95 per cent of the universe but cannot be measured or accounted for, this type of conditioning occurs in the interaction between the work itself, its oral performance, and the neurological processes of its audiences; it can only be imperfectly glimpsed by scholars who now have access only to the written work.

## Hanging Grendel's arm

On the morning after his defeat by Beowulf, Grendel's severed arm is hung in Heorot and the narrator observes,

> Þæt wæs tācen sweotol,
> syþðan hildedēor hond ālegde,
> earm ond eaxle—þǣr wæs eal geador
> Grendles grāpe—under gēapne hr(ōf).[15]

(That was a clear token, when the one brave in battle laid the hand, the arm and the shoulder—there was all together Grendel's grip— under the vaulted roof.)

---

[13] *Ruling Women*, p. 123.

[14] Daniel Donoghue, *How the Anglo-Saxons Read Their Poems* (Philadelphia: University of Pennsylvania Press, 2018), p. 12.

[15] Lines 833–6. All quotations from *Beowulf* in the original Old English are taken from *Beowulf and the Fight at Finnsburg*, edited Fr. Klaeber (Boston, MA: D.C. Heath, 1950), and are cited by line number. All translations are my own.

Although this description begins with an assertion that the meaning of the displayed arm is obvious, many scholars have found this statement intriguingly disingenuous: as Leslie Lockett points out, '[u]nlike other signs in *Beowulf*, this *tacen* has no stated referent, leaving the audience to ask, 'A clear sign *of what?*'[16] Much work has been dedicated to providing answers for this question, with the hanging of the arm variously interpreted as 'a symbolic element in inter-cultural warfare'; an initiator of suspense about the outcome of feud exchanges; part of a complex of references that, by linking hands and feasts, make 'the commonplace into something uncommonly savage'; the remnant of an Irish folktale tradition; symbolic of 'mund', the legal rights mandating control of territory; or a focus of 'reflections on the poet's craft and on the place of imaginative fiction in society'.[17] The sheer number of responses to the arm scene indicate that it has achieved in scholarly discourse the status of a 'touchstone' event, or an episode that is

---

[16] Leslie Lockett, 'The Role of Grendel's Arm in Feud, Law, and the Narrative Strategy of *Beowulf*', in *Latin Learning and English Lore: Studies in Anglo-Saxon Literature for Michael Lapidge*, edited by Katherine O'Brien O'Keeffe and Andy Orchard (Toronto: University of Toronto Press, 2005), pp. 368–88 at p. 368.

[17] Views espoused by, respectively John Edward Damon, '*De* *secto Capite Perfido*: Bodily Fragmentation and Reciprocal Violence in Anglo-Saxon England', *Exemplaria* 13 (2001): pp. 399–432, at p. 432; Lockett, 'Role of Grendel's Arm'; James L. Rosier, 'The Uses of Association: Hands and Feasts in *Beowulf*', *Publications of the Modern Language Association* 78 (1963): pp. 8–14, at p. 9; R. Mark Scowcroft, 'The Irish Analogues to *Beowulf*', *Speculum* 74 (1999): pp. 22–64; David Day, 'Hands Across the Hall: The Legalities of Beowulf's Fight with Grendel', *Journal of English and Germanic Philology* 98 (1999): pp. 1–24; Seth Lerer, 'Grendel's Glove', *English Literary History* 61 (1994): pp. 721–51, at p. 722. Other engagements with the hand in particular include J. J. Anderson, 'The "Cuþe Folme" in *Beowulf*', *Neophilologus* 67 (1983): pp. 126–30; Rolf H. Bremmer Jr, 'Grendel's Arm and the Law', in *Studies in English Language and Literature: 'Doubt Wisely'*, *Papers in Honor of E. G. Stanley*, edited by M. J. Toswell and E. M. Tyler (London: Routledge, 1996), pp. 121–32; Marilyn M. Carens, 'Handscoh and Grendel: The Motif of the Hand in *Beowulf*', in *Aeolian Harps: Essays in Literature in Honor of Maurice Browning Cramer*, edited by Donna G. Fricke and Douglas C. Fricke (Bowling Green: Bowling Green University Press, 1976), pp. 39–55; Stanley B. Greenfield, 'The Extremities of the Beowulfian Body Politic', in *Saints, Scholars and Heroes: Studies in Medieval Culture in Honour of Charles W. Jones*, edited by Margot H. King and Wesley M. Stevens (Collegeville: Hill Monastic Manuscript Library, 1979), pp. 1–14; Gale R. Owen-Crocker, 'Horror in *Beowulf*: Mutilation, Decapitation, and Unburied Dead', in *Early Medieval English Texts and Interpretations: Studies Presented to Donald G. Scragg*, edited by Susan Treharne and Elaine Rosser, vol. 252 (Tempe: Arizona Center for Medieval and Renaissance Studies, 2003), pp. 81–100, esp. p. 94, n. 23; L. Whitbread, 'The Hand of Æschere: A Note on Beowulf 1343', *Review of English Studies* 25 (1949): pp. 339–42.

interpreted as unlocking a meaning general to the narrative as a whole. In contrast to earlier more holistic readings of the poem, recent commentators make sense of *Beowulf*'s recursive, digressive and elliptical structure by concentrating on scenes overdetermined with interpretative signals. Thus it is that, by this more analogical approach, scholars have used the arm-hanging scene precisely to unite the fragmented corpus of the poem itself.[18] Of particular importance to these readings of the arm-hanging and sword-hilt scenes, as Seth Lerer notes, is that the external audience, modern and medieval, occupies the same interpretative space as the poem's characters.[19]

Although much scholarship has focused on determining the referent of the arm as *tacen*, it is important to note that the hand is not invested with any inherent meaning. Rather, the act of display itself opens a site of connection between the poem's internal and external audiences, and makes the hand into a token: 'þæt wæs tacen sweotol, *syþðan* hildedeor hond alegde, earm ond eaxle...under geapne hrof' (that was a clear token, after the one brave in battle laid the hand, arm and shoulder, under the steep roof).[20] By being placed, the matter of the arm is actually displaced, coming to stand in for, or token, something else. The poem suggests that the relation between the arm as sign and this something else it represents is metonymic by nature, by noting of the arm that 'þær wæs eal geador Grendles grape' (there was all together Grendel's grip).[21] If the arm represents Grendel's power in battle (a power based, like Beowulf's, largely on his strength of hand), then the severed hand stands for the annihilation of this power. As Mark Scowcroft notes, 'Grendel's "separation from life" must be "by arm"...because the arm in *Beowulf* also represents power and action, especially violent deeds...Disarming Grendel means quite explicitly to separate him from his deeds (*dæda getwæfan*, line 479b).'[22] In this way

---

[18] For methodologically similar readings of the sword hilt scene, see Allen Frantzen, *Desire for Origins: New Language, Old English, and Teaching the Tradition* (New Brunswick: Rutgers University Press, 1990), pp. 168–200; and Seth Lerer, *Literacy and Power in Anglo-Saxon Literature* (Lincoln: University of Nebraska Press, 1991), pp. 158–94.

[19] Lerer, *Literacy and Power*, p. 165.

[20] Lines 833–6, emphasis added.    [21] Lines 835–6.

[22] Scowcroft, 'Irish Analogues', p. 63.

the arm is metonymic of an event, Beowulf's victory over Grendel, and its display is intended to embody and authenticate this past action in the form of a present and visible sign. Thus the display is motivated and governed by a 'structure of desire' similar to that described by Susan Stewart in her study of collected objects, *On Longing: Narratives of the Miniature, the Gigantic, the Souvenir, the Collection*.[23] Within this structure objects function as supplements offering to bridge the gap between language and the experience it describes. Social, historical or intersubjective environments that elude representation are thus metonymically promised by collected objects that are, as James Clifford puts it, cut out of specific contexts and made to stand in for abstract wholes by their display.[24]

Although both Stewart and Clifford are writing about objects held in contemporary museum or souvenir collections, their work is helpful in considering *Beowulf* precisely because it accounts for the transformative effects of display on both the object and the viewer. Early medieval practices of display do need to be carefully differentiated from those available in the industrialized and capitalist societies in which museums flourish. However, the depiction, frequent within museum studies, of medieval culture as a time when relations to objects were more 'authentic' and 'simple' is also not adequate to describe the complexities of the period either. Within museum theory, mention of the pre-Conquest period is constrained to the generalized historical narrative of the development of museums, within which it is primarily distinguished for its collections of saints' relics and *Ubi sunt* passages, both of which are read as evidence of the proto-collecting impulse and a pervasive belief in the magical dimension of objects.[25] The origins of collecting proper are generally assigned to the sixteenth century with the development of the cabinet of curiosities which, as Tony Bennett among others has argued, functioned as part of the performance of royal power

---

[23] (Baltimore: Johns Hopkins Press, 1984).

[24] See especially, *The Predicament of Culture: Twentieth-Century Ethnography, Literature, and Art* (Cambridge, MA: Harvard University Press, 1988), pp. 189–251.

[25] See, for example, Susan Pearce, *Museums, Objects and Collections: A Cultural Study* (Washington, DC: Smithsonian Institution Press, 1992), pp. 43–6; Werner Muensterberger, *Collecting: An Unruly Passion* (Princeton: Princeton University Press, 1994), pp. 29–31.

before courtly society.[26] It was not until the eighteenth and nineteenth centuries that these collecting practices are seen to be co-opted and transformed in the service of the state, as part, in Bennett's argument, of a range of 'cultural technologies' designed to govern, as in shape and control, the populace's mandated free time. Thus, the role of the medieval within museum studies is similar to that it plays in nation or postcolonial theory—that is, an unproblematic, coterminous, and homogeneous origin, the distinctiveness of which serves to identify and characterize emergent modern practices. This methodological commonality is in fact unsurprising, given the influence of Foucault's epistemic theory, which has had the result of reinforcing period boundaries, on all three fields.[27] However, whereas this 'othering' of the medieval within national and postcolonial discourse has been noted and critiqued, that within museum studies has received little to no attention.

That the display of the arm in Heorot resembles, as Lockett puts it, 'a specimen in a museum' suggests that this act of display might serve similar functions in respect to its contemporary audience as exhibits in museums serve for their viewers.[28] Particularly important is what such 'morbid curiosity' reveals about the disposition of knowledge by and about groups, and the ways in which such knowledge serves to characterize those viewing as separate from those being viewed. This political function of display, which is widely recognized as a component of contemporary museums, is largely understood to be absent from medieval contexts, in which priority is given to the notion of an authentic encounter with objects rather than their role in constituting social relations. In contrast, modern museums are understood to carry, as Mark O'Neill puts it in his study of art museums, 'an ideological function' by 'reinforcing the power structures of society' and 'transforming visitors into willing acceptors of the status quo'.[29] O'Neill's

---

[26] Tony Bennett, *The Birth of the Museum: History, Theory, Politics* (New York: Routledge, 1995).

[27] For discussion of how Foucault's theory has reified traditional temporal divisions, see Kathleen Biddick, 'The Cut of Genealogy: Pedagogy in the Blood', *Journal of Medieval and Early Modern Studies* 30.3 (2000): pp. 449–62, at pp. 450–2.

[28] 'Role of Grendel's Arm', p. 371.

[29] Mark O'Neill, 'The Good Enough Visitor', in *Museums, Society, Inequality (Museum Meanings)*, edited by R. Sandell (New York: Routledge, 2002), pp. 24–40, at p. 25.

work is representative of a general trend within the field to characterize museums as coercive structures that replicate class divisions, in the ways in which exhibits are staged and rendered accessible or inaccessible to certain populations. Without assuming that the display of the arm is directly equivalent to that of museum objects, the distribution of the same elements within each field (strategic display, group viewing, interpretation) suggests that each serves a similar purpose of socialization within their various contexts.

As Stewart intimates, the force driving the display of significant objects, whether in a museum or a souvenir collection, is the perceived inadequacy of language to call up the diversity and multiplicity of experience itself, a conduit to which is promised by the tangible materiality of the object. Typically, however, the displayed object is made to 'speak' its meaning in conjunction with words, in the form of personal stories, in the case of souvenirs, or explanatory textual labels for museum objects. This kind of linguistic supplement to the arm is provided in *Beowulf* in the form of speeches given by Hrothgar and Beowulf, and bracketed by references to looking at the arm:

> Hrōðgār maþelode—hē tō healle gēong,
> stōd on stapole, geseah stēapne hrōf
> golde fāhne ond Grendles hond—:...
> Beowulf maþelode,...
> Ðā wæs swīgra secg, sunu Ec[g]lāfes,
> on gylpspræce gūðgeweorca,
> siþðan æþelingas eorles cræfte
> ofer hēanne hrōf hand scēawedon.[30]

(Hrothgar made a speech—he went to the hall, stood on the steps, saw the high roof decorated with gold and Grendel's hand... Beowulf made a speech... Then was the man more silent, Ecglaf's son, in boasting speech of battle-works, after the nobles had examined the hand above the vaulted roof, by the skill of the warrior.)

That the verbal responses to the hanging of the arm should so obviously accompany the visual act of looking at it indicates that the

---

[30] Lines 925–7, line 957, lines 980–3.

speeches are intended to supplement a point already made by the arm itself. Hrothgar's speech even begins with a reference to sight: 'Ðisse ansȳne Alwealdan þanc lungre gelimpe!' (For this sight may thanks to the Almighty be quickly forthcoming!)[31] Beowulf's speech, which describes the fight with Grendel and the rending of the arm, terminates quite literally with the silencing of language by visual spectacle, forcefully indicating that the arm is offered as a bridge between the narrative of the fight and the experience of it: 'Ða wæs swigra secg...' (then was the man more silent).[32] Whereas Lerer has argued that the severed body parts in the poem function as the cause and origin of public discourse, the arm here seems to work in the opposite fashion by silencing discussion in favour of spectacle.[33] The importance of the visual dimension is made more obvious by the unusually detailed description of the arm that immediately follows Beowulf's silence:

> foran ǣghwylc wæs,
> stīð[r]a nægla gehwylc stȳle gelīcost,
> hǣþenes handsporu hilderinces
> egl[u] unhēoru.[34]

(At each end was one hard nail most like steel, the terrible monstrous hand-spur of the heathen warrior.)

As both the warriors and the poem's external audience linger over the appearance of the arm, this scene suggests that looking is more eloquent than talking when it comes to accessing the event of Grendel's death: seeing is believing.

Although the eloquence of the arm as object is not unique within *Beowulf*, the particular vocabulary used to designate the act of looking at the hand, along with aspects of its display, do make the scene distinctive. That certain objects are invested with intense meaning, in particular as a result of their past use, is a well-recognized and well-studied aspect of heroic culture. In *Beowulf*, the role of the sword placed upon Hengest's lap in the Finnsburg digression epitomizes the fact that heroic weaponry brings its past with it, a past that impinges on and

---

[31] Lines 928-9.    [32] Line 980.
[33] 'Grendel's Glove', p. 742.    [34] Lines 984-90.

determines the present. Hengest—having agreed to live amicably at
Finn's court without avenging the death of his lord, Hnæf, at the hands
of the Frisians—is reminded of his thegnly duty to take vengeance by a
sword:

> Swā hē ne forwyrnde w[e]orodrǣden*de*,
> Þonne him Hūnlāfing hildelēoman,
> Billa sēlest on bearm dyde;
> Þæs wǣron mid Ēotenum ecge cūðe.[35]

(Thus he did not refuse the ruler of the host, when Hunlaf's son laid
the battle-light Hunlafing, the best of swords, in his lap; the edges of
which were known among the Jutes.)

The sword worn by the Danish warrior in Freawaru's retinue is made
to speak a similarly eloquent message about the necessity to avenge
old wrongs by the ancient Heathobard warrior (2041–61). The use of,
as Elisabeth Van Houts puts it, 'objects as pegs for memory' in this
way was customary in early medieval English culture, in which tap-
estries, clothing, or jewellery accumulated historical resonance as they
were willed from one generation to the next.[36] In contrast to these
objects, however, the hoisting of the severed arm in *Beowulf* involves
the self-conscious display of an otherwise useless artefact not crafted
from metal but ripped from the body of an opponent. The arm,
devoid of the use and aesthetic value that generally characterizes a
worthy object in heroic culture, is converted entirely into display
value, and thus may serve as a reflective focus for the shared identity
of those viewing it. Like the museum object, the transformation of the

---

[35] Lines 1142–5. This passage contains two words difficult of interpretation: 'Hūnlāf-
ing' and 'w[e]orodrǣden*de*'. The former could be a patronymic meaning 'son of Hunlaf'
or could be the name of the sword, as it is with Nægling and Hrunting, although most
scholars assume the former. 'W[e]orodrǣden*de*', with the translation 'ruler of the host'
referring to Finn, is an emendation from the manuscript's 'woroldrǣdenne', which is
often retained and translated as 'worldly custom'. For a summary of the issues, see
Klaeber, *Beowulf*, pp. 175–6.

[36] Elisabeth Van Houts, *Memory and Gender in Medieval Europe 900–1200* (Toronto:
University of Toronto Press, 1999), pp. 93–120. Objects could also be commissioned to
commemorate an event, such as the tapestry given by ealdorman Byrhtnoth's widow
Ælfflæd to the monastery at Ely (Van Houts, *Memory,* pp. 102–3; Mildred Budny, 'The
Byrhtnoth Tapestry or Embroidery', in *The Battle of Maldon AD 991*, edited by Donald
Scragg [Oxford: Basil Blackwell, 1991], pp. 263–78). This tapestry, which no longer
survives, apparently depicted Byrhtnoth's martial achievements.

arm into an object of knowledge (in this case about the outcome of the fight) also functions to identify and unify the viewing group, both as viewers and as different from the viewed. The somatic configuration of this boundary between the known and the knowing in fact gives the display of the arm much in common with the dynamics of the freak show, in which the spectacle of unusual bodies actually strengthens the viewers' sense of themselves as civilized, human, gendered subjects.[37]

## *Sceawian*: seeing and showing

That the arm hanging is a type of freak show—an observation that opens up possibilities for thinking about it as a venue for socialization—is signalled by the particular use of the verb *sceawian* for *to look*, which signals the nature of sight in this episode. Even though, as Lerer notes, it appears in both the arm and sword hilt scenes, and would thus seem to be a verb of quite particular significance, few attempts have been made to distinguish the meaning and range of use for *sceawian* from that of other verbs for looking, such as *locian* or *starian*. Customarily translated as *look at, examine, inspect, gaze*, or *behold, sceawian* is used in Old English translations to render a range of Latin verbs including *considerere, intendere, conspicere, contemplari, videre, intueor*, and *scrutari*.[38] As Andy Orchard has noticed, it frequently appears in *Beowulf* in proximity to the element *wundor-*, as it does also in the *Letter of Alexander to Aristotle*, but in no other texts of

---

[37] See, for example, Rosemary Garland-Thomas's study of the display of the Mexican Indian woman Julia Pastrana in nineteenth- and twentieth-century America, an exhibition that 'was less about her, and more about who her spectators imagined themselves to be' ('Making Freaks: Visual Rhetorics and the Spectacle of Julia Pastrana', in *Thinking the Limits of the Body*, edited by Jeffrey Jerome Cohen and Gail Weiss [Albany: State University of New York Press, 2002], pp. 129–43 at p. 142).

[38] See the entry for *sceawian* in *An Anglo-Saxon Dictionary*, edited by Joseph Bosworth and T. Northcote Toller (Oxford: Clarendon, 1898), pp. 827–8, for Latin equivalents. Bosworth-Toller offers the following translations: to look; to look at, observe, behold, see; to look at, look on with favour, to regard, have respect to, to look at with care, consider, inspect, examine, scrutinize, reconnoitre; to look out, seek for, select, choose, provide; to show (favour, respect, etc.), to grant.

the *Beowulf*-manuscript, and infrequently in the corpus in general, indicating that these two works likely have some previous scribal or manuscript association.[39] Even though Orchard's interest here is predominantly in vocabulary use as an indicator of textual association and not in the meaning of *sceawian*, which he translates as 'gazed upon' or 'examined', the link he observes between *sceawian* and *wundor* is suggestive of semantic range. He observes, in addition, that *sceawian* designates 'a strikingly limited set of objects' within *Beowulf*, all with 'monstrous, uncanny, or otherworldly associations'.[40] In particular, it is used to designate looking at tracks or omens; at bodies or at body parts; and at treasure.

Six instances of the word refer either to tracks or to omens: it is used for the examination of Grendel's footprints after his first attack on Heorot (line 132); when the Geats consider omens before Beowulf's departure for Denmark (line 204); twice in the description of how the Danes gather to look at Grendel's tracks away from Heorot after his fateful battle with Beowulf (lines 840 and 843); once as Beowulf urges Hrothgar out of his misery by encouraging him to look at the tracks of Grendel's Mother (line 1391); and finally of the scout's action in seeking out the path to the mere (line 1413).[41]

---

[39] Andy Orchard, *A Critical Companion to Beowulf* (Cambridge: D.S. Brewer, 2003), pp. 27–9.

[40] Ibid., p. 27.

[41] The relevant full quotations follow: 'Mǣre þēoden, æþeling ǣrgōd, unblīðe sæt, þolode ðrȳðswȳð, þegnsorge drēah, syðþan hīe þæs lāðan lāst scēawedon' (The glorious prince, the peerless noble, sat joyless, the mighty one suffered after they *scēawedon* the track of the hateful one); 'hwetton hige(r)ōfne, hǣl scēawedon' (They encouraged the brave one, *scēawedon* omens); 'fērdon folctogan feorran ond nean geond wīdwegas wundor scēawian, lāþes lāstas' (People-leaders came from far and near throughout the wide-ways to *scēawian* the wonder, the tracks of the hateful one); 'Nō his līfgedāl sārlīc þūhte secga ǣnegum þāra þe tīrlēases trode scēawode' (Not at all his death seemed sorrowful to any of the men who *scēawode* the tracks of the vanquished one); 'Ārīs, rīces weard, uton hraþe fēran, Grendles māgan gang scēawigan' (Arise, guardian of the kingdom, let us quickly go to *scēawigan* the track of Grendel's kin); 'hē fēara sum beforan gengde wīsra monna wong scēawian oþ þæt hē fǣringa fyrgenbēamas ofer hārne stān hleonian funde' (He went before with a few wise men to *scēawian* the place until he suddenly found mountain-trees leaning over the grey stone). Although 'wong' in this last example might more conventionally be translated as 'place', the connotation of the word here seems to be 'way', 'track', and thus *sceawian* designates the same process of following a track as in other examples within this category.

The word is used five times to describe looking at bodies or body parts: in reference to Grendel's hand (line 983); to the *nicor* killed by the Geats at the mere (line 1440); to the dragon, as the Geats set out to battle him (line 2402); to the corpse of Beowulf (line 3008); and to the *wundur* that is the bodies of Beowulf and the dragon lying together on the headland (line 3032).[42] Interestingly, all the uses of *sceawian* within this category refer to dead bodies or body parts, apart from the use of it to designate Beowulf's 'seeking' of the dragon following news of its ravages (the third listed above). This example might fit more comfortably within the use of the verb for tracking, which is the sense that Roy Liuzza implies in his translation, 'Grim and enraged, the lord of the Geats/ took a dozen men to seek out the dragon.'[43] The sense of movement implied by this particular use of the verb is supported by the translation of Latin 'perambulare' by 'sceawigan' in section 36 of *The Letter of Alexander to Aristotle*.[44]

Finally, *sceawian* is used a further six times to denote the action of viewing treasure: when Hrothgar looks at the ancient sword hilt that Beowulf has brought back from Grendel's mere (1687); for the lord's glance at the cup that his wretched servant rifled from the dragon's hoard (2285); twice in Beowulf's instructions to Wiglaf, after the fight with the dragon, that he go and look at the dragon's hoard (2744, 2748), and once when he looks at the gold that Wiglaf brings back to him (2793); once in a narrative reference to the hoard (3075); and finally, twice in Wiglaf's speech to the Geatish retainers (3084, 3104).[45] The

---

[42] The full quotations are as follows: 'Đā wæs swīgra secg, sunu Ec[g]lāfes, on gylpspræce gūðgeweorca, siþðan æþelingas eorles cræfte ofer hēanne hrōf scēawedon' (Then was the man more silent, the son of Ecglaf, in boasting speech of battle works, after the nobles, by the skill of the warrior, over the high roof *scēawedon* the hand); 'weras scēawedon gryrelīcne gist' (The men *scēawedon* the terrible stranger); 'Gewāt þā twelfa sum torne gebolgen dryhten Gēata dracan scēawian' (One of twelve, the lord of the Geats departed then, enraged with anger, to *scēawian* the dragon); 'Nū is ofost betost, þæt wē þēodcyning þǣr scēawian' (Now is haste best, that we *scēawian* the people-king there); 'Weorod eall ārās; ēodon unblīðe under Earnanæs wollentēare wundur scēawian' (The troop all arose; went unhappily under the eagles' headland with gushing tears to *scēawian* the wonder).

[43] *Beowulf: A New Verse Translation* (Peterborough, Ontario: Broadview Press, 2000).

[44] Noted by Orchard, *Critical Companion*, p. 29.

[45] The meaning of line 3075 is obscure; Klaeber echoed previous editors in calling it a 'locus desperatus' (*Beowulf*, line 227); it is clear, however, that 'gescēawod' in this line means to look (with the implication either favourably or accurately). Full quotations for *gescēawian*

frequent collocation of *wundur* and *sceawian* in application to these objects, as well as its appearance in the description of the monstrous encounters of Alexander's troops in *The Letter of Alexander to Aristotle*, indicates that tracks, omens, bodies (including those of exotic peoples and animals), and treasures are all understood to have something in common; each is viewed as having a heightened significance, the encounter with which takes a specifically visual form.[46] That this visual element is a conceptual detail particular to the Old English context is suggested by Orchard's comparison of the vernacular version of the *Letter* to the Latin, where he finds that 'of its ten occurrences in the text, the Old English *Letter* exhibits some form of the verb *sceawian* some six times where either the word translated has no visual connotations or there is no equivalent term in the Latin at all'.[47]

Although the frequent collocation with *wundur* is not paralleled in the corpus more generally, the limited range of usage for *sceawian* within *Beowulf* does seem to be characteristic of other texts, where the word is most frequently used to denote an examination of treasure, place, work, or the body.[48] For instance, the use of *sceawian* in reference to tracks in *Beowulf* is also attested in *The Old English Martyrology* for the act of looking at Christ's footprints left at the Church of the

---

used in reference to treasure are as follows: 'Hrōðgār maðelode—hylt scēawode, ealde lāfe, on ðǣm wæs ōr writen fyrngewinnes' (Hrothgar spoke, *scēawode* the hilt, the old remnant, on which was written the origin of ancient strife); 'Frēa scēawode fira fyrngeweorc forman sīðe' (The lord *scēawode* the ancient work of men for the first time); 'Nū ðū lungre geong hord scēawian under hārne stān, Wīglāf lēofa' (Now you quickly go to *scēawian* the hoard under the grey stone, dear Wiglaf); 'Bīo nū on ofoste, þæt ic ǣrwelan, goldǣht ongite, gearo scēawige swegle searogimmas' (Be now in haste that I might perceive the ancient wealth, the gold-treasure, may *scēawige* well the precious jewels); 'gomel on giohðe—gold scēawode' (The old man in sorrow *scēawode* the gold); 'næfne goldhwǣte gearwor hæfde Āgendes ēst ǣr gescēawod' (unless the one greedy for gold had better gescēawod the gift of the owner); 'hord ys gescēawod, grimme gegongen', (the hoard is gescēawod, grimly got); 'ic ēow wīsige, þæt gē genōge nēon scēawiað bēagas ond brād gold' (I will guide you so that nearby you may *scēawiað* many rings and broad gold).

[46] Orchard, *Critical Companion*, p. 28; for table of forms, see p. 29.
[47] Ibid., p. 28.
[48] *Dictionary of Old English Corpus.*

Ascension on the Mount of Olives.[49] Elsewhere the verb is frequently used to designate literal or metaphorical examinations of the body or soul in order to ascertain their physical or spiritual condition. Bald's *Leechbook* furnishes a number of examples of the former, such as this description of how to examine a person with 'healf deadan adle', or hemiplegia, a condition in which one half of the body is paralyzed: 'þonne seo adl cume ærest on ðone mannan þonne ontyne þu his muð sceawa his tungan þonne bið heo on þa healfe hwittre þe seo adl on beon wile' (when the sickness first comes on the man, then open his mouth, examine his tongue, then it is whiter on the half which the disease will be on).[50] Whereas, in this instance, *sceawian* refers to a close inspection of the body in order to read the future course of illness, homiletic texts provide a surfeit of instances where the verb is used for meditative examinations of the heart, mind, or soul as part of a process of self-knowledge or judgement. *Sceawian* is also used for the process of scrutinizing the wounds of Christ in order to verify the miracle of his resurrection, and it frequently occurs in translation narratives for the witnessing of a saint's incorrupt body. For instance, Ælfric, in his life of St Æthelthryth, describes how the doctor who lanced the saint's neck tumour before her death eagerly 'sceawode' the site of the wound when she is disinterred years later. In a related life, that for St Edmund, Ælfric again uses *sceawian* in the context of a complex set of issues, and narratives, concerned with verification. Like Æthelthryth, Edmund also suffered a neck wound (although his resulted from the severing of his head by the Vikings) that miraculously healed after his death to leave only a thin red scar. In the course of relating the grisly ends that thieves and doubters met when they attempted to penetrate Edmund's tomb, Ælfric is reminded of what Gregory the Great wrote about St Lawrence:

> þæt menn woldon sceawian symle hu he lage .
> ge gode ge yfele . ac god hi gestilde .
> swa þæt þær swulton on þære sceawunge ane

[49] 'mihton men ufan beorhtlice sceawian Drihtnes fota swaðe' ('the people from above could clearly see the Lord's footprints'). See Günter Kotzor, ed., *Das altenglische martyrologium* (Munich: Bayerische Akademie der Wissenschafter, 1981), ii.86.15–16.

[50] Thomas Oswald Cockayne, ed., *Leechdoms, Wortcunning and Starcraft of Early England*, rev. ed. (1864–6; repr. London: Holland Press, 1961), 2: 281.

seofon menn ætgædere . þa geswicon þa oþre
to sceawigenne þone martyr mid menniscum gedwylde.[51]

(That men, both good and evil, always wanted to examine how he lay,
but God stopped them so that there died in the looking once seven
men together; then the others ceased examining the martyr with
human error.)

The use of *sceawian* for looking both at the body and at tracks left by
the body suggests that the verb designates a specific type of visual
encounter with matter: a variety of looking motivated by inquiry and
directed toward understanding, whether that be the confirmation of a
past action such as the resurrection, a physical ailment, or an altered
spiritual condition such as sanctity. As the unfortunate fate of those
who wish to scrutinize Lawrence's body indicates, *sceawian* involves a
type of looking undertaken for specific reasons. Performing this type of
scrutiny with improper motivation yields deadly results, since it can
serve to identify the observers as members of the 'wrong' group, the
group of unbelievers or heretics who are cast out from knowledge of the
saint's perfection. In contrast, the doctor's glance at Æthelthryth's neck
serves to authenticate her sanctity and to indicate his membership
within an authorized group of observers, including the clerical guard-
ians of Æthelthryth's body. The fact that *sceawian* often serves to
designate interpretive communities in this way suggests that its meaning is close to that of *rædan*, or to read.[52] Indeed, the verb is used
several times unambiguously to indicate the interpretation of written
text in particular. In the same life of St Edmund, for example, Ælfric
describes how Bishop Theodred comes to regret so brusquely con-
demning to death a group of thieves who had threatened Edmund's
church: 'Eft þa ðeodred bisceop sceawode his bec syððan behreowsode
mid geomerunge . þæt he swa reðne dóm sette' (Since Bishop Theodred
examined his books, he afterwards regretted with melancholy that he
had set such a harsh judgement). The combination of *sceawian* and *boc*

---

[51] Original quoted from Walter W. Skeat, ed., *Ælfric's Lives of Saints*, Early English
Text Society o.s., 82 (London: Oxford University Press, 1881–5), p. 332. Translation is my
own.
[52] While Bosworth-Toller does not list this as a potential meaning, the *OED* entry
(clearly substantially based on Bosworth-Toller) does include 'to "see", read, find (in a
book)' (*Oxford English Dictionary*, 2nd ed., s.v. 'show').

occurs elsewhere in Ælfric's homiletic prose writing, in the metrical preface to Wærferth's translation of Gregory's *Dialogues*, and in the Old English Orosius. However, if *sceawian* denotes something close to *rædan*, then it is a type of reading that involves an extraordinary level of material engagement and risk on the part of the reader.

If *sceawian* designates such an act of reading, then the significance of its use for the act of looking at the arm has been underestimated by scholars. The description of how the nobles 'sceawedon' the arm following Beowulf's speech would suggest that their gaze both entangles them with the arm-object and functions to unite them as a viewing and knowing group: as a reading community of a kind. The bodily ravages that Grendel has performed in the hall for twelve years are here matched by the Danes' architectural incorporation of his arm: where he ate a thane 'feet and hands', the collected Danes and Geats visually consume Grendel's arm.[53] The arm is rendered part of the hall's structure—that is, it is consumed by the hall—as suggested by the comment that Hrothgar 'geseah steapne hrof/ golde fahne ond Grendles hond' (saw the high roof, decorated with gold, and Grendel's hand), lines 926-7. Although 'hond' is not dependent on 'fahne' here, so it is not 'decorated with Grendel's hand', the sentence as a whole suggests a certain equivalence between the adornment of the hall and the hand, signalling the distance of the hand from its original context as part of Grendel's body and its reincorporation as part of the visual structure of the hall itself.

The reflexive nature of this act—the fact that looking at the arm has an effect on the group looking—is also contained in the use of *sceawian*. The *OED* indicates that the verb was not used with a causative sense until around the year 1200, when a 'sudden' and 'hard to account for' change in usage and meaning occurred that pushed the word toward the connotation of Modern English *to show*. Although preserved in relatively late examples, the verb *sceawian* is used several times already

---

[53] The episode of Grendel consuming the sleeping thane had occurred at the beginning of the fight with Beowulf: 'ac he gefeng hraðe forman siðe/ slæpendne rinc, slat unwearnum,/ bat banlocan, blod edrum dranc,/ synsnædum swealh; sona hæfde/ unlyfigendes eal gefeormod,/ fet ond folma' (but he quickly seized at the first time a sleeping warrior, slit eagerly, bit the bonelocks, drank the blood from the veins, swallowed in huge morsels; immediately he had completely consumed the unloving one, feet and hands), lines 740-5.

in Old English with this meaning of *show* or *display*, which suggests that it may have been subject to transition earlier than the *OED* claims. For example, *sceawian* is used with the sense of *show* in the anonymous Old English homilies contained in MS. Bodley 343, all of which were composed in the early eleventh century, although they are preserved only in a later manuscript.[54] For example, from the homily on the transfiguration of Christ: 'Ðe godspellere cwæð þæt Crist wolde her on worlde sceawen his agene ansyne his leorningcnihtæs swa beorhtlice and swa þrymlice swa hine alle halige on heofenæ rice iseon sceolden' (the gospeller said that Christ here in the world wanted to show his own countenance to his disciples [?] as brightly and as gloriously as all the holy in the kingdom of heaven should see him). The *OED* discounts the use of the verb in the E-text of the *Anglo-Saxon Chronicle* because it can equally well indicate 'provided' as 'showed': '1048 . . . Þa wyrnde him mann ðera gisla, 7 sceawede him mann .v. nihta grið ut of lande to farenne' (then he was denied the hostages, and was offered five nights' truce to go out of the land).[55] Although these are isolated and ambiguous examples of the verb form being used with the meaning *show*, the related nouns *sceawung* and *sceawere* are already in Old English seeding the movement towards the later meaning. *Sceawung* is defined by Bosworth-Toller as both 'looking at, contemplation' and 'spectacle, show . . . appearance, pretence'. *Sceawere* is used to gloss Latin *speculea* (variant *speculia*), with the meaning either 'watchtower' or 'mirror'. Both definitions suggest that the *sceaw-* stem describes a relationship between the observer and the observed that is not entirely one-sided, but that what is seen also serves to show; that what is looked at in some way looks back, in the form of a reflection from a mirror or the surveillance from the watchtower.

As the assembled Danes and Geats *sceawedon* the displayed arm, therefore, it produces their coherence and identity as a group of interpreters: it shows them something about themselves. The fact that

---

[54] Susan Irvine, ed., *Old English Homilies from MS. Bodley 343*, Early English Text Society, o.s., 302 (Oxford: Oxford University Press, 1993).

[55] Susan Irvine, ed., *MS E*, vol. 7, *The Anglo-Saxon Chronicle: A Collaborative Edition* (Cambridge: D.S. Brewer, 2004), p. 82.

the arm happens to be a grisly remnant of an alien being suggests that the persistent linking of Old English *sceawian* and *wunder* in both *Beowulf* and *The Letter of Alexander to Aristotle*, observed by Orchard, could be a vernacular exploration of Latin *monstrum*, or *monster*, with its root in *monstrare* (to show, to inform), and *monere* (to teach, to point out, to remind).[56] What the arm shows the Danes and Geats is therefore not only their victory but also their membership in a human group.

# Taking the *tacen*

If the *sceawian–wundor* collocation is conceptually related to *monstrum*, then it likely connotes not only revelation but also admonition, since *monere* also means *to warn*. Certainly the horrible fate of those brazen observers of Edmund's tomb, who desired to examine the saint's body for the wrong reasons, would suggest that the action designated by *sceawian* is one not entirely benign. Their deaths, after all, function as a warning to others of the perils of impertinent looking: 'there died in the looking once seven men together; then the others ceased examining the martyr with human error'.[57] The aim of the watchtower, or *sceawere*, is similarly threatening, serving as much to warn against attack as literally to guard against it, and implicitly relying on an internalized fear on the part of the observer that someone is watching, whether they actually are or not.[58] This notion of potential deception is central to the use of *sceawere*, often in compound forms, for *spy*. For example, when Beowulf and the Geats first arrive at the Danish shore, the coastguard counsels that he will not allow them to proceed further as 'leassceaweras on land Dena' (spies into the land of the Danes).[59] By extension, a *sceawere* can also be a buffoon, glossing Latin *scurra*, or a poet, one

---

[56] The etymology of *monster* is rehearsed in much scholarship; see for instance, Michael Uebel, *Ecstatic Transformation: On the Uses of Alterity in the Middle Ages* (New York: Palgrave Macmillan, 2005), p. 19.

[57] *Lives of Saints*, pp. 332–3.

[58] See Foucault's classic discussion of the panopticon in *Discipline and Punish: The Birth of the Prison*, translated by Alan Sheridan (New York: Pantheon Books, 1977), pp. 195–228.

[59] Line 253.

who can use words both to trick and to mock. Thus the nightingale, or jay, riddle of the Exeter Book collection describes a mimic speaking in 'mongum reordum' (many voices) and singing 'sceawendwisan' (songs of jesters), like an '[e]ald æfensceop' (old poet in the evening).[60] These uses of the *sceaw-* stem suggest a type of looking, or interpretation, which both troubles and menaces its audience.

Beowulf's initial speech after hoisting the arm into the roof of Heorot has something of this anxiety. While the gathered audience of Danes and Geats understand the arm to mark Beowulf's successful completion of his boast to the Danes, Beowulf himself seems to find it insufficient when he tells Hrothgar, 'Uþe ic swiþor,/ Þæt ðu hine selfne geseon moste,/ feond on frætewum fylwerigne!' (I would prefer that you himself might see, the enemy in his adornments, weary in his fall!)[61] Thus Beowulf begins the formal speech following his victory with a wish that things were different. Indulging for a moment in the fantasy of Hrothgar looking at the whole corpse, the fantasy of a perfect correspondence between sign and event, Beowulf's comment raises a spectre of doubt about the stability of the body part as an epistemological site. For him, at least, its signifying function seems far from unambiguous, specifically because the body must stand in partial and metonymic relation to the event of Grendel's death and, thus, the completion of his boast. Passing and ill-founded as his anxiety proves to be, Beowulf's momentary dissatisfaction with the hand here is instructive, it seems, when considering the function of the hanging of the arm within the poem as a whole. As anyone familiar with the plot knows, this act is far from the ending that Hrothgar and the Danes believe it to be—the unequivocal sign that Beowulf has 'ealle gebette, inwidsorge, þe hie ær drugon' (completely remedied their sorrow, which they previously suffered)—but instead begins a second violent episode culminating in the Geats' return to the hall with Grendel's bloodied head.[62] Fuelled not by the 'sweotol' nature of the sign but

[60] Craig Williamson, ed., *The Old English Riddles of the* Exeter Book (Chapel Hill: University of North Carolina Press, 1977), p. 72.

[61] Lines 960–2. Most scholars have assumed that the internal audience's reaction to the arm is entirely positive (for example, Lockett, 'Role of Grendel's Arm', p. 379, but see also p. 368 for a slightly different view); Susan Deskis, Beowulf *and the Medieval Proverb Tradition* (Tempe: Medieval and Renaissance Texts and Studies, 1996), p. 32.

[62] Lines 830–1.

precisely by a sense of its menacing inadequacy, an inadequacy given rhetorical expression in Beowulf's '[u]þe ic swiþor' (I would prefer), the sequence of events following the display of the arm explores this notion of the co-opted body part as instable material marker of the bounds of civilized society.

The intrusion of Grendel's Mother into Heorot marks the potential instability of the arm's meaning, for with her theft of the hand she also takes away the Danes' certainty that their troubles are at an end: 'Hream wearð in Heorote; heo under heolfre genam/ cuþe folme; cearu wæs geniwod,/ geworden in wicun. Ne wæs þæt gewrixle til,/ Þæt hie on ba healfa bicgan scoldon/ freonda feorum!' (An outcry broke out in Heorot; she under [covered in] gore took the [well-] known arm; care was renewed, returned to the dwellings. That was not a good exchange that they on both sides should pay for with the lives of friends!)[63] It is worth stretching beyond the anthropomorphic in analysing why it is that Grendel's Mother takes the hand from Heorot. The text conceptualizes the act in terms of exchange: Æschere's life (the thane taken by Grendel's Mother) in exchange for Grendel's; the arm for renewed strife in the hall. More specifically, it is the 'cuþe', the known or well-known arm that is taken and exchanged. Where before the Danes and Geats were the knowing audience and the hand was known through its display, Grendel's Mother's removal of the arm eradicates its signifying and identificatory function within the hall. Taking the arm is as significant to Grendel's Mother's attack as is taking Æschere.

The reciprocity characteristic of the theft of the arm, the 'gewrixle', is also operative in Grendel's Mother's casual dropping of Æschere's head on the clifftop for the Danes to stumble over: 'Denum eallum wæs,/ Winum Scyldinga weorce on mode/ To geþolianne, ðegne monegum,/ Oncyð eorla gehwæm, syðþan Æscheres/ On þam holmclife hafelan metton' (For all the Danes, the men of the Scyldings, it was work in spirit to suffer, for many a thane, grief to the nobles, after they found Æschere's head on the sea cliff).[64] This act, rather than simply denoting

---

[63] Lines 1302–6. Not all scholars agree that Grendel's Mother actually takes the arm with her: J. J. Anderson, for instance, argues that the 'cuþe folme' is a metonymic reference to Æschere ('Cuþe Folme').

[64] 1417–21.

a horrifying carelessness on the part of Grendel's Mother, can be understood as a key part of the poem's investigation of how displayed bodies can function to outline social and cultural bounds. As many scholars have carefully delineated, the Grendelkin's underground 'nið-sele' shares many of the qualities of Heorot (warmth, firelight, dryness, the presence of treasure) but inverts these positively coded character-istics in the fact that it is underground, inhabited by non-humans, and ruled by a female.[65] Since the top of the sea cliff has the same relation to Grendel's Mother's underwater hall as the external roof of the hall to Heorot, the head on the clifftop operates as a form of counter display doubling and parodying the arm in the hall. As Lockett notes of Grendel's Mother, '[a]lthough the killings committed by her son are without just cause and are therefore kept concealed, her slaying of Æschere is—at least from her perspective—a legitimate requital of her own son's death, for which reason she prominently displays the head at the entrance of her own home, on high ground at the edge of the mere.'[66] Her dropping of Æschere's head on the cliff-top is thus equivalent to the Danes' hanging of the arm, and should be read as a similarly charged display. These unburied body parts and corpses, as Gale R. Owen-Crocker points out, would have been particularly dis-turbing and noteworthy to the original audience, especially in the context of tenth- and eleventh-century prescriptions about the neces-sity for Christian burial.[67]

While reciprocity, or an effect of doubling, is not unique to this episode—in fact, scholars have repeatedly observed its presence within the poem—it does serve a particular purpose here, notably to initiate a critique of appropriative assertions of identity, such as the display of the arm. That Beowulf and Grendel are peculiarly reciprocal characters with many similarities has, in particular, been meticulously noted by

---

[65] Daniel G. Calder, 'Setting and Ethos: The Pattern of Measure and Limit in *Beowulf*', *Studies in Philology* 69 (1972): pp. 21–37, esp. pp. 21–7; Rosier, 'Uses of Association', p. 12; Scowcroft, 'Irish Analogues', pp. 46–7.

[66] Lockett ('Role of Grendel's Arm', p. 372) and Damon ('*Desecto Capite Perfido*', p. 402) are the only other scholars I know of to read this act as a display. Whitbread notes the parallel situation of the arm and Æschere's head, but distinguishes between accident and intent as motivating factors ('The Hand of Æschere', p. 341).

[67] 'Horror in *Beowulf*', pp. 91–3.

scholars, who have read such overlap as integral to the poem's evaluation of heroic ideals and a human society structured on such ideals. Particular attention has been paid to the meaning of terms used to denote Grendel, such as *wiht*, *aglæca*, *wræc*, which are used also of men; physical correspondences between Grendel and Beowulf, such as excessive strength of hand, are also often noted.[68] Stanley Greenfield even links reciprocity at the level of plot and character with the uses the poem makes of the body in order to find a coherent body-politic motif running throughout: as he writes, 'these three struggles—between thane and anti-thane, between avenger and mock avenger, and between king and anti-king—have their bodily objective correlatives: the hand, the head, and the heart respectively'.[69] As Linda Georgianna puts it, 'The brave hero kills the monster, but the monsters keep on coming, and more and more the outsiders come to resemble the kin and folk whom the hero would protect.'[70] While the reciprocal emphasis of the poem is thus generally interpreted as the mark of a social investigation—an analysis of what it means to live in human community—it is less often observed that not until the entry of Grendel's Mother does the situation facing the Danes become something more than a group versus an individual. Although the audience is aware that Grendel, like the Scandinavian warriors who oppose him, has a lineage (albeit monstrous), they do not know that he has living kin until Grendel's Mother appears in the hall. Her arrival makes this a conflict not only between the social and its abjected solitary other but between one community and another.

At the same time, her seizure of Æschere and the arm, followed by her display of the head on the cliff, represents an act of performative reciprocity that differs in kind from the situational or physical similarity observed between Grendel and Beowulf. While their likeness in

---

[68] See, in particular, S. L. Dragland, 'Monster-Man in *Beowulf*', *Neophilologus* 61 (1977): pp. 606–18; and Katherine O'Brien O'Keeffe, '*Beowulf*, Lines 702b–836: Transformations and the Limits of the Human', *Texas Studies in Literature and Language* 23 (1981): pp. 484–94. As Klein notes, the 'very thin line demarcating the boundary between militancy and monstrosity' is encapsulated in the poem's use of the term *eotena* for the Jutes in the Finnsburg episode, since this term can mean both 'Jutes' and 'giants' (for bibliography see *Ruling Women*, p. 97).

[69] 'Body Politic', p. 11. See also Whitbread, 'Hand of Æschere', p. 340.

[70] Linda Georgianna, 'King Hrethel's Sorrow and the Limits of Heroic Action in *Beowulf*', *Speculum* 62 (1987): pp. 829–50, at pp. 847–8, and see also n. 61.

strength of hand and prodigious achievement served to undercut any fast distinction between hero and otherworldly opponent, it is predominantly Grendel's Mother's actions, rather than her appearance or attributes, that uncannily double those of human society. Indeed she forces an awareness, as Homi Bhabha puts it, that '[t]erms of cultural engagement, whether antagonistic or affiliative, are produced performatively' and that the 'representation of difference must not be hastily read as the reflection of pre-given ethnic or cultural traits'.[71] If she is ultimately more troubling to Beowulf, as his difficult fight against her seems to suggest, it is because she is precisely, as Greenfield styled it, a 'mock-avenger', one whose actions undermine the norms of heroic culture specifically by mocking or replicating them. Taking the token of cultural identity, the arm, from the hall and leaving in its stead Æschere's head on the sea cliff represents, in this respect, a hybrid act, or one that subversively 'turns the discursive conditions of dominance into the grounds of intervention'.[72] Grendel's Mother's actions thus reveal her as a type of colonized subject who, in duplicating the act authenticating culture, radically destabilizes the valence or internal coherence of the entire system of identification.[73] As Bhabha describes them, such acts of mimicry make explicit the split foundational to the colonizer identity, constructed in relation to a colonized other imagined as 'less than one but double', as unequal to but aspiring to be like the colonizer. For the colonized, the repetition of acts that function to assert cultural difference as an epistemological absolute reveals that cultural difference is in fact a product of this staging rather than an essence to be revealed. For Bhabha, these hybrid acts of mimicry thus have a liberatory and innovative potential: they function to 'turn the gaze of the discriminated back upon the eye of power' by co-opting and thus revealing the 'emptiness' of the colonizer's representational strategies.[74]

---

[71] Homi K. Bhabha, *The Location of Culture* (New York: Routledge, 2004; repr. 2005, 2006), p. 3.

[72] Ibid., p. 160. For a reading of Gerald of Wales' use of mimicry, see Jeffrey Jerome Cohen, 'Hybrids, Monsters, Borderlands: The Bodies of Gerald of Wales', in *The Post-Colonial Middle Ages*, edited by Jeffrey Jerome Cohen (St Martin's Press, 2000; repr. New York: Palgrave, 2001), pp. 85–104.

[73] Bhabha, *Location*, esp. pp. 121–74.

[74] Ibid., p. 160.

Notwithstanding the markedly hybrid nature of Grendel's Mother's display of the arm on the cliff, it might seem anachronistic or strained to conceptualize her as a colonial subject, if it were not for the fact that other aspects of the encounter between the Scandinavian tribes and the Grendelkin were structured according to a colonial logic. From the beginning of the poem, the paradigm of a successful heroic people is patterned on an imperial model, in which lordship over neighbouring territories is offered as a marker of the 'god cyning':

> Oft Scyld Scefing sceaþena þreatum,/ monegum mægþum meodose-
> tla ofteah,/ egsode eorl[as] ... he þæs frofre gebad,/ weox under
> wolcnum weorðmyndum þah,/ oð þæt him æghwylc ymbsittendra/
> ofer hronrade hyran scolde,/ gomban gyldan'[75]

> (Scyld Scefing often deprived troops of enemies, many peoples, of
> meadbenches, terrified nobles, ... he experienced comfort of that,
> prospered under the skies, thrived in honours, until each of the
> neighbouring peoples over the whale-road had to obey him, to give
> tribute.)

Grendel and his Mother are, apparently, not quite *ymbsittend*, but 'mearcstapan' (boundary-steppers; line 1348), whose somewhat independent territory has an ambiguous status as both inside and outside of the Danish realm. That they hold a territory seems clear: Grendel's Mother, for instance, is described as 'se ðe floda begong heorogifre beheold hund missera' (the one who, voracious, held the mingling of waters for half a hundred years; lines 1497–8). But the watery, permeable, and flowing nature of this territory complicates and inverts the Danes' land-based territorial model. Located in the undesirable 'westen' or 'mor', the home of the Grendelkin apparently holds no attraction or utility for the Danes, and in fact its repellent otherness is part of its functionality in marking the bounds of the social, from which it is excluded.[76] Grendel and his Mother are therefore maintained in a position of marginality in relation to the metropole of the Danish hall: as colonial subjects both a part of and apart from human society. Grendel's desire to inhabit Heorot is, in this context, a manifestation of

---

[75] Lines 4–11.
[76] Waste, desert, wilderness (line 1265); marsh, wasteland, desert (lines 103, 162, 710, 1348, and 1405).

the colonized subject's desire to be like the colonizer, a desire which configures the bounds of the relation, while at the same time troubling the colonizer's essentializing assumptions about difference. Such a relationship is suggested by the poem's allusive description of Grendel's twelve years of lonely nights spent in the hall, emptied of its occupants by his nightly ravages:

> Heorot eardode,
> sincfāge sel sweartum nihtum;—
> nō hē þone gifstōl gretan mōste,
> māþðum for Metode, nē his myne wisse.—
> Þæt wæs wræc micel wine Scyldinga,
> mōdes brecða.[77]

(He occupied Heorot, the treasure-patterned hall by dark nights—not at all might he approach the gift-throne, treasures from the creator, nor now his intention—that was a great trouble to the lord of the Scyldings, grief of spirit.)

Grendel here indulges in the 'fantasy of the native', as Bhabha puts it, dreaming of occupying 'the master's place while keeping his place in the slave's *avenging* anger'.[78] While he can physically occupy the hall, he cannot penetrate the cultural practices that the hall represents; in fact his very presence renders such communal practices of gift-giving and reward impossible. Hanging Grendel's arm is, for the Danes, the reassertion that follows the troubling intrusion of this desiring colonial subject—a reassertion that, in taking the form of a public display, yokes

---

[77] Lines 166–70. This passage is problematic, with scholars unsure whether to interpret the 'gifstol' as belonging to Hrothgar or God. Liuzza, following Fred C. Robinson in 'Why is Grendel's not Greeting the *gifstol* a *wræc micel*', in *Words, Texts, and Manuscripts: Studies in Anglo-Saxon Culture Presented to Helmut Gneuss on the Occasion of his Sixty-Fifth Birthday*, edited by Michael Korhammer (Cambridge: D.S. Brewer, 1992), pp. 257–62, translates as 'he saw no need to salute the throne, he scorned the treasures; he did not know their love', which does not destroy the distinction drawn in this passage between the physical space of Heorot, which Grendel can inhabit, and its practices, which he cannot. Robinson argues that his reassessment of the lines clarifies Grendel's 'outlaw status' (p. 259).

[78] Bhabha, *Location*, pp. 63–4. See also Jeffrey Jerome Cohen, *Medieval Identity Machines* (Minneapolis: Minnesota University Press, 2003), p. 136.

the scopic and exhibitionist modes characteristic of colonial discourse.[79]

The appropriateness of thinking about the hanging and taking of the arm as a type of colonial encounter is lent support by the dual valence of the verb *sceawian* that I explored above. Primarily designating the acquisition of knowledge through looking, the menacing underside of *sceawian*—its association with surveillance, deception, and mockery—encapsulates the duality inherent to the colonial relationship, in which the colonizer simultaneously requires and is threatened by the ambiguous alterity of the colonized subject. In this respect, Beowulf's sense of the arm's inadequacy as a sign, his notion that he would have preferred Hrothgar to see Grendel's dead body whole, is a response to the hybridity of the arm, which fails to embody the other as difference. This hybridity is evident in the lengthy physical description given of the hand, in which its alien qualities, or 'unlikeness', are expressed in terms of likeness to familiar domestic substances such as steel.[80] While the principle of resemblance, which is common to Old English descriptions of the exotic and unusual, functions to make these categories explicable and imaginable, it also troubles the boundary between self and other that these kinds of descriptions work to maintain. The hybrid nature of the arm, exposed by Grendel's Mother's mimicking display of Æschere's head, then motivates the warriors toward the acquisition of a replacement. It is for this reason that, after Beowulf has travelled to the mere and killed Grendel's Mother, it is with Grendel's head and not hers that he returns.[81] As James Rosier summarizes, '[t]he triumph of the dam's visit to Heorot is represented most gruesomely in the head of Æschere which she leaves for the stricken Hrothgar; Beowulf's triumph is similarly betokened by Grendel's head which he brings back to the king. For whatever reason … the … configuration of these scenes of inimical visitation is in many ways uniform.'[82] The fact that Beowulf returns to the hall after the second fight with what he wanted to have after the first—Grendel's head—indicates that the exchange of body

---

[79] Bhabha, *Location*, p. 109 and p. 166.

[80] Lines 984–90. Quotation given in full above on page p. 154.

[81] For a comparison between this episode and execution cemeteries, see Gale Owen-Crocker, '*Horror in* Beowulf', p. 93.

[82] Rosier, 'Uses of Association', p. 12.

parts is about something more than the series of fights themselves, to which the body parts do not correspond. These encounters are rather about the ways in which bodies are made to display the presence of social categories, and to draw a boundary between the inside and the outside of groups. As such, the exchange of body parts is a working out of sovereignty, with Beowulf's abilities to kill Grendel and his Mother giving him the power also to make meaning from their corpses. The 'uniform' forms by which this meaning is expressed, however—with Beowulf's decision to take Grendel's head mirroring Grendel's Mother's theft of Æschere's head—reveal that such sovereignty is far from absolute, but is itself a product of reciprocal acts.

## Violent plots: *Beowulf* and Englishness

The two readings I have offered of the hanging and taking of the arm, as similar in kind first to the ideologically motivated display of objects in museums and second to the encounter between settler and colonized, are in effect two sides of the same coin, and it is the similarity between them that brings both into alignment with the concerns of early eleventh-century England. In the modern context, especially during the late eighteenth and nineteenth centuries, the freak show and the museum functioned to stage the colonial encounter with otherness for the benefit, and the repeated production, of the national democratic subject from within the bounds of the nation itself.[83] Nations are thus always, in some sense, imperial, partaking of the same split consciousness that characterizes the colonial relationship also, as I have explored above. The identity of the national subject is, according to Bhabha, made manifest in a continuous process of vacillation, ambiguity and anxiety, produced in the catch between the nation as a structure, on the one hand, of great antiquity and, on the other, of perpetual newness. Thus the national people experience themselves both as an already-constituted historical presence, what Bhabha calls a 'pedagogical object', and a continuously constituted performance in which they must always engage.[84] This temporal rift in the nation's identity, akin

---

[83] Garland-Thomas, 'Making Freaks'.
[84] Bhabha, *Location*, p. 211.

to the position of the anthropologist looking at the ethnographic scene of which he or she is also part, means that '[o]nce the liminality of the nation-space is established, and its signifying difference is turned from the boundary "outside" to its finitude "within", the threat of cultural difference is no longer a problem of "other" people. It becomes a question of otherness of the people-as-one.'[85] In the early stages of nationhood in particular, this otherness within the 'people as one' is particularly marked, as territories experience what Robert Bartlett designates as 'internal expansion': '[n]ation-states coalesce, that is, through overland expansion, annexing adjacent territories and gradually achieving legitimacy.'[86] Incorporating these outlying regions thus represents an interior form of colonization that serves to exercise and make visible the duality that is characteristic of national consciousness. The throes attendant on the attempted incorporation may be worked out on the imaginary level by staging situations of difference and assimilation either in literary or spectacular form. The museum and the freak show are such venues: places where the modern observer can repeatedly reconstitute themselves as a national subject through the visual encounter with and consumption of the exotic and different. Or, in other words, they are places where the observer can experience marginality within the geographical confines of the nation itself.

If we understand the modern museum as responding to the need for an environment that can harness the force of spectacle to the reproduction of social forms, then it is not difficult to see *Beowulf* in relation to a similarly configured need in the eleventh century. As much recent archaeological work has thoughtfully considered, the presence of Scandinavians within early medieval England is not easily observable, mostly because their settlements, grave-sites, and material possessions are hybridized to the extent that they represent a new form of social expression that overlaps with, permeates, and is frankly difficult to distinguish from something that we could reasonably call 'English'. In particular, work on new items found by metal detectorists is revealing

---

[85] Ibid., p. 215.

[86] Robert Bartlett, *The Making of Europe: Conquest, Colonization, and Cultural Change 950–1350* (London: Penguin, 1993), p. 2; Barbara Fuchs, 'Imperium Studies: Theorizing Early Modern Expansion', in *Postcolonial Moves: Medieval through Modern*, edited by P. Ingham and M. Warren (New York: Palgrave Macmillan, 2003), pp. 71–90.

the ways in which certain common and highly visible artefacts were being used for self-conscious expression of group identity within tenth- and eleventh-century England. Gabor Thomas, for instance, concludes that strap-ends and disc-brooches seem to have been particularly central to the development of what he calls a 'new hybrid cultural tradition', precisely because they 'would have been one of the most immediately recognizable and familiar elements of their respective dress traditions'.[87] New types of mass production, such as the York craft workshops, seem to have allowed for the wide distribution of such accessories which, because they were made of cheap materials, were probably worn by many in the population rather than only being available to the nobility (as much of the earlier and well-studied jewellery of the period must have been). As Thomas asserts, the frequent occurrence of combined English and Scandinavian elements in the form and decoration of later metalwork, along with the lack of finds exemplifying a traditional Scandinavian style within England, is a sign of 'the selective use of material culture to facilitate the process of cultural integration'. As he explains at greater length:

> [i]n the context of Scandinavian settlement, it is possible that those aspects of costume and dress which represented a 'foreign' unfamiliar identity may have been actively abandoned in favour of other aspects of material culture which could be used to express unity and cultural likeness.[88]

Thomas's insights suggest that tenth- and eleventh-century metalwork was being used by individuals to make their own bodies an expression of cultural integration.

The evidence, of both material culture and texts, therefore suggests that the turn of the eleventh century witnessed increased awareness and use of the body as an interactive site for expression of group identity, and that such expression was locally driven from the bottom up rather than being the mandate of a centralized elite, either religious or secular. The concern of such local displays of ethnic identity was, apparently, an

[87] Gabor Thomas, 'Anglo-Scandinavian Metalwork from the Danelaw: Exploring Social and Cultural Interaction', in *Cultures in Contact: Scandinavian Settlement in England in the Ninth and Tenth Centuries*, edited by Dawn M. Hadley and Julian D. Richards (Turnhout: Brepols, 2000), pp. 237–55, at p. 252.

[88] Thomas, 'Metalwork', p. 252.

incorporation achieved by the management of a dual affiliation to both Scandinavian and English culture. At the same time, the political fortunes of Æthelred's reign involve the complex negotiation of differences between English and Scandinavian, ally and enemy, south and north, in which the alignment of opposing terms was far from constant. Æthelred's government too, then, was deeply concerned with issues of incorporation and of duality. *Beowulf*, for its audiences around the year 1000, is part of this broader scene of cultural evolution, with its complex narrative of severed and displayed body parts allowing audiences to explore and play with the role of bodies in both the drawing and experience of boundaries between groups.

# Conclusion

## *What Matters*

The story of how Germanic tribes migrated to the island of Britain sometime in the fifth century, settled, fought each other, took over each other's territories and that of the Britons, and became something new has been debated and narrated countless times since Bede told it. Traditional understandings of cultural syncretism have shown us that the conversion of the early medieval English in the late sixth century would have played a key role in this process by bringing Latin learning and religious practices to bear upon native ideas and customs, and thus generating Englishness as a new and unique identity position with rich historical and cultural dimensions. And as Nicholas Howe demonstrated in *Migration and Mythmaking*, this new culture was founded on acts of remembrance that the English had come from elsewhere. But this book has aimed to return to this story the ways that material and cultural facets intersect and conflate, rather than being separate concerns, arguing that Englishness during the early medieval period is more than an ideological product. I have examined instances when early medieval texts and artefacts evince that the syncretism between history, geography, and religion, which makes Englishness, is a side effect of a much larger interaction between matter and discourse.

*Materializing Englishness in Early Medieval Texts*. Jacqueline Fay, Oxford University Press.
© Jacqueline Fay 2022. DOI: 10.1093/oso/9780198757573.003.0006

In short, like a number of other recent scholars in the field of early medieval studies, I have tried to shift the point of view elsewhere from the human in order to account for the active engagement of other material entities in the story. Whether it be soil, stone, or plants, the early medieval body is permeable and actively engaged with substances that are both external and internal to it. The bodies that I have considered are thus not simply textual, functioning to represent and externalize abstract social constructs like ethnicity or nation, as would be the case, for example, with the metaphor of the body politic. In contrast, the texts examined in the book indicate that the bodies of the early medieval English are engaged in and by the materiality of language, the book, and their surroundings, provoking audiences to experience themselves as permeated by history and geography—or, rather, to be permeated by history and place. Books, bodies, and other material elements are not treated here as discrete and mutually exclusive entities but, as would make sense in manuscript culture, are revealed to be *intra*-acting with each other, Barad's term for a type of activity that occurs in entanglement rather than in the space between.

However, as Tom Williamson notes, we are doubly estranged from the material world of the past: not only does matter exist in a constant state of transformation, but also the highly urban and technological mode of existence in the twenty-first century decisively distances most of us from the agrarian rhythms and concerns of earlier time periods.[1] For Williamson, a 'conscious effort of the imagination' is required to overcome or short circuit the changes wrought by time on our mode of living in relation to the environment. What Williamson, a pre-eminent landscape historian, seems to advocate here is an engaged relation to landscape involving information and observation, learning and sensing. In certain ways Williamson's 'imagination' is similar to new materialist theorist Jane Bennett's recommendation that we practise a 'countercultural kind of perceiving'—that is, 'a cultivated, patient, sensory attentiveness to nonhuman forces operating outside and inside the human body'.[2] For Bennett, modern and postmodern literature by

---

[1.] Tom Williamson, *Environment, Society and Landscape in Early Medieval England: Time and Topography* (Woodbridge: Boydell Press, 2015), p. 4.

[2] Jane Bennett, *Vibrant Matter: A Political Ecology of Things* (Durham, NC: Duke University Press, 2010), p. xiv.

Kafka, Thoreau, and other writers can be of assistance in developing this countercultural perception by surprising us into viewing anew the material world, which we have become overly accustomed to see as a passive container for active human subjects. The work of both Bennett and Williamson, in different ways, identifies the need for a reorientation towards the material world that, in particular, involves acknowledging and experiencing human engagement in/with it. Their combined insights show that in certain respects we are no less alienated from the material world at our finger tips—or inside our own bodies—than we are from the fields, homesteads, and rivers of the past: access to either requires an intentional effort on our parts. But whereas medievalists might very well find reading Kafka or Thoreau helpful in their efforts to reorient themselves towards the materiality of past and present, the connection between medieval matters and contemporary concerns is not always recognized as flowing in the opposite direction. Transcendentalism and existentialism, among other philosophical and textual movements, are very effective at producing recognition of those deeply embedded modes of viewing the material world as inactive and less important than humanity. But other ways to provoke an experience of alienation that both occurs in and impacts the present could include the exercise of 'imagination' mentioned by Williamson as necessary to the study of medieval landscapes and, by extension, medieval materiality in general.

That this possibility is not more generally recognized is indicative of the dominant paradigms within which relevance can be accrued and communicated in the academy. Kathleen Davis's work, along with that of many other medievalists, has done much to further the recognition that 'we have never been modern', as Bruno Latour famously put it in 1993. Davis's insightful study demonstrates that periodization, especially the establishment of a categorical boundary between medieval and modern, functions as a 'political technique—a way to moderate, divide, and regulate' that is maintained by and in the service of the present moment.[3] The question of how studying or teaching the early medieval period is relevant, with the frequent assumption that it is

---

[3] Kathleen Davis, *Periodization and Sovereignty: How Ideas of Feudalism and Secularization Govern the Politics of Time* (Philadelphia: University of Pennsylvania Press, 2008), p. 5.

not, emerges from the periodized entrenchment of 'units such as sacred-medieval-feudal and secular-modern-capitalist (or democratic)' that allows only certain configurations to be recognizable as political, as being fully vibrant in the sense of touching lives. And yet while the notion of an abrupt shift between the medieval and modern periods has been theoretically discredited, in practice much of the structure of assumed difference between the two periods lingers in conversations and questions, in who reads our work or attends our talks and who does not, in what courses we teach and what purpose they are thought to serve in our curricula.

Early medievalists have followed a number of strategies in attempting to avoid the historicist problem articulated by Nicholas Howe when he noted that '[i]f we fail to make Pre-Conquest England a subject of interest, even in a quietly modest way, we risk trivializing ourselves as antiquarians who collect lore about the past as magpies collect bright, shiny objects.'[4] The conclusion to Heide Estes' *Anglo-Saxon Literary Landscapes* is particularly well thought-out and direct in this regard, pointing out that the type of 'environmentally inflected literary study' in which she engages necessarily has an 'activist component' and enjoining readers to 'divest from fossil fuels, invest in public transit, seek ways to sequester the carbon we have released by burning things, and stop consuming so much stuff'.[5] Her final striking sentences, 'These are not just words. This is a call to action. Stop. Think. Reverse course', are unusual for a volume analysing Old English texts. As Estes makes clear, investigating the way earlier periods characterize, describe, and name other entities that are not people—a task to which the whole volume is dedicated—is crucial to recognizing and understanding the deeply engrained modes of understanding that govern behaviours and decision-making in the modern world: as she puts it, '[e]xamining how people of the distant past told stories about their environments can help us to understand contemporary stories.'[6] Neither the original texts examined nor the analysis of them are 'just words'.

---

[4] Nicholas Howe, 'Historicist Approaches,' in *Reading Old English Texts*, edited by Katherine O'Brien O'Keeffe (Cambridge: Cambridge University Press, 1997), p. 82.

[5] Estes, *Anglo-Saxon Literary Landscapes: Ecotheory and the Environmental Imagination* (Amsterdam: Amsterdam University Press, 2017), p. 192.

[6] Ibid., p. 190.

Cultivating a relationship with the past as 'a subject of interest' rather than an object for antiquarianism necessitates challenging the way that the past is usually conceived of as influencing the present. The relationship between the past and the present is only partially captured when it is inscribed in terms of a genealogy of ideas, words, and narrative structures that still resonate in the present and during all the times in between the present and the past. More compelling is what Patricia Ingham describes as 'a self-conscious historicism that insists that we can understand something crucial about then and now by recasting the medieval record in terms resonant to our own moment'.[7] Ingham suggests that studies written in this mode involve 'a deliberate turn, insisting that the past might be translated into terms usable in the present',[8] an intentional about-face that equates to Estes's 'Stop. Think. Reverse.' This approach harnesses the surprise of a past—specifically one that contemporary audiences are largely unfamiliar with or have misconceptions about—to the project of revealing something generally unrecognized in the present. In attempting this resonant mode of historicism in this volume, I have aimed to tell a different story about words and matter in early medieval England, a story with roots also in the now. As scholars, we have paid most attention to representational strategies: to symbolism, words, and ideas. But being attentive to the wider interactions of these words seems truer to the way matter and text are conceived of in early medieval England, where you could be changed by consuming soil, where words could be written and washed into a bowl and then drunk, where loaves could be buried in a field and interact with speech to make seeds grow.

---

[7] Patricia Clare Ingham, *The Medieval New: Ambivalence in an Age of Innovation* (Philadelphia: University of Pennsylvania Press, 2015), p. 27.
[8] Ibid.

# BIBLIOGRAPHY

## Primary Texts

Adamnan. *De Locis Sanctis*, edited by Denis Meehan. Scriptores Latini Hiberniae 3 (Dublin, 1958. Repr. 1983).

Aldhelm. *The Prose Works*, edited and translated by Michael Lapidge and Michael Herren (Ipswich: D.S. Brewer, 1979).

Aldhelm. *The Poetic Works*, translated by Michael Lapidge (Cambridge: D.S. Brewer, 1985).

Ælfric. *The Homilies of the Anglo-Saxon Church: The Sermones Catholici or Homilies of Ælfric*, edited and translated by Benjamin Thorpe. Vol. 1 (London, 1844. Repr. New York, 1971).

Ælfric. *Lives of Saints*, edited by Walter W. Skeat. Early English Text Society, o.s., 82 (London: Oxford University Press, 1881–5).

*Ancient Christian Commentary on Scripture: New Testament Ia, Matthew 1–13*, edited by Manlio Simonetti (Downers Grove, IL: Intervarsity Press, 2001).

*The Anglo-Saxon Chronicle: A Collaborative Edition.*

*MS A.* Vol. 3, edited by Janet Bately (Cambridge: D.S. Brewer, 1986).

*MS C.* Vol. 5, edited by Katherine O'Brien O'Keeffe (Cambridge: D.S. Brewer, 2001).

*MS D.* Vol. 6, edited by G. P. Cubbin (Cambridge: D.S. Brewer, 1996).

*MS E.* Vol. 7, edited by Susan Irvine (Cambridge: D.S. Brewer, 2004).

*The Bayeux Tapestry*, edited by Martin K. Foys (Leicester: Scholarly Digital Editions, 2003).

Bede. *Two Lives of Saint Cuthbert: A Life by an Anonymous Monk of Lindisfarne and Bede's Prose Life*, edited and translated by Bertram Colgrave (Cambridge: Cambridge University Press, 1940).

Bede. *Bedae uenerabilis de locis sanctis*, edited by J. Fraipont. *Corpus christianorum series Latina* 175 (Turnhout: Brepols, 1965).

Bede. *Ecclesiastical History of the English People*, edited by Bertram Colgrave and R. A. B. Mynors (Oxford: Clarendon Press, 1969).

Bede. *Bede: A Biblical Miscellany*, translated by W. Trent Foley and Arthur G. Holder (Liverpool: Liverpool University Press, 1999).

*Beowulf and the Fight at Finnsburg*, edited by Fr. Klaeber (Boston, MA: D.C. Heath, 1950).

*Beowulf: A New Verse Translation*, translated by Roy Liuzza (Peterborough, Ontario: Broadview Press, 2000).

Biggam, C. P. 'The True Staff of Life: The Multiple Roles of Plants'. In *The Material Culture of Daily Living in the Anglo-Saxon World*, edited by Maren Clegg Hyer and Gale R. Owen-Crocker (Exeter: University of Exeter Press, 2011), pp. 23–48.

Bosworth, Joseph, and T. Northcote Toller. *An Anglo-Saxon Dictionary* (Oxford: Clarendon, 1898). http://bosworth.ff.cuni.cz.

Byrthtferth. *Byrhtferth's Manual*, edited and translated by S. J. Crawford. Early English Text Society, 177 (London: Oxford University Press, 1929).

Byrthtferth. *Byrhtferth's Enchiridion*, edited by Peter S. Baker and Michael Lapidge. Early English Text Society, s.s., 15 (Oxford: Oxford University Press, 1995).

Cockayne, Thomas Oswald, ed. *Leechdoms, Wortcunning and Starcraft of Early England*. Rev. ed. (1864–6. Repr. London: Holland Press, 1961).

*The Dictionary of Old English Corpus*. http://libproxy.uta.edu:2506/o/oec/.

*The Dictionary of Old English Plant Names*, edited by Peter Bierbaumer and Hans Sauer with Helmut W. Klug and Ulrike Krischke. 2007–2009. http://oldenglish-plantnames.org.

*The Electronic Sawyer: Online Catalogue of Anglo-Saxon Charters*. http://www.esawyer.org.uk/about/index.html.

*Epigrammata Damasiana*, edited by Antonius Ferrua (Rome: Pontifico Istituto di Archeologia Cristiana, 1942).

Gaimar, Geffrei. *Lestorie des Engles solum la translacion Maistre Geffrei Gaimar*, edited by Thomas Duffus Hardy and Charles Trice Martin (London: Rolls Series, 1888). Vol. 1.

Gaimar, Geffrei. *Lestorie des Engles solum la translacion Maistre Geffrei Gaimar*, edited by Thomas Duffus Hardy and Charles Trice Martin (London: Rolls Series, 1899). Vol. 2.

Gaimar, Geffrei. *L'Estoire des Engleis*, edited by Alexander Bell (Oxford: Anglo-Norman Text Society, 1960).

Gregory the Great. *Dialogues*, edited by Adalbert de Vogüé and translated by Paul Antin. Sources Chrétiennes, 260 (Paris: les Éditions du Cerf, 1979).

Kotzor, Günter, ed. *Das altenglische martyrologium* (Munich: Bayerische Akademie der Wissenschaften, 1981).

*Old English Homilies from MS. Bodley 343*, edited by Susan Irvine. Early English Text Society, o.s. 302 (Oxford: Oxford University Press, 1993).

*The* Old English Martyrology: *Edition, Translation and Commentary*, edited and translated by Christine Rauer (Rochester: Boydell and Brewer, 2014).

*The Old English Riddles of the* Exeter Book, edited by Craig Williamson (Chapel Hill: University of North Carolina Press, 1977).

*The Old English Version of Bede's Ecclesiastical History of the English People*, edited and translated by Thomas Miller. Early English Text Society, o.s., 95 (London: N. Trübner, 1890).

*The Old English Version of the Gospels*, edited by R. M. Liuzza. Early English Text Society, o.s., 504 (Oxford: Oxford University Press, 1994).

*Oxford English Dictionary.* 2nd ed. (Oxford: Oxford University Press, 1989). http://www.oed.com.

*Regesta regum anglorum: A Searchable Edition of the Corpus of Anglo-Saxon Royal Diplomas 670–1066.* http://www.trin.cam.ac.uk/chartwww/NewRegReg.html.

Sulpicius Severus. 'Life of Martin'. In *Early Christian Lives*, edited and translated by Carolinne White (London: Penguin, 1998), pp. 131–59.

Wigram, Spencer Robert, ed. *The Cartulary of the Monastery of St Frideswide at Oxford.* 2 vols. Oxford Historical Society 28, 31 (Oxford: Clarendon Press, 1895–6).

Wilson, H. A., ed. *The Calendar of St Willbrord from MS. Paris Lat. 10837: A Facsimile with Transcription, Introduction, and Notes.* Henry Bradshaw Society 55 (1918. Repr. London: Boydell Press, 1998).

## Secondary Texts

Alaimo, Stacy. *Bodily Natures: Science, Environment, and the Material Self* (Bloomington: Indiana University Press, 2010).

Alaimo, Stacy, and Susan Hekman, eds. *Material Feminisms* (Bloomington: Indiana University Press, 2008).

Anderson, J. J. 'The 'Cuþe Folme' in *Beowulf*'. *Neophilologus* 67 (1983): pp. 126–30.

Ayoub, Lois. 'Old English *wæta* and the Medical Theory of the Humours'. *Journal of English and Germanic Philology* 94 (1995): pp. 332–46.

Baker, Peter. 'More Diagrams by Byrhtferth of Ramsey'. In *Latin Learning and English Lore: Studies in Anglo-Saxon Literature for Michael Lapidge*, edited by Katherine O'Brien O'Keeffe and Andy Orchard (Toronto: University of Toronto Press, 2005), pp. 53–73.

Banham, Debby. *Food and Drink in Anglo-Saxon England* (Stroud: Tempus Publishing, 2004).

Banham, Debby. 'A Millennium in Medicine? New Medical Texts and Ideas in England in the Eleventh Century'. In *Anglo-Saxons: Studies Presented to Cyril Roy Hart*, edited by Simon Keynes and Alfred P. Smyth (Dublin: Four Courts Press, 2006), pp. 230–42.

Banham, Debby. 'Race and Tillage: Scandinavian Influence on Anglo-Saxon Agriculture?' In *Anglo-Saxons and the North*, edited by Matti Kilpio, Leena Kahlas-Tarkka, Jane Roberts, and Olga Timofeeva (Tempe: Arizona Center for Medieval and Renaissance Studies, 2009), pp. 165–91.

Banham, Debby. '"In the Sweat of Thy Brow Shalt Thou Eat Bread": Cereals and Cereal Production in the Anglo-Saxon Landscape'. In *The Landscape Archaeology of Anglo-Saxon England*, edited by Nicholas J. Higham and Martin J. Ryan (Woodbridge: Boydell Press, 2010), pp. 175–92.

Banham, Debby. 'The Staff of Life: Cross and Blessings in Anglo-Saxon Cereal Production'. In *Cross and Cruciform in the Anglo-Saxon World*, edited by Sarah Larratt Keefer, Karen Louise Jolly, and Catherine E. Karkov (Morgantown: West Virginia Press, 2010), pp. 279–318.

Banham, Debby. '*Lectun* and *Orceard*: A Preliminary Survey of the Evidence for Horticulture in Anglo-Saxon England'. In *The Anglo-Saxons: The World through Their Eyes*, edited by Gale R. Owen-Crocker and Brian W. Schneider (Oxford: BAR British Series, 2014), pp. 33–48.

Banham, Debby, and Rosamond Faith. *Anglo-Saxon Farms and Farming* (Oxford: Oxford University Press, 2014).

Barad, Karen. *Meeting the Universe Halfway: Quantum Physics and the Entanglement of Matter and Meaning* (Durham, NC: Duke University Press, 2007).

Bartlett, Robert. *The Making of Europe: Conquest, Colonization, and Cultural Change 950–1350* (London: Penguin, 1993).

Bately, Janet. 'The Compilation of the Anglo-Saxon Chronicle, 60 BC to AD 890: Vocabulary as Evidence'. *Proceedings of the British Academy* 64 (1978): pp. 93–129.

Bately, Janet. 'The Compilation of the Anglo-Saxon Chronicle Once More'. *Leeds Studies in English* 16 (1985): pp. 7–26.

Bately, Janet. 'Manuscript Layout and the Anglo-Saxon Chronicle'. *John Rylands University Library Bulletin* 70 (1988): pp. 21–43.

Bately, Janet. *The Anglo-Saxon Chronicle: Texts and Textual Relationships* (Reading: Reading Medieval Studies Monograph, 1991).

Bennett, Jane. *Vibrant Matter: A Political Ecology of Things* (Durham, NC: Duke University Press, 2010).

Bennett, Tony. *The Birth of the Museum: History, Theory, Politics* (New York: Routledge, 1995).

Berschin, Walter. '*Opus deliberatum ac perfectum*: Why Did the Venerable Bede Write a Second Prose Life of St Cuthbert?' In *St Cuthbert, his Cult and his Community to AD 1200*, edited by Gerald Bonner, David Rollason, and Clare Stancliffe (Woodbridge: Boydell Press, 1989), pp. 95–102.

Bhabha, Homi K. *The Location of Culture* (New York: Routledge, 2004. Repr. 2005, 2006).

Biddick, Kathleen. 'The Cut of Genealogy: Pedagogy in the Blood'. *Journal of Medieval and Early Modern Studies* 30.3 (2000): pp. 449–62.

Biddle, Martin. 'Excavations at Winchester 1965: Fourth Interim Report'. *Antiquaries Journal* 46 (1966): pp. 308–32.

Bintley, Michael. Review of Heide Estes, *Anglo-Saxon Literary Landscapes: Ecotheory and the Environmental Imagination*. *The Medieval Review* (18 November 2006).

Bjork, Robert E., and Anita Obermeier. 'Date, Provenance, Author, Audiences'. In *A Beowulf Handbook*, edited by Robert E. Bjork and John D. Niles (Exeter: University of Exeter Press, 1996), pp. 13–34.

Blair, John. 'A Saint for Every Minster? Local Cults in Anglo-Saxon England'. In *Local Saints and Local Churches in the Early Medieval West*, edited by Alan Thacker and Richard Sharpe (Oxford: Oxford University Press, 2002), pp. 455–94.

Blair, John. *The Church in Anglo-Saxon Society* (Oxford: Oxford University Press, 2005).

Blurton, Heather. *Cannibalism in High Medieval English Literature* (New York: Palgrave Macmillan, 2007).

Bonner, Gerald. 'St Cuthbert at Chester-le-Street'. In *St Cuthbert, his Cult and his Community to AD 1200*, edited by Gerald Bonner, David Rollason, and Clare Stancliffe (Woodbridge: Boydell Press, 1989), pp. 387–95.

Bonner, Gerald, David Rollason, and Clare Stancliffe, eds. *St Cuthbert, his Cult and his Community to AD 1200* (Woodbridge: Boydell Press, 1989).

Braidotti, Rosi, and Maria Hlavajova, eds. *The Posthuman Glossary* (London: Bloomsbury, 2018).

Bredehoft, Thomas. *Textual Histories: Readings in the Anglo-Saxon Chronicle* (Toronto: University of Toronto Press, 2001).

Bredehoft, Thomas. *The Visible Text: Textual Production and Reproduction from Beowulf to Maus* (Oxford: Oxford University Press, 2014).

Bremmer Jr, Rolf H. 'Grendel's Arm and the Law'. In *Studies in English Language and Literature: 'Doubt Wisely', Papers in Honor of E. G. Stanley*, edited by M. J. Toswell and E. M. Tyler (London: Routledge, 1996), pp. 121–32.

Brown, Peter. *The Cult of the Saints: Its Rise and Function in Latin Christianity* (Chicago: University of Chicago Press, 1981).

Bruns, Gerald. 'The Originality of Texts in a Manuscript Culture'. *Comparative Literature* 32 (1980): pp. 113–29.

Budny, Mildred, ed. 'The Byrhtnoth Tapestry or Embroidery'. In *The Battle of Maldon AD 991*, edited by Donald Scragg (Oxford: Basil Blackwell, 1991), pp. 263–78.

Bynum, Caroline. 'Why All the Fuss about the Body? A Medievalist's Perspective. *Critical Inquiry* 22 (1995): pp. 1–33.

Calder, Daniel G. 'Setting and Ethos: The Pattern of Measure and Limit in *Beowulf*. *Studies in Philology* 69 (1972): pp. 21–37.

Cameron, Kenneth. *English Place-names* (London: B.T. Batsford, 1961).

Cameron, M. L. *Anglo-Saxon Medicine* (Cambridge: Cambridge University Press, 1993).

Campbell, James. 'England, France, Flanders and Germany: Some Comparisons and Connections'. In *Ethelred the Unready: Papers from the Millenary Conference*, edited by David Hill (Oxford: British Archaeological Series, 1978), pp. 255–70.

Campbell, James. 'What Is Not Known about the Reign of Edward the Elder'. In *Edward the Elder, 899–924*, edited by N. J. Higham and D. H. Hill (London and New York: Routledge, 2001), pp. 12–24.

Carens, Marilyn M. 'Handscoh and Grendel: The Motif of the Hand in *Beowulf*'. In *Aeolian Harps: Essays in Literature in Honor of Maurice Browning Cramer*, edited by Donna G. Fricke and Douglas C. Fricke (Bowling Green: Bowling Green University Press, 1976), pp. 39–55.

Carver, Martin. 'Burial as Poetry: The Context of Treasure in Anglo-Saxon Graves'. In *Treasure in the Medieval West*, edited by Elizabeth M. Tyler (York: York Medieval Press, 2000), pp. 25–48.

Chase, Colin, ed. *The Dating of* Beowulf (Toronto: University of Toronto Press, 1981).

Chen, Mel Y. *Animacies: Biopolitics, Racial Mattering, and Queer Affect* (Durham, NC: Duke University Press, 2012).

Clark, Cecily. 'The Narrative Mode of the *Anglo-Saxon Chronicle* before the Conquest'. In *England before the* Conquest, edited by Peter Clemoes and Kathleen Hughes (Cambridge: Cambridge University Press, 1971), pp. 215–35.

Clarke, Catherine. *Literary Landscapes and the Idea of England, 700–1400* (Cambridge: D.S. Brewer, 2006).

Clemoes, Peter. 'Language in Context: *Her* in the 890 *Anglo-Saxon Chronicle*'. *Leeds Studies in English* 16 (1985): pp. 27–36.

Clifford, James. *The Predicament of Culture: Twentieth-Century Ethnography, Literature, and Art* (Cambridge, MA: Harvard University Press, 1988).

Cohen, Jeffrey Jerome. 'Hybrids, Monsters, Borderlands: The Bodies of Gerald of Wales'. In *The Post-Colonial Middle Ages*, edited by Jeffrey Jerome Cohen (St Martin's Press, 2000. Repr. New York: Palgrave, 2001), pp. 85–104.

Cohen, Jeffrey Jerome. *Medieval Identity Machines* (Minneapolis: Minnesota University Press, 2003).

Cohen, Jeffrey Jerome. *Stone: An Ecology of the Inhuman* (Minneapolis: University of Minnesota Press, 2015).

Coole, Dianna, and Samantha Frost. *New Materialisms: Ontology, Agency, and Politics* (Durham, NC: Duke University Press, 2010).

Cooper, Marion, and Anthony W. Johnson. *Poisonous Plants in Britain and their Effects on Animals and Man* (London: Her Majesty's Stationery Office, 1984).

Corradini, Richard. 'The Rhetoric of Crisis: *Computus* and *Liber annalis* in Early Ninth-Century Fulda'. In *The Construction of Communities in the Early Middle Ages: Texts, Resources and Artefacts*, edited by Richard Corradini, Max Diesenberger, and Helmut Reimitz (Leiden: Brill, 2003), pp. 269–321.

Cramp, Rosemary. 'The Making of Oswald's Northumbria'. In *Oswald: Northumbrian King to European Saint*, edited by Clare Stancliffe and Eric Cambridge (Stamford: Paul Watkins, 1995), pp. 17–32.

Cranfield University. *The Soils Guide*. Available at www.landis.org.uk (Cranfield University, UK, 2016).

Crook, John. 'The Enshrinement of Local Saints in Merovingia and Carolingian Francia'. In *Local Saints and Local Churches in the Early Medieval West*, edited by Alan Thacker and Richard Sharpe (Oxford: Oxford University Press, 2002), pp. 189–224.

Cross, J. E. 'The Apostles in the Old English Martyrology'. *Mediaevalia* 5 (1979): pp. 15–59.

Dale, Corinne. *The Natural World in the Exeter Book Riddles*. Woodbridge: D.S. Brewer, 2017.

Damon, John Edward. 'Deseco Capite Perfido: Bodily Fragmentation and Reciprocal Violence in Anglo-Saxon England'. *Exemplaria* 13 (2001): pp. 399–432.

Davis, Kathleen. 'National Writing in the Ninth Century: A Reminder for Post-Colonial Thinking about the Nation'. *Journal of Medieval and Early Modern Studies* 28 (1998): pp. 611–37.

Davis, R. H. C. 'Alfred the Great: Propaganda and Truth'. *History* 56 (1971): pp. 169–82.

Day, David. 'Hands across the Hall: The Legalities of Beowulf's Fight with Grendel'. *Journal of English and Germanic Philology* 98 (1999): pp. 1–24.

Delany, Sheila. *Impolitic Bodies: Poetry, Saints, and Society in Fifteenth-Century England* (Oxford: Oxford University Press, 1998).

Deskis, Susan. Beowulf *and the Medieval Proverb Tradition* (Tempe: Medieval and Renaissance Texts and Studies, 1996).

Dolley, Michael. 'An Introduction to the Coinage of Æthelræd II'. In *Ethelred the Unready: Papers from the Millenary Conference*, edited by David Hill (Oxford: British Archaeological Series, 1978), pp. 115–33.

Doyle, Conan. *Anglo-Saxon Medicine and Disease: A Semantic Approach*. Unpubl. PhD dissertation. University of Cambridge, 2011.

Dragland, S. L. 'Monster-Man in *Beowulf*'. *Neophilologus* 61 (1977): pp. 606–18.

Dumville, David. '*Beowulf* Come Lately: Some Notes on the Palaeography of the Nowell Codex'. *Archiv für das Studium der Neueren Sprachen und Literaturen* 225.1 (1988): pp. 49–63.

Earl, James W. 'Violence and Non-Violence in Anglo-Saxon England: Ælfric's "Passion of St Edmund"'. *Philological Quarterly* 78 (1999): pp. 125–49.

Edson, Evelyn. *Mapping Time and Space: How Medieval Mapmakers Viewed Their World* (London: British Library, 1997).

Estes, Heide. *Anglo-Saxon Literary Landscapes: Ecotheory and the Environmental Imagination* (Amsterdam: Amsterdam University Press, 2017).

Fanon, Franz. *The Wretched of the Earth*, translated by C. Farrington (Harmondsworth: Penguin, 1969).

Fay, Jacqueline. 'Becoming an Onion: The Extra-Human Nature of Genital Difference in the Old English Riddling and Medical Traditions'. *English Studies* 101.1 (2020): pp. 60–78.

Fay, Jacqueline. 'The Farmacy: Wild and Cultivated Plants in Anglo-Saxon England'. *Interdisciplinary Studies in Literature and the Environment* 28.1 (2021): pp. 186–206.

Ferhatović, Denis. *Borrowed Objects and the Art of Poetry: Spolia in Old English Verse* (Manchester: Manchester University Press, 2019).

Firbank, L. G. 'Agrostemma githago L (Lychnis githago (L.) Scop.)'. *Journal of Ecology* 76 (1988): pp. 1232–46.

Fleming, Robin. *Britain after Rome: The Fall and Rise, 400–1070* (London: Penguin, 2010).

Foot, Sarah. 'The Making of Angelcynn: English Identity before the Norman Conquest'. *Transactions of the Royal Historical Society* 6 (1996): pp. 25–49.

Foucault, Michel. *Discipline and Punish: The Birth of the Prison*, translated by Alan Sheridan (New York: Pantheon Books, 1977).

Frantzen, Allen. *Desire for Origins: New Language, Old English, and Teaching the Tradition* (New Brunswick: Rutgers University Press, 1990).

Fuchs, Barbara. 'Imperium Studies: Theorizing Early Modern Expansion'. In *Postcolonial Moves: Medieval through Modern*, edited by P. Ingham and M. Warren (New York: Palgrave Macmillan, 2003), pp. 71–90.

Garland-Thomas, Rosemary. 'Making Freaks: Visual Rhetorics and the Spectacle of Julia Pastrana'. In *Thinking the Limits of the Body*, edited by Jeffrey Jerome Cohen and Gail Weiss (Albany: State University of New York Press, 2002), pp. 129–43.

Georgianna, Linda. 'King Hrethel's Sorrow and the Limits of Heroic Action in *Beowulf*'. *Speculum* 62 (1987): pp. 829–50.

Gledhill, David. *The Names of Plants* (Cambridge: Cambridge University Press, 2002).

Gransden, Antonia. *Historical Writing in England c.550 to c.1307* (Ithaca: Cornell University Press, 1974).

Greenfield, Stanley B. 'The Extremities of the Beowulfian Body Politic'. In *Saints, Scholars and Heroes: Studies in Medieval Culture in Honour of Charles W. Jones*, edited by Margot H. King and Wesley M. Stevens (Collegeville: Hill Monastic Manuscript Library, 1979), pp. 1–14.

Grosz, Elizabeth. *Volatile Bodies: Toward a Corporeal Feminism*. Bloomington: Indiana University Press, 1994.

Gunn, Victoria A. 'Bede and the Martyrdom of St Oswald'. *Studies in Church History* 30 (1993): pp. 57–66.

Hadley, Dawn. '"Cockle amongst the Wheat": The Scandinavian Settlement of England'. In *Social Identity in Early Medieval Britain*, edited by William O. Frazer and Andrew Tyrrel (London: Leicester University Press, 2000), pp. 111–35.

Hadley, Dawn. *Death in Medieval England* (Stroud: Tempus, 2001).

Hadley, Dawn. *The Vikings in England: Settlement, Society and Culture* (Manchester: Manchester University Press, 2006).

Hadley, Dawn, and Julian D. Richards, eds. *Cultures in Contact: Scandinavian Settlement in England in the Ninth and Tenth Centuries* (Turnhout: Brepols, 2000).

Hahn, Cynthia. *The Reliquary Effect: Enshrining the Sacred Object* (London: Reaktion Books, 2017).

Hall, Allan. 'The Fossil Evidence for Plants in Mediaeval Towns'. *Biologist* 33 (1986): pp. 262–7.

Hardy, Gavin, and Laurence Totelin. *Ancient Botany* (London: Routledge, 2016).

Harris, Anne F. 'Hewn'. In *Inhuman Nature*, edited by Jeffrey Jerome Cohen (Washington, DC: Oliphaunt Books, 2014), pp. 17–38.

Harris, Stephen. *Race and Ethnicity in Anglo-Saxon Literature* (New York: Routledge, 2003).

Harris, Stephen. 'An Overview of Race and Ethnicity in Pre-Norman England'. *Literature Compass* 5 (2008): pp. 740–54. DOI: 10.1111/j.1741-4113.2008.00560.x

Hart, Cyril. 'The B Text of the *Anglo-Saxon Chronicle*'. *Journal of Medieval History* 8 (1982): pp. 241–99.

Healey, Antonette DiPaulo. 'Perplexities about Plant Names in the Dictionary of Old English'. In *Old Names, New Growth*, edited by Peter Bierbaumer and Helmut W. Klug (Frankfurt am Main: Peter Lang, 2009), pp. 99–120.

Higgitt, John. 'The Dedication Inscription at Jarrow and its Context'. *Antiquaries Journal* 59 (1979): pp. 343–74.

Hill, David, ed. *Ethelred the Unready: Papers from the Millenary Conference* (Oxford: British Archaeological Series, 1978).

Hines, John. 'The Becoming of the English: Identity, Material Culture and Language in Early Anglo-Saxon England'. *Anglo-Saxon Studies in Archaeology and History* 7 (1994): pp. 49–59.

Hooda, P. S., C. J. K. Henry, T. A. Seyoum, L. D. M. Armstrong, and M. B. Fowler. 'The Potential Impact of Soil Ingestion on Human Mineral Nutrition'. *Science of the Total Environment* 333 (2004): pp. 75–87.

Hostetter, Aaron. 'Disruptive Things in *Beowulf*'. *New Medieval Literatures* 17 (2017): pp. 34–61.

Howard, Ian. *Swein Forkbeard's Invasions and the Danish Conquest of England 991–1017* (Woodbridge: Boydell Press, 2003).

Howe, Nicholas. *Writing the Map of Anglo-Saxon England: Essays in Cultural Geography* (New Haven and London: Yale University Press, 2008).

Innes, Matthew. 'Danelaw Identities: Ethnicity, Regionalism, and Political Allegiance'. In *Cultures in Contact: Scandinavian Settlement in England in the Ninth and Tenth Centuries*, edited by Dawn M. Hadley and Julian D. Richards (Turnhout: Brepols, 2000), pp. 65–88.

Iovino, Serenella, and Serpil Oppermann. 'Introduction: Stories Come to Matter'. In *Material Ecocriticism*, edited by Serenella Iovino and Serpil Opperman (Bloomington: Indiana University Press, 2014), pp. 1–17.

Iovino, Serenella, and Serpil Opperman, eds. *Material Ecocriticism* (Bloomington: Indiana University Press, 2014).

Jolly, Karen. 'Magic, Miracle, and Popular Practice in the Early Medieval West: Anglo-Saxon England'. In *Religion, Science, and Magic: In Concert and In Conflict*, edited by Jacob Neusner, Ernest S. Frerichs, and Paul Virgil McCracken Flesher (Oxford: Oxford University Press, 1989), pp. 166–82.

Jolly, Karen. 'Father God and Mother Earth: Nature-Mysticism in the Anglo-Saxon World'. In *The Medieval World of Nature: A Book of Essays*, edited by Joyce E. Salisbury (New York: Garland, 1993), pp. 221–52.

Justice, Stephen. 'Did the Middle Ages Believe in Their Miracles?' *Representations* 103 (2008): pp. 1–29.

Keynes, Simon. 'The Declining Reputation of King Æthelred the Unready'. In *Ethelred the Unready: Papers from the Millenary Conference*, edited by David Hill (Oxford: British Archaeological Series, 1978), pp. 227–54.

Keynes, Simon. *The Diplomas of King Æþelred 'The Unready'* (Cambridge: Cambridge University Press, 1980).

Keynes, Simon. 'Royal Government and the Written Word in Late Anglo-Saxon England'. In *The Uses of Literacy in Early Medieval Europe*, edited by Rosamund McKitterick (Cambridge: Cambridge University Press, 1990), pp. 226–57.

Kiernan, Kevin. *Beowulf and the Beowulf Manuscript* (Ann Arbor: University of Michigan Press, 1981. Rev. ed. 1996).

King, Helen. 'Female Fluids in the Hippocratic Corpus: How Solid Was the Humoral Body?' In *The Body in Balance: Humoral Medicines in Practice*, edited by Peregrine Horden and Elisabeth Hsu (New York: Berghahn Books, 2013), pp. 25–52.

Kingsbury, John M. *Poisonous Plants of the United States and Canada* (Englewood Cliffs: Prentice Hall, 1964).

Klein, Stacy. *Ruling Women: Queenship and Gender in Anglo-Saxon Literature.* (Notre Dame: University of Notre Dame Press, 2006).

Lacapra, Dominick. *History and Criticism* (Ithaca: Cornell University Press, 1985).

Laistner, M. L. W. *A Hand-List of Bede Manuscripts* (Ithaca: Cornell University Press, 1943).

Lapidge, Michael. 'Some Remnants of Bede's Lost *Liber Epigrammatum*'. *English Historical Review* 90 (1975): pp. 798–820.

Lapidge, Michael. 'Bede's Metrical *Vita S. Cuthberti*'. In *St Cuthbert, his Cult and his Community to AD 1200*, edited by Gerald Bonner, David Rollason, and Clare Stancliffe (Woodbridge: Boydell Press, 1989), pp. 77–93.

Lapidge, Michael. *Anglo-Latin Literature 600–899* (London: Hambledon Press, 1996).

Lapidge, Michael. 'The Archetype of *Beowulf*'. *Anglo-Saxon England* 29 (2000): pp. 5–41.

Lapidge, Michael. 'The Saintly Life in Anglo-Saxon England'. In *The Cambridge Companion to Old English Literature* (Cambridge: Cambridge University Press, 2006), pp. 243–63.

Lapidge, M., and R. Love. 'The Latin Hagiography of England and Wales (600–1550)'. In *Hagiographies: Histoire internationale de la littérature hagiographique latine et vernaculaire en Occident des origines à 1550/International History of the Latin and Vernacular Hagiographical Literature in the West from Its Origins to 1550*, edited by Guy Philippart. 4 vols. (Turnhout: Brepols, 1994–2006), III, pp. 203–325.

Lavezzo, Kathy, ed. *Imagining a Medieval English Nation* (Minneapolis: University of Minnesota Press, 2004).

Lees, Clare, and Gillian Overing. 'Before History, Before Difference: Bodies, Metaphor, and the Church in Anglo-Saxon England'. *Yale Journal of Criticism* 11.2 (1998): pp. 315–34.

Lees, Clare, and Gillian Overing. 'In Ælfric's Words: Conversion, Vigilance and the Nation in Ælfric's *Life of Gregory the Great*. In *A Companion to Ælfric*, edited by Hugh Magennis and Mary Swan (Leiden: Brill, 2009), pp. 271–96.

Lerer, Seth. *Literacy and Power in Anglo-Saxon Literature* (Lincoln: University of Nebraska Press, 1991).

Lerer, Seth. 'Grendel's Glove'. *English Literary History* 61 (1994): pp. 721–51.

Leyerle, John. 'The Interlace Structure of *Beowulf*'. *University of Toronto Quarterly* 37 (1967): pp. 1–17.

Lockett, Leslie. 'The Role of Grendel's Arm in Feud, Law, and the Narrative Strategy of *Beowulf*'. In *Latin Learning and English Lore: Studies in Anglo-Saxon Literature for Michael Lapidge*, edited by Katherine O'Brien O'Keeffe and Andy Orchard (Toronto: University of Toronto Press, 2005), pp. 368–88.

Lockett, Leslie. *Anglo-Saxon Psychologies in the Vernacular and Latin Traditions* (Toronto: University of Toronto Press, 2011).

Marder, Michael. *The Philosopher's Plant: An Intellectual Herbarium* (Columbia: Columbia University Press, 2014).

Marder, Michael. *Dust* (London: Bloomsbury, 2016).

Martin, Angela K. and Sandra Kryst. 'Encountering Mary: Ritualization and Place Contagion in Postmodernity'. In *Places through the Body*, edited by Heidi Nast and Steve Pile (London: Routledge, 1998), pp. 153–70.

Mawer, A. and F. M. Stenton. *The Place-Names of Bedfordshire and Hunting-donshire*. English Place-Name Society 3 (Cambridge: Cambridge University Press, 1926).

McKitterick, Rosamund. *History and Memory in the Carolingian World* (Cambridge: Cambridge University Press, 2004).

Meaney, Audrey L. 'St Neots, Æthelweard and the Compilation of the *Anglo-Saxon Chronicle*: A Survey'. In *Studies in Earlier Old English Prose*, edited by Paul E. Szarmach (Albany, NY: State University of New York Press, 1986), pp. 193–243.

Metcalf, D. M. 'The Ranking of the Boroughs: Numismatic Evidence from the Reign of Æthelred II'. In *Ethelred the Unready: Papers from the Millenary Conference*, edited by David Hill (Oxford: British Archaeological Series, 1978), pp. 159–201.

Mink, Louis. 'Narrative Form as a Cognitive Instrument'. In *The Writing of History: Literary Form and Historical Understanding*, edited by Robert H. Canary and Henry Kozicki (Madison: University of Wisconsin Press, 1978), pp. 129–49.

Muensterberger, Werner. *Collecting: An Unruly Passion* (Princeton: Princeton University Press, 1994).

Musselman, John Lytton. 'Zawan and Tares in the Bible'. *Economic Botany* 54 (2000): pp. 537–42.

National Science Foundation. 'New Answer to MRSA, Other "Superbug" Infections: Clay Minerals?' (17 July 2014). http://www.nsf.gov/discoveries/disc_summ.jsp?cntn_id=132052&org=NSF.

Niles, John D. Beowulf: *The Poem and Its Tradition* (Cambridge, MA: Harvard University Press, 1983).

NSRI Staff. 'Glossary of Soil-related Terms' (Cranfield University, UK: National Soil Resources Institute, 2011).

O'Brien O'Keeffe, Katherine. '*Beowulf*, Lines 702b–836: Transformations and the Limits of the Human'. *Texas Studies in Literature and Language* 23 (1981): pp. 484–94.

O'Brien O'Keeffe, Katherine. 'Body and Law in Late Anglo-Saxon England'. *Anglo-Saxon England* 27 (1998): pp. 209–32.

O'Brien O'Keeffe, Katherine. *Visible Song: Transitional Literacy in Old English Verse* (Cambridge: Cambridge University Press, 2006).

Ó Carragáin, Éamonn. 'The City of Rome and the World of Bede'. Jarrow Lecture, 1994 (NP), p. 7.

Okasha, Elisabeth. 'The Non-Runic Scripts of Anglo-Saxon Inscriptions'. *Transactions of the Cambridge Bibliographical Society* 4 (1968): pp. 321–8.

Okasha, Elisabeth. *Hand-List of Anglo-Saxon Non-Runic Inscriptions* (Cambridge: Cambridge University Press, 1971).

Okasha, Elisabeth. 'A Supplement to *Hand-List of Anglo-Saxon Non-Runic Inscriptions*'. *Anglo-Saxon England* 11 (1983): pp. 83–118.

Okasha, Elisabeth. 'Vernacular or Latin? The Languages of Insular Inscriptions, AD 500–1100'. In *Epigraphik 1988: Fachtagung für mittelalterliche und neuzeutliche epigraphic. Graz, 10–14 Mai 1988*, edited by Walter Koch (Wien: Verlag der österreichischen Akademie der Wissenschaften, 1990), pp. 139–62.

Okasha, Elisabeth. 'A Second Supplement to *Hand-List of Anglo-Saxon Non-Runic Inscriptions*'. *Anglo-Saxon England* 21 (1992): pp. 37–85.

Okasha, Elisabeth. 'The Commissioners, Makers and Owners of Anglo-Saxon Inscriptions'. *Anglo-Saxon Studies in Archaeology and History* 7 (1994): pp. 71–7.

Okasha, Elisabeth. 'A Third Supplement to *Hand-List of Anglo-Saxon Non-Runic Inscriptions*'. *Anglo-Saxon England* 33 (2004): pp. 225–81.

Okasha, Elisabeth. 'Memorial Stones or Grave-Stones?' In *The Christian Tradition in Anglo-Saxon England: Approaches to Current Scholarship and Teaching*, edited by Paul Cavill (Cambridge: D.S. Brewer, 2004), pp. 91–101.

O'Neill, Mark. 'The Good Enough Visitor'. In *Museums, Society, Inequality (Museum Meanings)*, edited by R. Sandell (New York: Routledge, 2002), pp. 24–40.

Opperman, Serpil. 'From Ecological Postmodernism to Material Ecocriticism: Creative Materiality and Narrative Agency'. In *Material Ecocriticism*, edited by Serenella Iovino and Serpil Opperman (Bloomington: Indiana University Press, 2014), pp. 21–36.

Orchard, Andy. *The Poetic Art of Aldhelm* (Cambridge: Cambridge University Press, 1994).

Orchard, Andy. *A Critical Companion to Beowulf* (Cambridge: D.S. Brewer, 2003).

Owen-Crocker, Gale R. 'Horror in *Beowulf*: Mutilation, Decapitation, and Unburied Dead'. In *Early Medieval English Texts and Interpretations: Studies Presented to Donald G. Scragg*, edited by Susan Rosser and Elaine Treharne. *Medieval and Renaissance Texts and Studies*. Vol. 252 (Tempe: Arizona Center for Medieval and Renaissance Studies, 2003), pp. 81–100.

Page, R. I. 'How Long Did the Scandinavian Language Survive in England? The Epigraphical Evidence'. In *England before the Conquest: Studies in Primary Sources presented to Dorothy Whitelock*, edited by Peter Clemoes and Kathleen Hughes (Cambridge: Cambridge University Press, 1971), pp. 165–81.

Page, R. I. *An Introduction to English Runes* (London: Methuen, 1973).

Parkes, Malcolm. 'The Palaeography of the Parker Manuscript of the Chronicle, Laws and Sedulius, and Historiography at Winchester in the Late Ninth and Tenth Centuries'. *Anglo-Saxon England* 5 (1976): pp. 149–71.

Paz, James. 'Æschere's Head, Grendel's Mother, and the Sword that Isn't a Sword: Unreadable Things in *Beowulf*'. *Exemplaria* 25 (2013): pp. 231–51.

Paz, James. *Nonhuman Voices in Anglo-Saxon Literature and Material Culture* (Manchester: Manchester University Press, 2017).

Pearce, Susan. *Museums, Objects and Collections: A Cultural Study* (Washington, DC: Smithsonian Institution Press, 1992).

Poole, Reginald L. *Chronicles and Annals: A Brief Outline of Their Origin and Growth* (Oxford: Clarendon Press, 1926).

Preston, Christopher D., David A. Pearman, and Allan R. Hall. 'Archaeophytes in Britain'. *Botanical Journal of the Linnean Society* 145 (2004): pp. 257–94.

Ray, Roger. 'Bede's *Vera Lex Historiae*'. *Speculum* 55 (1980): pp. 1–21.

Reynolds, Andrew. *Later Anglo-Saxon England: Life and Landscape* (Stroud: Tempus, 1999).

Richards, Julian. *Viking Age England* (Stroud: Tempus, 2004).

Richardson, Peter R. 'Making Thanes: Literature, Rhetoric and State Formation in Anglo-Saxon England'. *Philological Quarterly* 78 (1999): pp. 215–32.

Ridyard, Susan J. *The Royal Saints of Anglo-Saxon England* (Cambridge: Cambridge University Press, 1988).

Rigby, Kate. 'Earth, World, Text: On the (Im)possibility of Ecopoiesis'. *New Literary History* 35 (2004): pp. 427–42.

Roberts, Jane, Christian Kay, and Lynne Grundy. *A Thesaurus of Old English in Two Volumes* (Atlanta, GA: Rodopi, 2000).

Robinson, Fred C. Beowulf *and the Appositive Style* (Knoxville: University of Tennessee Press, 1985).

Robinson, Fred C. 'Why is Grendel's not Greeting the *gifstol* a *wræc micel*'. In *Words, Texts, and Manuscripts: Studies in Anglo-Saxon Culture Presented to Helmut Gneuss on the Occasion of his Sixty-Fifth Birthday*, edited by Michael Korhammer (Cambridge: D.S. Brewer, 1992), pp. 257–62.

Rollason, David. *Saints and Relics in Anglo-Saxon England* (Oxford: Blackwell, 1989).

Rosier, James L. 'The Uses of Association: Hands and Feasts in *Beowulf*'. *Publications of the Modern Language Association* 78 (1963): pp. 8–14.

Rossi-Reder, Andrea. 'Embodying Christ, Embodying Nation: Ælfric's Accounts of Saints Agatha and Lucy'. In *Sex and Sexuality in Anglo-Saxon England: Essays in Memory of Daniel Calder*, edited by Carol Braun Pasternack and Lisa M. C. Weston (Tempe: Arizona Center for Medieval and Renaissance Studies, 2004), pp. 183–202.

Saldanha, Arun. 'Reontologising Race: The Machinic Geography of Phenotype'. *Environment and Planning D: Society and Space* 24 (2006): pp. 9–24.

Schardl, Christopher L., Robert B. Grossman, Padmaja Nagabhyru, Jerome R. Faulkner, and Uma P. Mallik. 'Loline Alkaloids: Currencies of Mutualism'. *Phytochemistry* 68 (2007): pp. 980–96.

Schumann, G. L., and S. Uppala. 'Ergot of Rye'. *The Plant Health Instructor* (2000, updated 2017). DOI: 10.1094/PHI-I-2000-1016-01.

Scowcroft, R. Mark. 'The Irish Analogues to *Beowulf'. Speculum* 74 (1999): pp. 22–64.

Semper, Philippa. 'Doctrine and Diagrams: Maintaining the Order of the World in *Byrhtferth's Enchiridion*'. In *The Christian Tradition in Anglo-Saxon England: Approaches to Current Scholarship and Teaching*, edited by Paul Cavill (Cambridge: D.S. Brewer, 2004), pp. 121–37.

Sharpe, Richard. 'Martyrs and Local Saints in Late Antique Britain'. In *Local Saints and Local Churches in the Early Medieval West*, edited by Alan Thacker and Richard Sharpe (Oxford: Oxford University Press, 2002), pp. 75–154.

Sharpe, Richard. 'King Ceadwalla's Roman Epitaph'. In *Latin Learning and English Lore: Studies in Anglo-Saxon Literature for Michael Lapidge*, edited by Katherine O'Brien O'Keeffe and Andy Orchard (Toronto: University of Toronto Press, 2005), pp. 171–93.

Sheppard, Alice. *Families of the King: Writing Identity in the Anglo-Saxon Chronicle* (Toronto: University of Toronto Press, 2004).

Shiba, Takuya, Koya Sugawara, and Akira Arakawa. 'Evaluating the Fungal Endophyte *Neophytodium occultans* for Resistance to the Rice Leaf Bug, *Trigonotylus caelestialium*, in Italian Ryegrass, *Lolium multiflorum*'. *Entomologia experimentalis at applicata* 141.1 (2011): pp. 45–51.

Sims-Williams, Patrick. 'Milred of Worcester's Collection of Latin Epigrams and Its Continental Counterparts'. *Anglo-Saxon England* 10 (1982): pp. 21–38.

Sims-Williams, Patrick. 'William of Malmesbury and *La Silloge Epigrafica di Cambridge*'. *Archivum Historiae Pontificiae* 21 (1983): pp. 9–33.

Sims-Williams, Patrick. *Religion and Literature in Western England 600–800* (Cambridge: Cambridge University Press, 1990).

Smith, Anthony. *The Ethnic Origin of Nations* (Oxford: Blackwell, 1986).

Smith, D. Vance. *The Book of the Incipit: Beginnings in the Fourteenth Century* (Minneapolis: Minnesota University Press, 2001).

Smyth, Alfred, ed. *King Alfred the Great* (Oxford: Oxford University Press, 1995).

Stafford, Pauline. 'The Reign of Æthelred II, A Study in the Limitations on Royal Policy and Action'. In *Ethelred the Unready: Papers from the Millenary Conference*, edited by David Hill (Oxford: British Archaeological Series, 1978), pp. 15–46.

Stafford, Pauline. *The East Midlands in the Early Middle Ages* (Leicester: Leicester University Press, 1995).

Stancliffe, Clare. 'Cuthbert and the Polarity between Pastor and Solitary'. In *St Cuthbert, his Cult and his Community to AD 1200*, edited by Gerald Bonner, David Rollason, and Clare Stancliffe (Woodbridge: Boydell Press, 1989), pp. 21–44.

Stancliffe, Clare. 'Oswald, "Most Holy and Victorious King of the Northumbrians"'. In *Oswald: Northumbrian King to European Saint*, edited by Clare Stancliffe and Eric Cambridge (Stamford: Paul Watkins, 1995), pp. 33–83.

Stancliffe, Clare. 'Where Was Oswald Killed?' In *Oswald: Northumbrian King to European Saint*, edited by Clare Stancliffe and Eric Cambridge (Stamford: Paul Watkins, 1995), pp. 84–96.

Stancliffe, Clare, and Eric Cambridge. 'Introduction'. In *Oswald: Northumbrian King to European Saint*, edited by Clare Stancliffe and Eric Cambridge (Stamford: Paul Watkins, 1995), pp. 1–12.

Stancliffe, Clare, and Eric Cambridge, eds. *Oswald: Northumbrian King to European Saint* (Stamford: Paul Watkins, 1995).

Stenton, F. M. 'The South-Western Element in the Old English Chronicle'. In *Preparatory to Anglo-Saxon England, being the Collected Papers of Frank Merry Stenton*, edited by D. M. Stenton (Oxford: Clarendon Press, 1970), pp. 106–15.

Stephenson, Rebecca. 'Scapegoating the Secular Clergy: The Hermeneutic Style as a Form of Monastic Self-Definition'. *Anglo-Saxon England* 38 (2009): pp. 101–35.

Stewart, Susan. *On Longing: Narratives of the Miniature, the Gigantic, the Souvenir, the Collection* (Baltimore: Johns Hopkins Press, 1984).

Steyn, D. G. 'Poisoning of Human Beings by Weeds Contained in Cereals (Bread Poisoning) and Senecio Poisoning in Stock. *Journal of the Royal Sanitary Institute* 56 (1935): pp. 760–8.

Stock, Brian. *Listening to the Text: On the Uses of the Past* (Philadelphia: University of Pennsylvania Press, 1996. Originally published by Johns Hopkins University Press in 1990).

Stodnick (Fay), Jacqueline. 'The Interests of Compounding: Angelcynn to Englaland in the Anglo-Saxon Chronicle' In *Anglo-Saxon Texts and Their Transmission: Essays in Honour of Donald G. Scragg [on the occasion of his seventieth birthday]*, edited by Hugh Magennis and Jonathan Wilcox (Morgantown: West Virginia University Press, 2006), pp. 337–67.

Story, Joanna. 'The Frankish Annals of Lindisfarne and Kent'. *Anglo-Saxon England* 34 (2005): pp. 59–109.

Thacker, Alan. '*Membra Disjecta*: The Division of the Body and the Diffusion of the Cult'. In *V/i>*, edited by Clare Stancliffe and Eric Cambridge *(Stamford: Paul Watkins, 1995), pp. 97–127.*

Thacker, Alan. '*Loca Sanctorum*: The Significance of Place in the Study of Saints'. In *Local Saints and Local Churches in the Early Medieval West*, edited by Alan Thacker and Richard Sharpe (Oxford: Oxford University Press, 2002), pp. 1–43.

Thacker, Alan. 'The Making of a Local Saint'. In *Local Saints and Local Churches in the Early Medieval West*, edited by Alan Thacker and Richard Sharpe (Oxford: Oxford University Press, 2002), pp. 45–72.

Thomas, Gabor. 'Anglo-Scandinavian Metalwork from the Danelaw: Exploring Social and Cultural Interaction'. In *Cultures in Contact: Scandinavian Settlement in England in the Ninth and Tenth Centuries*, edited by Dawn M. Hadley and Julian D. Richards (Turnhout: Brepols, 2000), pp. 237–55.

Thompson, Victoria. *Death and Dying in Later Anglo-Saxon England* (Woodbridge: Boydell Press, 2004).

Thormann, Janet. '*The Battle of Brunanburh* and the Matter of History'. *Mediaevalia* 17 (1994): pp. 5–13.

Thormann, Janet. 'The *Anglo-Saxon Chronicle* Poems and the Making of the English Nation'. In *Anglo-Saxonism and the Construction of Social Identity*, edited by Allen J, Frantzen and John D. Niles (Gainesville: University Press of Florida, 1997), pp. 60–85.

Tilghman, Benjamin C. 'On the Enigmatic Nature of Things in Anglo-Saxon Art'. *Different Visions: A Journal of New Perspectives on Medieval Art* 4 (2014): 1–43.

Tomlinson, P., and A. R. Hall. 'A Review of the Archaeological Evidence for Food Plants from the British Isles: An Example of the Use of the Archaeobotanical Computer Database (ABCD)'. *Internet Archaeology* 1 (1996). http://intarch.ac.uk/journal/issue1/tomlinson/toc.html. Accessed 30 October 2018.

Tompkins, Kyla Wazana. 'New Materialisms'. *Lateral 5.1* (2016). DOI: 10.25158/L5.1.8.

Tran, Nhiem, Aparna Mir, Dhriti Mallik, Arvind Sinha, Suprabha Nayar, and Thomas J. Webster. 'Bactericidal Effect of Iron Oxide Nanoparticles on Staphylococcus Aureus'. *International Journal of Nanomedicine* 5 (2010): pp. 277–83.

Treharne, Elaine. *Living through Conquest: The Politics of Early English, 1020–1220* (Oxford: Oxford University Press, 2012).

Tuana, Nancy. 'Viscous Porosity: Witnessing Katrina'. In *Material Feminisms*, edited by Stacy Alaimo and Susan Hekman (Bloomington: Indiana University Press, 2008), pp. 188–213.

Turville-Petre, Thorlac. *England the Nation: Language, Literature and National Identity, 1290–1340* (Oxford: Clarendon Press, 1996).

Tyler, Elizabeth. *Old English Poetics: The Aesthetics of the Familiar in Anglo-Saxon England* (York: York Medieval Press, 2006).

Uebel, Michael. *Ecstatic Transformation: On the Uses of Alterity in the Middle Ages* (New York: Palgrave Macmillan, 2005).

Van Houts, Elisabeth. *Memory and Gender in Medieval Europe 900–1200* (Toronto: University of Toronto Press, 1999).

Vincent, Peter. *The Biogeography of the British Isles: An Introduction* (London: Routledge, 1990).

Walker, Winifred. *All the Plants of the Bible* (New York: Doubleday, 1975).

Walker Bynum, Carolyn. *Christian Materiality: An Essay on Religion in Late Medieval Europe* (New York: Zone Books, 2011).

Walker Kirby, H. 'Ergot of Cereals and Grasses'. *Report on Plant Diseases* 107 (1998): pp. 1–4.

Wallach, Luitpold. 'Alcuin's Epitaph of Hadrian I'. *American Journal of Philology* 72 (1951): pp. 128–44.

Wallach, Luitpold. 'The Epitaph of Alcuin: A Model of Carolingian Epigraphy'. *Speculum* 30 (1955): pp. 367–73.

Wallach, Luitpold. 'The Urbana Anglo-Saxon Sylloge of Latin Inscriptions'. In *Poetry and Poetics from Ancient Greece to the Renaissance: Studies in Honor of James Hutton*, edited by G. M. Kirkwood (Ithaca: Cornell University Press, 1975), pp. 134–51.

Walsham, Alexandra. 'Introduction: Relics and Remains'. *Past and Present* 5 (2010): pp. 9–36.

Wheeler, Wendy. 'Natural Play, Natural Metaphor, and Natural Stories: Biosemiotic Realism'. In *Material Ecocriticism*, edited by Serenella Iovino and Serpil Oppermann (Bloomington: Indiana University Press, 2014), pp. 67–79.

Whitbread, L. 'The Hand of Æschere: A Note on Beowulf 1343'. *Review of English Studies* 25 (1949): pp. 339–42.

White, Hayden. 'The Value of Narrativity in the Representation of Reality'. In *On Narrative*, edited by W. J. T. Mitchell (Chicago: University of Chicago Press, 1991), pp. 1–23.

Whitelock, Dorothy. 'The Importance of the Battle of Edington, AD 878'. In *Report for 1975, 1976, and 1977 of the Society of Friends of the Priory Church of Edington, Wiltshire*, pp. 6–15. Reprinted in *From Bede to Alfred: Studies in Early Anglo-Saxon Literature and History* (London: Variorum Reprints, 1980).

Whitelock, Dorothy, ed. *English Historical Documents 500–1041*. Vol. 1 (New York: Routledge, 1996).

Wilcox, Jonathan. 'The St Brice's Day Massacre and Archbishop Wulfstan'. In *Peace and Negotiation: Strategies for Coexistence in the Middle Ages and Renaissance*, edited by D. Wolfthal (Turnhout: Brepols, 2000), pp. 79–91.

Williams, Ann. '"Cockles amongst the Wheat": Danes and English in the Western Midlands in the First Half of the Eleventh Century'. *Midland History* 11 (1986): pp. 1–22.

Williams, Howard. 'Introduction: The Archaeology of Death, Memory and Material Culture'. In *Archaeologies of Remembrance: Death and Memory in Past Societies*, edited by Howard Williams (New York: Kluwer Academic/Plenum Publishers, 2003), pp. 1–24.

Williams, Howard. *Death and Memory in Early Medieval Britain* (Cambridge: Cambridge University Press, 2006).

Williams, L. B., D. W. Metge, D. D. Eberl, R. W. Harvey, A. G. Turner, P. Prapaipong, and A. T. Poret-Peterson. 'What Makes Natural Clays Antibacterial?' *Environmental Science and Technology* 45 (2011): pp. 3768–73.

Williamson, Tom. *Shaping Medieval Landscapes: Settlement, Society, Environment* (Macclesfield: Windgather Press, 2003).

Williamson, Tom. *Environment, Society and Landscape in Early Medieval England: Time and Topography* (Woodbridge: Boydell Press, 2015).

Withers, Benjamin C. and Jonathan Wilcox, eds. *Naked before God: Uncovering the Body in Anglo-Saxon England* (Morgantown: West Virginia University Press, 2003).

Wormald, Francis. *English Kalendars before AD 1100*. Henry Bradshaw Society 72 (1934. Repr. London: Boydell Press, 1988).

Wormald, Patrick. 'Æþelred the Lawmaker'. In *Ethelred the Unready: Papers from the Millenary Conference*, edited by David Hill (Oxford: British Archaeological Series, 1978), pp. 47–80.

Wormald, Patrick. *The Making of English Law: King Alfred to the Twelfth Century* (Oxford: Blackwell, 1999. Reprinted 2000).

Young, Sera L. *Craving Earth: Understanding Pica* (New York: Columbia University Press, 2011).

Zupitza, Julius. 'Englisches aus Prudentiushandschriften'. *Zeitschrift für Deutsches Alterthum* 20 (1876): pp. 36–45.

# MANUSCRIPT INDEX

*Note*: Figures are indicated by an italic "*f*", respectively, following the page number.

For the benefit of digital users, indexed terms that span two pages (e.g., 52–53) may, on occasion, appear on only one of those pages.

# GENERAL INDEX

*Note*: Figures are indicated by an italic "*f*", respectively, following the page number.

For the benefit of digital users, indexed terms that span two pages (e.g., 52–53) may, on occasion, appear on only one of those pages.